The CD-ROM
Revolution

Devra Hall

PRIMA PUBLISHING

Rocklin, California

Managing Editor: Paula Munier Lee
Acquisitions Editor: Sherri Morningstar
Project Editor: Stefan Grünwedel
Cover Production Coordinator: Anne Flemke
Copyeditor: Peter Weverka
Production & Design: Susan Glinert, BookMakers
Indexer: Brown Editorial Service
Cover Designer: Page Design, Inc.

3DO, the 3DO logo, and Interactive Multiplayer are trademarks of The 3DO Company.
SIRS Discoverer is a trademark of SIRS, Inc.
Nickelodeon and its logo, titles, and related characters are trademarks of Viacom Incorporated.

Prima Publishing and the author have attempted throughout this book to distinguish proprietary trademarks from descriptive terms by following the capitalization style used by the manufacturer.

ISBN: 1-55958-515-3
Library of Congress Catalog Card Number: 93-87189

Printed in the United States of America
95 96 97 98 RRD 10 9 8 7 6 5 4 3 2 1

Prima Publishing, P.O. Box 1260BK, Rocklin, CA 95667

To family, friends, and even total strangers—those who choose to embrace evolution and revolution, pushing forward the cutting edge in their respective fields.

Contents

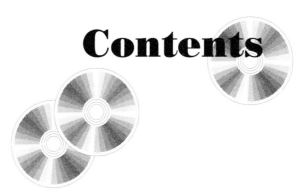

Preface

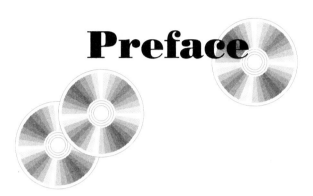

Just before this book went to press, I received a fax from Craig Rispin, vice president of sales and marketing at Big Hand Productions, Inc. His message read in part:

> Your book contains the information that every person or company wants to know about CD-based technology. I spend a lot of time speaking at computer- and multimedia-related trade shows, trying to give people the correct information about CD-based products—that is, the truth rather than things that many people *think* are true.
>
> *The CD-ROM Revolution* is the only place I know of to spell out, for the average person, the basis for CD-based technology. I can recommend this resource to anyone about to start a CD-based project, starting a company to produce interactive projects, or for the veteran in the industry that just forgot where we came from.

His timing was perfect, not just because I can use the endorsement, but because he reminded me that this book's intention is to present the basics— what these discs contain, how they are made, and why you might want to use them. It's a reminder I very much need at the moment, because my publisher wants to go to press and I keep wanting to add new material.

Every day I read or hear about some neat new application or technological advancement. Compact discs are definitely a hot topic these days. Even my local television station is featuring a special report on compact discs during their 5 p.m. broadcast every day this week.

U.S. News and World Report devoted 20 pages to technology in its November 28, 1994, issue. The "News You Can Use" section featured articles about buying the right personal computer for your needs), "stellar software" (most of the magazine's favorites were CDs), video gaming, hot products, and more.

And several computer magazines are featuring CD-ROMs on their covers. The December, 1994, cover of *NewMedia* magazine says "Editors Pick the Best: 50 Best CD-ROMs." *PC World*'s December, 1994, cover heralds a "Special Year-End Roundup: Best CDs of 1994 and All You Need to Run Them." And the November, 1994, cover of *PC/Computing* screams "CD-ROMs You Gotta Get!"

The only way I could stop adding material to this book was to leave town—leaving my magazines and research notes behind. I headed for Maui and while on the plane began to review the galley pages. The lady sitting next to me was a veteran school teacher, who, after reading Chapters 2 and 3 over my shoulder, engaged me in a lengthy conversation about how she and her colleagues might integrate CDs into their classroom activities.

Shortly after I got to my friend Laura-Lee's home in Hawaii, her seven-year-old nephew, Justin, called to thank her for an audio CD she had sent for Christmas. He told her that he had already figured out how to play it on the CD-ROM drive in his new computer. The next day, I met a lady and her daughter in a hardware store. They has just gotten a CD-ROM with a bundle of CD titles. When I asked her which ones, I found that I happened to have mentioned each and every one of them in this book.

The revolution is clearly in full swing, and it will continue for quite some time to come. In fact, it may never end.

Acknowledgments

I had a lot of help and support in getting this book to press. Family, friends, and colleagues were eager to share their thoughts and experiences. Because CD-ROMs have been receiving a tremendous amount of general press coverage, even people who have not yet become technologically savvy, like my mother, forwarded articles that proved to be quite useful. Phil Hopkins (one of my very techno-savvy friends) compiled quite a bit of research for me, and discussed ideas that factored greatly in the final product. Bjoern Hartsfvang, a man with professional research skills, also uncovered a lot of information for this book. Stuart Stuple, a friend who balances my perspective for me on a daily basis, was among those who reminded me that I don't live in a Windows-only world. And that leads me to thank my neighbors Patrick and Shirley Russ for allowing me to use their Macintosh system from time to time.

I also want to thank everyone at Prima Publishing, without whom you would not be reading this book. Thanks to Acquisitions Editor Sherri Morningstar, not only for getting the ball rolling, but for believing in readers like you who are interested in the big picture, not just the how-to. Without the tenacity and follow-through of one Juliana Aldous, Prima's *prima* acquisitions coordinator, we would not have been able to round-up all the photographs and screen shots that appear here. I've always thought of copyeditors as a necessary evil, but Peter Weverka is the best I've ever worked with, and *almost* changed my mind. A book passes through many other hands before it hits the shelf. Thanks go to the typesetter, Susan Glinert at BookMakers; Anne Flemke, cover production coordinator; indexer Lynn Brown of Brown Editorial Service; and the cover designers at Page Design, Inc. And last, but definitely not least, the man who managed to keep all the pieces together, Project Editor Stefan Grünwedel.

I'm going to stick my neck out here and try to acknowledge, by name, all of the industry professionals who contributed time and information—I just hope I don't leave anyone out. (If I do, please forgive me.) But before I tackle the list-at-large, I'd like to single out Craig Rispin, V.P. of sales and marketing, and Kimberly Rispin, press and marketing manager, at Big Hand Productions in Dallas, Texas. They feel, as I do, that the dissemination of factual and accurate information is the key to keeping the revolution going.

Several people graciously granted interviews: Greg Bestick (Electronic Arts), Eric Brown (*NewMedia*), Allen Chapel (Electronic Data Systems), Jill Croft (Disc Manufacturing Inc.), Rick Devine (Club Kidsoft), Mary W. Elings (Berkeley Custom Process), Warren Harmon (Dayton-Hudson Corporation), Anthony Hushion (Royal Ontario Museum), Robert Kersey (Optical Data Corporation), Rick King (Jostens Learning Corporation), Dennis Knott (U.S. Navy), Paul LeBlanc (Houghton Mifflin), Craig Rispin (Big Hand Productions, Inc.), Michael van der Kieft (Blockbuster Entertainment Group), John Velie (Spinnaker Communications), and Jay Wolff (Big Hand Productions, Inc.)

Other industry people that I'd like to acknowledge include: Sally Bowman Alden (Computer Learning Foundation), Daphne Allen (Portland State University Library), Stewart Alsop (*InfoWorld*), Chris Andrews (UniDisc), Susan Barron (Mammoth Micro Productions), Julia Blixrud (Council on Library Resources), Colleen Brady (Bureau of Electronic Publishing Inc.), Bob Bruce (Walnut Creek CDROM), Mary Frances Budig (Viacom New Media), Michael Carpenter (DiAMAR Interactive), Steve Case (America Online), Colleen Coletta (Optical Data Corporation), Beth Davidson (Bureau of Electronic Publishing Inc.), Claire Dean (Storm Software), Kim Dempster (Brøderbund), Jeff Dewey (SRDS), Michelle Dollarhide (Waggener Edstrom), Leslie Eicher (Jostens Learning Coporation), Mark Foster (Quanta Press), Adriana Getz (Philips Media), Mike Granger (TFPL Publishing), Ronnie Gunnerson (Turner Home Entertainment), Mark Hadlock (United Parcel Service), Ron Johnson (Prism Studios, Inc.), Ron Jones (Freeman Associates Inc.), Wallace Knief (Blockbuster

Entertainment Group), Michelle Kraus, Richard W. Krueger (Meridian Data, Inc.), Ron Kushnier (Veda, Inc.), Claire LaBeaux (Banner Blue Software), Laurie Labelle (Social Issues Resources Series, Inc.), Rita Lencioni (The Terpin Group), Steve Litzinger (IBM Multimedia Publishing Studio), Mark Logan (Spinnaker Communications), Andrew Lunde (Floyd Design), Laurie Lupo (Saphar & Associates), Lawrence Lyford (Naval Air Warfare Center), Cathy Maloney (Deep River Publishing), Andrea Marozas (Philips Media), Gerald A. McDonald (Mammoth Micro Productions), Pam McGraw (America Online), Rebecca Michaels (Adobe Systems), Maureen Miller (Social Issues Resources Series Inc.), John Monday (MusicWriter Inc.), Cindy Monticue (The Bohle Company), Reuel Moore (Allegro New Media), Joyce Murray (Pemberton Press), Suzie Nussel (Jostens Learning Corporation), Lynda Orban (Knowledge Adventure), Carol Parcels (Hewlett-Packard Company), Chip Partner (Saphar & Associates), Maryanne Piazza (Grolier Electronic Publishing Inc.), Bruce Polichar, Gina Privitere (Against All Odds Productions), Betsy Ramirez (Dialog Information Services Inc.), Eddie Ranchigoda (Sierra On-Line Inc.), Paul Reaume (Lester B. Pearson Senior High School), Denise Rocco (Against All Odds Productions), Sue A. Rowland (Reed Technology and Information Services), Loretta Sapino (Market Vision), Avra Shapiro (Beit Hashoah Museum of Tolerance), Laura Siegel (Viacom New Media), Yoav Sisley (Enigma), Wendy B. Smith (The 3DO Company), Greg Thompson (IBM/Eduquest), Jane Torbica (CompuServe Incorporated), Gail Uchida (Hewlett-Packard Company), Paul Wheaton (Dataquest), Sarah White (Software Publishers Association), Maggie Young (Club Kidsoft), and Laura Zawaski (Quality Education Data).

Thank you. Thank you. Thank you.

Chapter 1

CD-ROMs Are Everywhere

"The Information Revolution promises to touch—and in some cases radically transform—every aspect of life: our work and leisure, all manner of scientific techniques, and virtually every method for recording and transmitting knowledge, including books, newspapers, magazines, movies, television...." So heralded the introductory article in *Business Week*'s special issue devoted to "The Information Revolution 1994."

One of the key factors fueling this revolution is the advances in technology that provide the means for collecting, accessing, processing, distributing, and otherwise handling information. Advances in technology provide new tools that spawn new media and new ways of doing things.

The purpose of this book is simple. Audio CDs were just the tip of the iceberg. Compact-disc–based technologies now include CD-ROM (compact disc read-only memory), CD-i (compact disc–interactive), Photo CD, Video CD, and more, which represent a revolution in progress. This book is your guide to understanding what this medium represents, how it changes what we know, where we are going with it, and how to join the movement. In the first half of the book, I tell you about CD-based projects and products that are being used in schools, businesses, homes, libraries, museums, even in stores. And you'll hear the opinions of innovators, experimenters, and industry watchers. The second half of this book is devoted to the issue of using and producing *optical discs* (another term that applies to compact discs) for personal, business, educational, and entertainment uses. But first, a little perspective.

Evolution of the Revolution

For well over 500 years, books were the state-of-the-art technology for exchanging and storing massive amounts of text and graphics. After the invention of movable type, it wasn't long before these portable collections of entertainment, opinion, and just plain facts became common objects in our lives. Few would dispute the fact that the wide availability of organized information has had an enormous impact on the course of human history and our understanding of the world.

The personal computer emerged from the imagination of this information-transformed society, and with it came the need for powerful, convenient, and inexpensive information storage devices. In a culture strongly influenced by visions of the future, progress came to be measured by the yardstick of technological potential. These influences nurtured the mania to invent the ultimate "what-if" information storage medium, and out of the mania came the compact disc.

The concept of virtually unlimited portable information devices had its genesis in science fiction, but the real revolution began when Sony and Philips developed a way for the recording industry to put 74 minutes of distortion-free music on a 12-centimeter (about 4¾") platter. As the platter, dubbed the compact disc, rotates at high speed, a laser scans a tight spiral of microscopic pits on the disc's surface. This trail of cavities, representing data *bits*, allowed recorded music to be encoded digitally on a disc. As record companies soon discovered, it takes almost 5.5 trillion bits on an audio CD to make music sound good.

Once the music CD format was accepted by the audiophile marketplace, it didn't take long for a few bright people to realize that "bits are bits." In other words, what sold commercially as a media for high-quality recordings could also be used to store massive amounts of computer data. Each disc could hold up to 650 *megabytes* (MB) of data, which is a lot. In fact, 650MB is far more text than one person could expect to produce in a lifetime. As my friend Phil Hopkins points out, if you were to type continuously at the rate of 60 words per minute for every single minute of a 40-hour work week, it would take you 19 years to fill up a CD with text (and that's assuming you get a two-week vacation each year).

NOTE

In this book and in other literature, you may hear that CD-ROMs are capable of containing various amounts of data. A CD actually holds 681,574,400 bytes of data. Some people think this means that a CD holds approximately 680MB, based on the assumption that a megabyte is equal to 1 million bytes. Wrong. Technically speaking, a megabyte equals 1,048,576 bytes. When you divide 681,574,400 by 1,048,576, the result is 650MB—and that's the figure that I'll use throughout this book.

Soon personal computer software manufacturers pounced on the opportunities brought about by CDs. Manufacturers now had the capability to distribute productivity software, operating systems, reference information, games, and other storage-intensive products for minimal fabrication, packaging, and shipping costs. This new medium only needed three more things to be successful: a memorable name for the technology, a critical number of CD drives installed in computers to make the marketing of software worthwhile, and some products that people would want to buy.

Rumor has it that the first success factor, an easily remembered name, came courtesy of a columnist from a computer industry trade journal. But Stewart Alsop, editor-in-chief of *InfoWorld*, thinks the name originated with the Sony and Philips partnership. In fact, he remembers complaining about the name for being excessively obscure and technical. Moreover, the appellation "CD-ROM" bordered on being technically incorrect because *read-only memory* (ROM) typically referred to software hard-coded into silicon-based computer chips, while anything flat and round that spins was customarily classified as storage media. But the name had resonance among manufacturers and consumers alike, so it stuck.

Naming the technology was child's play compared to convincing consumers to buy an expensive piece of computer equipment that, at the time, offered few benefits other than spectacular potential. The situation was akin to manufacturers promoting color televisions during the time when stations broadcasted solely in black and white. The computer press began the buzz, but it wasn't until the consumer press caught on that the technology was deemed ready for prime time.

Software of all types was growing more sophisticated, and CD-ROMs seemed the ideal medium for diskette-intensive program distribution. Press releases gushed with statistics comparing the data capacity of a single CD-ROM disc with a garbage can full of diskettes, or a stack of books ten stories tall. But before consumers would care that the emerging technology could leap tall libraries in a single bound, there had to be products that really *needed* this type of volume storage.

Several early storage-intensive applications made history back in 1987. Chris Andrews was one of the early developers of CD-ROM applications. In his book, *The Education of a CD-ROM Publisher,* Andrews talks about the early days when Alldata Corporation created CD-ROMs that contained automotive repair and parts manuals that would have taken up, in book form, more than 100 feet of shelf space. That same year, Hewlett-Packard became the first company to create a CD-ROM for customer support. Their LaserROM disc contained thousands of paper documents for the HP-3000 minicomputer. And a similar product was created by KnowledgeSet that incorporated all the technical manuals for the Boeing 767 aircraft.

Hewlett-Packard Company's LaserROM for the HP 9000 Series 800 HP-UX enables users to search electronically through more than 10,000 pages of UNIX system support information and documentation. (Photo courtesy of Hewlett-Packard Company.)

Meridian Data's CD Publisher (left), a micro-based system that formats data for CD-ROM mastering. CD Professional (right) enables the user to print CD-ROM discs in an office environment. (Photos courtesy of Meridian Data, Inc.)

A year earlier, in 1986, a CD-ROM was first displayed on the cover of *Byte* magazine, and a company named Meridian Data made a name for itself with its CD Publisher, a system that formats data for CD-ROM mastering. By the late 1980s, CD-Recorders, sometimes referred to as *one-offs*, became available and were used by publishers to create test versions of their developing products. But only the big boys, such as Hewlett-Packard and Apple, could afford to play—CD Professional was a 600-pound system costing close to $100,000 that enabled users to print CD-ROM discs in an office environment.

Remarkably, no single application emerged that would single-handedly sell CD technology to the public. (When one product does have such an impact, it is known as a *killer app*, "app" being short for application.) As time went on, the companies that produced multimedia applications found that it was simply more economical to distribute their wares on CD-ROMs rather than on diskettes. So they did. Entrepreneurial catalog software distributors discovered that they could put a wide range of useful stuff on a lightweight CD-ROM and advertise it as a virtual software warehouse on a disc. So they tried it. Kodak, always looking for new opportunities to complement its core photographic products business, developed a new standard for storing still images on inexpensive CD-ROMs. The new standard, called Photo CD, appealed to professional photographers, desktop publishers, graphic designers, and, most importantly, consumers.

For the vast quantities of data that the government must make available both internally and to the public, the CD-ROM has become the way to go. In a 1992 article in *Byte* magazine, a production chief at the National Technical Information Service reported that the U.S. Government produced 2,000 CD-ROM titles that year. The year 1992 was also when CD-ROMs gained momentum in niche markets with titles geared to the medical and legal communities.

Finally the floodgates seem to have opened to self-publishing tools, technical and reference information, multimedia clip collections, entertainment, and games by the thousands. The compact disc is well on its way to being as common an object in our society as the book. Many who were around at the beginning of the revolution are wondering what took so long.

The Day Before Tomorrow

Prices are affordable, the drives are faster, the number of CD drives or players in use (known as the *installed base*) continues to grow by leaps and bounds, and titles are proliferating at an amazing rate. Today, with the dropping prices of CD recordable drives (CD-Rs) for in-house small-scale manufacturing, businesses are beginning to use the medium for disseminating internal communications, sales presentations, and just-in-time training.

With respect to CD-ROMs connected to a computer, the availability of information resources on these discs is increasing especially fast thanks to multi-disc jukeboxes and local area network (LAN) connectivity. Now that users on a network can simultaneously read data off a disc, and multi-disk jukeboxes make it possible for people to utilize many discs at once, access to useful data is increasing exponentially. Also, the amount of space available on a CD-ROM means developers can create and distribute dedicated program modules for all types of machines on the same disc. A disc with programs for more than one type of machine is called a *hybrid disc*. Macintosh and IBM-compatible computers on the same network (or individually) can use the same hybrid CDs. The CD-ROM disc is becoming a necessity for more and more computer users.

Mass storage technology is even changing the way educators teach courses. Teachers are already swapping traditional books for discs that give students access to a wealth of visual and audio information. The challenge for instructors is to teach students how to add value to the information they encounter. Although many teachers welcome the compact discs, others are afraid of what will happen when teachers are no longer the single source of learning in the classroom. However, CDs allow students to examine more information in greater depth, and they provide educators with a medium that enables the design and distribution of challenging and entertaining learning environments.

With competition among software publishers and hardware manufacturers, the cost of working with optical technologies seems to drop on a weekly basis. As prices fall, businesses are creating their own training materials, catalogs, manuals, presentations, and demos. As prices continue to fall, document archiving with CD-ROMs as a replacement for traditional microfilm and microfiche media becomes more enticing.

Book publishers, unwilling to stand idly by while their bread-and-butter intellectual property is transformed into new market commodities by others, are jumping onto the bandwagon by creating new departments to produce and market compact disc titles. Reference books like the *Physician's Desk Reference* and the *American Heritage Dictionary* have long been known to pay the operating expenses of major publishing companies, if only by virtue of their long life spans. Titles like these are perennial sellers, with consumers coming back for regular updates and enhancements. So it is not surprising that reference works were some of the first titles to appear in CD-ROM format.

Movie and record companies can also be described as publishers. Along with organizations such as like the Mayo Clinic and the U.S. Government, movie and record companies are finding that CD-based multimedia software is an excellent, and lucrative, way to market their wares to consumers—whether it be movie footage, musical applications, census data, or health care information.

Companies specializing in computer games, meanwhile, see the cost benefits of CDs as a strategic advantage, permitting them to design intricate and storage-intensive adventures while keeping distribution costs under control. And like it or not, even publishers of adult entertainment materials realize that there is money to be made in repackaging their images and prose in a conveniently discreet, cost-effective format. It appears that everybody is doing it with CDs.

Is the CD Here to Stay?

If sales statistics and projections are any indication, there is definitely a disc in your future. Dataquest, an international company of the Dun & Bradstreet Corporation, projects that the international installed base of CD-ROM drives will approach 60 million by 1996. Prices of CD-ROM titles for these machines are already dropping due to stiff competition and tight shelf space.

Despite impressive statistics, however, there are those who believe that these little discs are just a transitional medium, a short-lived delivery system that will drop by the wayside when most homes are plugged into broadband digital delivery systems. ("Broadband" refers to the amount of data that can be transmitted at once. Our current telephone and cable lines are too "narrow." They weren't designed to handle the vast amounts of video, audio, and graphical data that interactive television demands.) Estimates of when that will be range from two, to five, to ten years from now. The technology is here, but the economic conditions do not yet favor massive use of broadband systems.

Online services connected to PCs by phone lines are gaining in popularity. However, some of these services are difficult to use, and others are not yet affordable. The Internet, for example, is not easy to navigate, and even the "free" services often have toll-call charges that can add up if you download megabytes of data with even with the speediest of modems. Today, CDs are the way to go for affordable local or mass market delivery of large amounts of pre-formatted content.

"Modem-based online services and CD-based multimedia applications are both growing rapidly, but so far they have developed separately," says Steve Case, President and CEO of America Online. "As a result, online services lack pizzazz, and CD-ROM titles lack connectivity. We'll be creating hybrid offerings that marry the best attributes of each for mass market appeal. These hybrid CD/online and cable/PC offerings will serve as the training wheels for an eventual broadband world."

CD naysayers complain about the slow speed of CDs (relatively speaking, that is), and their read-only status. Proponents, on the other hand, believe that there will always be a need for portable storage media that can deliver data to a single user without the benefit of a network or a mainframe computer. Also, many consumers still prefer to own a copy of the information that they use on a frequent basis.

Buy the Numbers

The pace of CD-ROM market penetration is increasing at a remarkable rate. Infotech, a Vermont-based research firm, projects that CD-ROM publishers will generate $30 billion in worldwide revenues by 1995. The Software Publishers Association reported that more discs were sold in the last quarter of 1993 than the prior three quarters combined.

Industry analysts cite a number of factors for this growth rate, including:

- A booming home PC market
- Improved multimedia software
- Advances in the computing power of the average PC
- A steady flow of new titles
- Decreasing software prices
- Decreasing replication costs
- Decreasing CD-ROM drive prices (of course)

CD-ROM and Multimedia Titles

CD-ROMs first gained entry into the library market in the form of large reference databases and bibliographic archives. Corporations and government offices were next to reap the benefits afforded by the low-cost data storage techniques of the CD and the ease with which data can be accessed and retrieved. Selling information has always been profitable, and these applications, while not glamorous, were no exception.

These less-than-glamorous applications are described in TFPL Publishing's *Facts & Figures 94* as "data-intensive applications—phone directories, legal references and financial market data, to name a few—whose value and utility is improved only marginally or not a whit by multimedia content." TFPL's figures indicate these titles represent 74 percent of the all CD titles.

The remaining applications are classified as "multimedia titles," and while they represent only 26 percent of all titles, the glamour of multimedia has became the focus of the consumer market. The Software Publishers Association reported that the breakdown of 1993 consumer retail sales is as follows: 40 percent of CD-ROM titles are reference oriented, 30 percent are games and entertainment, 24 percent are directed specifically at the home and education markets, and 6 percent are classified as "Other."

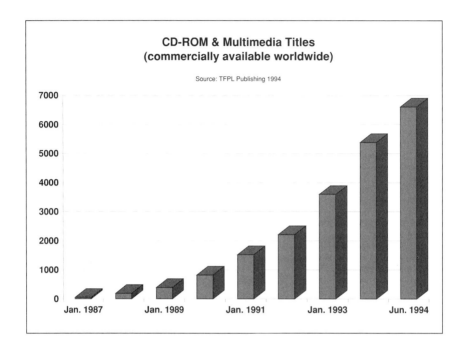

The above figure shows the growth of commercially available CD-ROM and multimedia titles. The very first edition of *The CD-ROM Directory* (December, 1986), also published by TFPL, catalogued only 48 CD titles available worldwide. By the beginning of 1992, the list contained 2,212 titles produced by 2,600 companies. The number jumped to 5,379 titles by the beginning of 1994, and the June, 1994 *CD-ROM Directory* shows 6,605 CD-ROM titles available worldwide—an increase of 300 percent, or three times as many as were available in 1992.

And these are only the commercially available titles. According to InfoTech's Optical Publishing Industry Assessment report, the number of CD-ROM titles in print representing worldwide aggregate totals for all market segments will come close to 14,000 in 1995. These include commercial titles for corporate, professional, library, educational, and consumer use, plus not-for-sale titles created in-house.

Increases of this magnitude may sound like hyperbole, but seem entirely realistic in light of the diversity of software titles in general, and the fact that, according to Dataquest, the installed base of CD-ROM drives reached 26.3 million in 1994. This number represents a dynamic sales environment, with only

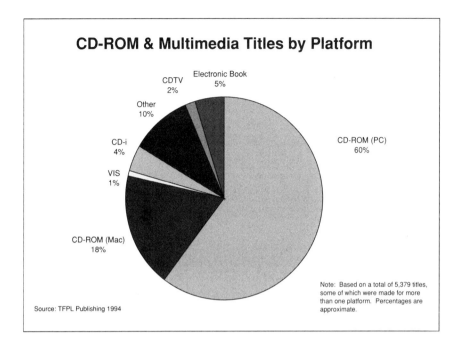

a fraction of the potential market currently enjoying the benefits of the technology. But that too will change, and soon.

Computers and Set-Top Boxes

There are actually a number of different *platforms* for CD technology, the computer being the platform for CD-ROMs. TV-based multimedia game-players connected to television sets originally played only cartridges rather than CDs, but that is changing, and now there are other types of CDs, such as Commodore's CDTV, Philips' CD-i, Tandy's VIS, and Kodak's Photo CD, Video CD, and 3DO. The above figure shows the percentage of titles developed for each platform.

These technologies are related. All are based on the original audio CD specifications, each with different enhancements and alterations. Appendix A briefly explains the evolution of these technologies. It also contains a layman's description of each format.

If it hasn't happened already, expect to see 486-based personal computers with integrated CD-ROM drives selling for less than $1000 in mass-merchandise outlets. CD-ROM drives are now being promoted as standard features on most of Apple Computer's product lines, and multimedia upgrades are selling like hot-cakes on systems not initially configured for multimedia.

In August of 1994, Dataquest projected that 17.5 million CD-ROM drives would ship in that year alone. This would represent a 250-percent growth over 1993, when 6.7 million drives were shipped. For CD-ROM drives shipped prior to 1993, Dataquest reports a total of 3 million drives for all years combined. They predict that in 1996 the percentage of desktop PCs that have CD-ROM drives will reach between 35 and 40 percent, almost double the 19.4 percent reported for 1994.

Then there are the machines dedicated solely to games. In the boom-and-bust game business, manufacturers like Sega Enterprises, Philips, and Panasonic currently feature CD titles that run on proprietary game machines. This trend toward basing game titles on compact disc media will accelerate anew when computer and entertainment giants like Sony introduce their own game lines employing this technology. In fact, Sony has formed a business unit to market a 32-bit CD-ROM-based video game machine in 1995. Reportedly, the system will feature full-motion video, processors for sound and graphics, and technologies to facilitate "3-D" video. It will be a far cry from Game Boy, and it won't be the only system like it on the market.

The Amiga CD32, Commodore's 32-bit game machine that came to market in the spring of 1994, sported an optional MPEG full-motion video cartridge that allowed the machine to play Video CDs, Movie CDs, and Karaoke CDs with up to 74 minutes of video and CD-quality audio on a single disc. When the CD32 was launched in Europe the previous fall, 100,000 units were reportedly sold before Christmas, four times the unit sales of the Sega machine.

Industry watchers at *NewMedia* magazine describe the playing field for game machines as generational. They see Nintendo as the main platform for kids and young teens, and Sega as the platform for high school and college-age consumers. 3DO is winning over some of the teen market while going after the MTV generation. Apparently the Macintosh and PC market is primarily the choice of people over 30.

The video games market was largely responsible for getting new technology (in the form of games machines) into many homes, especially homes with children. And while it is true that CDs can't compare with the speed of the silicon-based cartridges, the CD market has its place. Even Sega has plans for a CD drive plus cartridge in its upcoming Saturn player. Today, it is the growth of multimedia titles, coupled with the technology's benefits for educational and business use, that is propelling the compact disc into all facets of our lives.

Goldstar, Panasonic, and Sanyo 3DO interactive multiplayer systems. (Photo courtesy of The 3DO Company.)

Changing Channels

So if CDs are to become as common as books, where will you buy them? Well, in bookstores, video and music shops, toy stores, specialty stores, and virtually any other place where information and entertainment titles are retailed. Most bookstores already carry at least a handful of CD-ROM titles. Software publishers never had access to the booksellers retail channel, so now they are forming alliances with those who do. Random House, for example, is now distributing Knowledge Adventure's software titles to bookstores.

One of the underlying forces driving the CD revolution is the convenience and flexibility of the technology. A compact disc isn't marketed just as a way to store data anymore. It's a book, it's a game, it's a greeting card. Will you see a rack of cheery multimedia CDs at Hallmark? Perhaps, but most of the reference and educational titles will more likely be sold at bookstores and newsstands, while games will be available at a wider variety of retailers.

In April of 1994, *Investors Business Daily* reported that retailers were only stocking about 10 percent of the available consumer titles. The majority of the rest were available through direct mail catalogs and specialty publishers. But that has begun to change. Until the fourth quarter of 1993, most people did not actively shop for CD-ROM titles. David Trembley, Software Publishers Association's research director, says, "The third quarter of 1993 will likely be remembered as the 'lift-off' point for CD software sales. For the first time, consumers started going out and buying individual CD titles, rather than just acquiring them as part of a package bundled with their new computer or add-on multimedia kit."

Renting CDs

It should come as no surprise that multimedia discs rent well. Need, not novelty, has become the criterion for today's discriminating CD-ROM shopper, who appreciates the opportunity to sample the wares before purchasing them. Furthermore, these rental programs stimulate the marketplace. Reports from both *Gaming* and *Game Pro* magazines show that four out of five people prefer to rent game cartridges and CD-ROMs before making a purchase.

Blockbuster Entertainment Corporation launched a pilot rental program in the San Francisco Bay Area where consumers could rent a multimedia title (CD-ROMs and games, with the required game-player if needed). Titles available for a three-night rental included games and adventure, educational, edutainment, and reference. Early on in the pilot program, Mike van der Kieft, Blockbuster's director of business development and manager of new media markets, reported that educational titles were already mirroring the game model, where consumers were renting titles before deciding to purchase them.

The typical Blockbuster consumer profile is a multimedia publisher's dream: a family with parents in their mid-thirties and a median income of more than $50,000. Furthermore, the percentage of Blockbuster customers who have personal computers at home is twice the national average. The slogan at Blockbuster is, "See it, try it, buy it." They clearly believe in a lucrative future for interactive media, and plan to position themselves as a source for multimedia products.

Data collection for the first Blockbuster trial period ended in June, 1994. When their evaluations are complete, van der Kieft said they plan to reevaluate and fine-tune the program before launching it in other locations. "There are several hundred Blockbuster stores that match the profile for a potentially profitable rollout. It's a question of how aggressive we want to be in going into those other stores." In fact, there might already be a multimedia CD available for rent at a store near you.

Blockbuster is not the only company to see a future for rental CDs. CD-publisher Compton's NewMedia provided twenty compact disc titles to Major

Display kiosks at a Blockbuster retail outlet during their pilot rental program. (Photo courtesy of Blockbuster Entertainment Corporation.)

Video Concepts, the second largest video distributor after Blockbuster, for a joint trial rental venture.

Some are concerned that CD rentals could have a negative impact on publishers' revenues while the rental outlets fill their coffers. For example, if Blockbuster rents a CD-ROM title for approximately $4, they will quickly recover the cost of the disc and begin making a profit. Unless it is damaged, a compact disc is expected to perform to factory specifications for decades. So under typical use CDs could turn a profit through hundreds or even thousands of rental cycles, theoretically depriving the software publisher of sales.

Under these conditions, software piracy also becomes a major concern. The threat of an unlimited number of knock-off CDs is somewhat minimized by the nature of the technology itself, but remains a vexing problem for software product publishers. The concerns of software publishers sound very much like those voiced by movie studios when video rentals began, and as we all know, while video rentals is still a booming business, so too is the theater box office.

Shopping by Mail

Besides retail shops, shopping by mail is a significant factor in CD market penetration. Software catalogs on CD-ROM represent significant competition to computer superstores and mail-order companies. For example, programs on a disc containing several, or several hundred, commercial software packages can be sampled, then selectively decrypted with a purchased password. Potential buyers can kick the tires, then buy only what they need from the disc.

Despite the still relatively limited channels for distribution, the potential sales of a hit compact disc title are already up from about 20,000 units in 1992 to approximately 200,000 units, a tenfold increase in just two years. *Myst*, with reported sales of 500,000 units, is considered a megahit. This explosion in potential sales revenues is due, in part, to growing consumer awareness and interest, as well as the decreasing costs of hardware and software. Altogether, these factors continue to fuel the growth of the installed base.

Around the World

The Information Revolution is not only a United States phenomenon. International developers are placing multilingual information kiosks in airports, train stations, subways, shopping arcades, and other high-profile locations. In fact, an article in *NewMedia* magazine cites a report by TFPL Publishing of London which said that 1,343 companies in Europe were working on CD-ROM titles in 1993, compared to only 1,166 in the United States during that same time period.

Many of these projects involve national government sponsorship, while others are the brainchildren of telecommunications companies, banks, travel agencies, and catalog shopping services. Some of these efforts, like the networked CD-ROM transaction applications installed by Interactive Transaction Partners in France, involve alliances with American corporations.

Furthermore, Europe's cultural history makes the continent a rich source of historical content. Title developers both here and abroad seek out usage rights to the artworks in museums and private collections. You can already buy such CD-ROM titles as Microsoft's *Art Gallery: The Collection of the National Gallery, London*. In short, in addition to being an excellent source of material, the overseas market for home and business CD drives and titles is enormous.

The market in China, on the other hand, is barely tepid. Optical Data Corporation executives and researchers told *CD-ROM World* magazine that they expect the installed base to grow rapidly, but so far it's hardly noticeable. But with such a large population, you can bet that China will become a very hot market. It's just a matter of time.

Nothing Is Perfect

With all these technological benefits and a growing worldwide market, compact discs are hardly the perfect medium. CD-ROMs transfer data relatively slowly from disc to computer monitor. CD-i (compact disc-interactive) is faster, but when publishers start experimenting with multimedia performance "solutions" (that means software), all CD platforms can suffer from compatibility problems, and currently the discs are limited to *only* 650MB of storage capacity.

On the other hand, compact discs are a powerful medium. They enable artists to create virtual worlds, educators to lead multimedia excursions into history, journalists to research every topic under the sun, designers to produce luminous, three-dimensional effects, and the general public to enjoy an absorbing game or other entertainment. CDs also provide convenient, relatively inexpensive access to the most interesting lanes of the celebrated but still mythical information superhighway—that as-yet undefined means of quickly exchanging massive amounts of information among a multitude of people.

In *1984*, George Orwell predicted a world in which memory would be eradicated. Instead, memory has become enormous, and everything can be recorded for future generations. The compact disc is only one of many useful, new technologies to come down the pike. But as a tool of the Information Revolution, it facilitates access to the collective memory of our species and enhances our lives in many wonderful, subtle ways. Put simply, it changes everything.

Chapter 2

CD-ROMs
in the Schools

CD-ROMs and interactive multimedia figure prominently in the revolution called educational reform—more commonly referred to in educational circles as "restructuring." The technology is providing electronic tools that make it possible to restructure the classroom and teaching techniques, reach more students with individualized instruction, and foster active learning.

In this chapter I talk not only about educational CD-ROM products, but also a bit about philosophies and attitudes concerning the use of computer technology in schools. I also talk briefly about topics such as student motivation, the role of teachers, and the difficulties of implementing this new type of learning in the classroom. In the next chapter I'll discuss different types of CD titles, preschool through post-graduate, and describe a few examples. You'll hear the opinions of experts and be privy to interesting statistics compiled by industry analysts.

A Little History

In 1985, CD-ROMs were being touted as the newest way to solve the problem of storing massive amounts of textual data. By the following year, CD-ROMs had entered the educational market in a big way, with the release of more than 50 database and reference resources, including *The New Grolier Electronic Encyclopedia.*

In early 1989, *Grolier* was still among the educational titles being touted in education-related magazines. Other titles mentioned at that time included the *Oxford English Dictionary* from Tri-Star Publishing, and a program called Science Helper K-8 that offered close to 1,000 lesson plans.

As CD-ROM technology continued to evolve, and as the information age took hold, educational technologists began to describe ideal students as "knowledge navigators," and software developers began to deliver increasingly rich learning environments.

Teachers have long augmented text books with recordings, photos, films, and videos. In the early days of educational technology, "multimedia" meant supplementing text book material with film strips or slide shows, usually with live narration read in the dark by a frustrated teacher. The first software programs were only available on floppy disks and were incapable of holding the large files that multimedia requires. In fact, most of the early programs were drill-and-practice exercises. They were little more than automated worksheets and were used too often as electronic baby-sitters.

When CD-ROM technology made it possible to store hundreds of megabytes of digital data on a single affordable disc, some developers saw the light. Drill-and-practice programs, less affectionately known as "drill-and-kill" programs, began to give way to robust multimedia databases and interactive environments for exploration. Unfortunately, quite a few drill-and-practice programs are still out there.

Greater storage capacity not only made room for more content, but also for new software innovations. One such innovator was Knowledge Adventure, a company that developed innovative compression techniques for its early multimedia programs on floppy disks. Examples of Knowledge Adventure's software innovations include its Virtual Object Control technology. With this technology, users can rotate an object and zoom in on it as part of a dynamic learning experience. Knowledge Adventure has also developed proprietary 3-D software for creating true stereo 3-D still images and movies, including full-screen movies, on a standard PC equipped with a VGA monitor and a CD-ROM or hard drive.

Of course, the evolution of educational software was not caused by technology alone. It is interesting to note that, as educational technology products evolved, learners began to assume more control, moving from rote drills, to following predetermined instructional paths, to analysis. And the evolution continues.

Many educators believe that children learn best when they are involved in activities that both encourage them and allow them to discover new information. Once a teacher has created a context in which learning can occur (it could be a small group research assignment, for example), he or she can then point students to the right resources (compact disc titles, books, people) and encourage them to strike out on their own.

To this way of thinking, it is better, for example, to teach children to *be scientists* than to teach them *about science* by presenting scientific facts. Instead of presenting facts and theories and expecting kids to internalize them at an abstract level, encouraging students to engage themselves in activities and providing them the tools for exploration is thought to be more conducive to learning. The content of many interactive multimedia titles is based on just such a premise.

Multimedia is no longer simply a delivery method. As a medium, it has the ability to communicate and bring into being new contexts for learning. In a journal article titled "Multimedia: The Essential Elements," Allan Kaprow suggests that educational multimedia ought to include, "a robust database in different forms, a consistent but rich interface owning full human-computer interactivity, a multilayered and dynamic navigational system that permits freedom to explore but not get lost, and a well-thought-out presentation of what is available to the user." This is more than a notion, as you'll see later in this book when I talk about what's involved in creating a CD title.

That's the rosy picture, and it really only describes one stream of thought in education, a stream of thought that some consider the minority view. The "back to basics" approach, and the belief in programmed instruction, still have many followers in the schools. The innovators are making a lot of noise and garnering attention, but the majority may still be using Apple IIs and teaching only keyboarding skills.

Basic Math

Today's educational software market is a lucrative one. Market Vision, a multimedia market research publisher in Santa Cruz, California, says that between 1993 and 1994 multimedia revenues, with an emphasis on educational multimedia applications, increased by about 40 percent, jumping from $485 million to $676 million. Market Vision president Robert Aston projects that revenues in the educational multimedia market will reach $1.37 billion in 1997.

John Kernan, CEO of Jostens Learning Corporation, speaks of far larger figures, starting with $4.2 billion in 1993. These figures are higher because they include ILS and text-based products that are not considered part of the multimedia market. Charlie Finnie, a representative of Volpe, Welty & Company, a San Francisco-based market analysis firm, says that over 15,000 elementary and secondary schools in the U.S. collectively spent over $4 billion on computer-based learning materials in 1993.

It's an industry where all types of alliances are made, and joint ventures have become the norm. For example, movie director Steven Spielberg has an equity stake in Knowledge Adventure and will be working with the company to develop educational multimedia products. And Knowledge Adventure also has an alliance with Random House to create, produce, and market multimedia titles, including the *Random House Kid's Encyclopedia*.

Microsoft has joined with Scholastic Corporation to create CD-ROMs based on Scholastic books, such as its *Magic School Bus* series. Davidson and Associates has an agreement with Simon & Schuster whereby Davidson will develop curriculum-based software, and Simon & Schuster will contribute financing and handle distribution to the educational marketplace. And that's just the tip of the iceberg—it doesn't take into account the affiliate-label programs and licensing deals.

According to Quality Education Data (QED), the growth in the use of CD-ROMs for instruction has been dramatic. In the 1988–89 school year, only three percent of districts used CD-ROMs. By the 1993–94 school year, this figure increased to 43 percent, a growth of more than 1,500 percent. The most dramatic part of this increase, however, occurred in just one year when usage jumped from 19 percent of school districts in the 1992–93 school year to 43 percent the following year, far outstripping the penetration of videodisc players.

The 43 percent of school districts that used CD-ROMs in 1992–93, represents 67 percent of all public schools and nearly three-fourths (72 percent) of all public school students. Viewed from another perspective, 23 percent of U.S. public elementary schools used CD-ROMs during the scholastic year 1993–94, as did 36 percent of middle and junior high schools, and 46 percent of senior high schools.

QED cited several reasons for this growth, including the dropping price of multimedia-capable computers (computers that not coincidentally come with bundled software, including one or more CD-ROMs), an increase in software availability, ease of use, and the proliferation of audio CDs, which made consumers less afraid of CD-ROMs.

QED research also shows that multimedia technologies are used to enhance four primary types of learning:

- **Active learning,** where students take personal responsibility for how and what they learn
- **Cooperative learning,** where students work in interactive groups
- **Interdisciplinary learning,** also referred to as cross-curriculum instruction, where subjects that were traditionally kept separate, such as history and science, are integrated
- **Individualized learning,** where instruction is customized to the needs and learning styles of individual students

In the beginning, multimedia software consisted primarily of reference titles, such as electronic encyclopedias, so most school CD-ROM drives were placed in the library beside the other reference materials. Sometimes CD-ROMs were placed in the computer lab in schools with more equipment and a technology specialist on hand. The April, 1994, issue of *Multimedia Monitor* analyzed more of the details provided in the QED report. *Multimedia Monitor* reported that "on average, 50 percent of a school's CD-ROM drives are still located in a library. Twenty-five percent are situated in classrooms; 20 percent in computer labs; and 5 percent elsewhere in the school."

Multimedia Monitor also reported that, while 86 percent of school districts with CD-ROMs use CD-ROM-based reference titles, content has expanded into other areas of the curriculum. For example, 68 percent of the districts used CD-ROMs to study science, 65 percent used them in social studies, and 47 percent used them for language arts. These categories and others are shown in the bar chart on the next page.

Issues and Arguments

These statistics may prove to be deceptive. Yes, it's true that the percentage of schools that use CD-ROM drives continues to increase at a rapid rate. And yes, it's true that more and more educational titles are not only flooding the market, but being purchased. However, the history of technology in education—in the early 1900s with film, the 1920s with radio, and the 1950s with television—

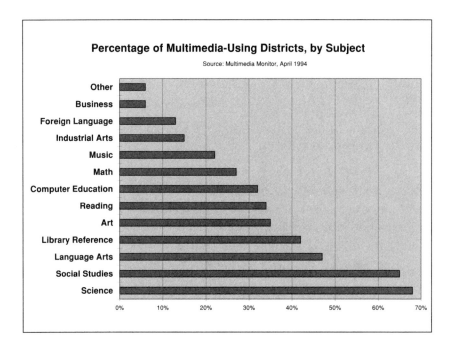

Percentage of Multimedia-Using Districts, by Subject

Source: Multimedia Monitor, April 1994

repeatedly shows that, lack of accessibility notwithstanding, increased access does not automatically lead to increased usage. Statistics from school districts and schools may or may not accurately reflect what is going on inside the classroom.

It's Greek to Me

There are still plenty of teachers who, excited by the possibilities, are also overwhelmed by the prospect of integrating a new technology. Some feel threatened by computers. With access to so much information, it is now possible for students to know more than their teachers. In an April, 1994, *Multimedia World* article titled "Classroom Education + Interactive Multimedia = Formula for Revolution," Dr. Peter Kneedler, a consultant with California's Educational Technology Office, says, "Teachers have to adopt the attitude that it's okay for students to know more than they do."

Time and ease of use are also major factors in determining whether computer technology gets used in the classroom. After the routines required for basic classroom maintenance, little if any time is left for developing alternative

MS. BROWN'S 4TH GRADE
SCHOOL SUPPLIES LIST
• #2 PENCILS   • 486 PC (OR BETTER)
• BALLPOINT PENS   • WRIST REST
• 3-RING BINDER   • WORD PROCESSOR
• LINED PAPER   • 10 3½ INCH FLOPPIES
• RULER   • CD-ROM DRIVE

© 1994 John Grimes

instructional materials. Other practicality issues include how difficult it is to set up the hardware, whether or not the hardware is easily accessible, and whether "canned materials" can be integrated into prescribed lesson plans.

Despite the obstacles, however, there is evidence that kids are using CD-ROMs in school. Jostens Learning Corporation was able to overcome teacher resistance by providing curriculum-based applications that were part of a *turnkey* system. A turnkey system is one that includes software, hardware, lots of support and training options, and is ready to use when it arrives. Today Jostens is the biggest player in the school arena. Another inroad to the schools is through the homes, which I discuss in the next chapter.

But if there's so much resistance, what's all the fuss about?

The Benefits of CD-ROMs in the Classroom

Skeptics believe in the old fashioned way, the "no pain, no gain" philosophy. So what if it takes hours and hours to pour through dozens of books to find the data you need? Advocates talk about interest, impact, interactivity. In a letter to the editor in the April, 1994, issue of *NewMedia* magazine, a middle school teacher wrote, "Multimedia has become a tool by which research has become fun where it was drudgery. I wish [you] could see the delight in the middle school students when they are able to access information using the CD-ROM format....The multimedia format has given students a new lease on the learning process."

Should educators have to compete with MTV? When it's put that way, it's easy to take sides. Either you demand discipline and don't give in, or you fight fire with fire. But when you consider it in terms of motivation, it becomes a less volatile issue. Kathleen Wilson is one of many experts who not only believe that motivation is a crucial aspect of teaching and learning, but who are also comfortable and confident with the idea of multimedia as a motivating force. Back in June of 1989, during Wilson's tenure as multimedia director at the Bank Street Center for Children and Technology, *Electronic Learning* magazine quoted her as follows: "One of the major difficulties teachers face is motivating their students. And that's the first thing that must be done if learning is to occur. Unquestionably, multimedia motivates kids, even the learner-phobic."

Multimedia is also touted for its emotional impact and realism. Multimedia can connect students with people, places, and events beyond their small communities, and bring world events directly into the classroom. Just as in the boardroom, visual presentations in the classroom bring events to life and have the capability to evoke emotional responses. Providing multiple viewpoints and interpretations, another area that multimedia is good at, is also vital to proper education.

Emerging Technology's Richard Pollak believes that, to change education as it exists today, emphasis must be placed on manipulating information as opposed to simply accessing information. In other words, emphasis must be placed on "interactivity."

Interactivity can be defined in more than one way. When a student using a disc-based program moves from screen to screen with the click of a mouse, some say that's interactive. Others say that clicking a mouse is no more interactive than turning the pages of a book. For many, interactivity is a relative term, to be assessed by the level or amount of control the user has over the program. Of course, some people say that unless a student is creating something, the learning experience is not truly interactive.

Hypermedia also has something to do with interactivity, and you may hear the term from time to time. *Hypermedia* describes interactive multimedia programs where various thoughts, themes, facts, etc. are connected to one another by programmed links. When the student clicks on a word and a dictionary definition or picture appears, for example, the word is said to be "linked" to the definition or picture. It's a matter of association, and people think by association, not linearly. For this reason, some theorize that hypermedia applications are good for teaching because they contain modularized content connected by links, and as such they mirror our thought processes.

When information is easy to access, and presented in an interactive form, students' attention to learning tasks increases, promoting better comprehension and increased retention. Of course, multimedia and interactivity don't automatically create an educational experience, just as product availability does not guarantee usage.

A New Role for Teachers

In an article written for a publication called *Technology and Learning,* D. Kinnaman wrote about the potential for change in American education. He pointed out that technology can be used to perpetuate and entrench "the traditional approach" or to "embrace reform." Technology itself provides only potential, and there are myriad ways to integrate technology so that it becomes a new tool for both teaching and learning. Integrating technology in the classroom will require a major effort on the part of teachers.

When the teacher's role changes from that of expert or primary knowledge source to that of facilitator or knowledge guide, students will discover information beyond the teacher's own areas of expertise. Unfortunately, some teachers, fearing the loss of personal contact or the loss of classroom control, may resist the role change. Many teachers will wish for the old days when they were more involved in every moment of their students' growth and enlightenment and they had complete control over the classroom.

Many teachers fear being replaced by technology, but multimedia packages cannot replace teachers. The teacher's expertise is required to incorporate these new tools into the learning process, and to motivate and guide students as they explore and search for knowledge. Teachers must concern themselves with covering the requisite content, breadth as well as depth, to ensure that students get the big picture. Teachers are the ones who translate global objectives into classroom specifics.

While controversy among educators concerning the strengths and weaknesses of multimedia persists, students and teachers all across the country are using CDs. Teachers use the medium as a teaching aid or tool, citing the virtues of random access to make class presentations easy. Multimedia systems can provide information, instruction, and simulations, adding realism and depth that spark class discussion. Class presentations can be created by both teachers and students alike.

When the preference is for showing rather than telling, content from CD titles can be used to illustrate lectures, accompany oral reports, supplement laboratory work, and provide an environment for small group or whole class exploration. You don't have to provide a computer for every student. The available content of CDs is diverse, with many different viewpoints and inter-

A presentation cart can make it easy for teachers to work with small groups or the whole class. (Photo © Jostens Learning Corporation.)

pretations, enabling students to use these discs as a resource for research and problem solving.

Integrating Technology and the Curriculum

More and more multimedia programs for a variety of curricular areas are reaching the marketplace at an ever increasing pace. However, understanding the best ways to use multimedia technology in educational settings is proceeding at a much slower pace.

The mission statement of the Center for Children and Technology sets forth the premise that technology can only enhance classroom education if it is well-integrated with both the curriculum and with the processes of learning and instruction.

The Lester B. Pearson Senior High School in Calgary was designed with technology in mind. When it opened in 1991, it was Calgary's first new school building in 20 years. The prime directive of this high school was the complete integration of learning and technology. Computers were not to be isolated in computer labs and libraries. Every single classroom has at least one computer, and all computers are connected to a school network, which includes eight file servers and a 20-unit CD-ROM "stack" in the library. This is Pearson High's "information everywhere" approach. For example, a student can access a CD-ROM encyclopedia from anywhere in the school.

Networking a classroom, let alone a whole school, is no mean feat, and while I did not get to talk directly to the folks in Calgary who designed the Pearson High network, I did talk to some networking experts at Reed Technology and Information Services, the company formerly known as Online Computer Systems, and profiled in the January, 1994, issue of *CD-ROM World*. RTIS is a leading developer and provider of CD-ROM, networking, and electronic publishing products and services.

Schools can turn to companies such as RTIS to set up their CD-ROM networking systems. Besides providing hardware (CD-ROM storage units, towers, and jukeboxes) and Opti-Net, its own networking software, RTIS can help schools build a CD-ROM library. Because RTIS is also a software distributor, it carries a number of educational and reference CD-ROM titles that can be installed on a school network. Schools can, of course, add CD-ROM titles from other publishers to the network as well.

Among the reference titles available from RTIS for networking are: the *New Grolier Multimedia Encyclopedia, Microsoft Encarta Multimedia Encyclopedia, Time Almanac Reference Edition*, the *1994 Guinness Multimedia Disc of Records*, the *Multimedia Encyclopedia of Science & Technology, Microsoft Dinosaurs, Heinemann's Children's Multimedia Encyclopedia,* and *PC Globe Maps 'N' Facts*. RTIS also markets network licenses for a variety of edutainment titles, including *Forces & Motion, Leonardo: The Inventor,* the Brøderbund Living Books School Edition Series, and *Where in the World/USA is Carmen Sandiego?* Deluxe School editions.

This 20-unit CD-ROM "stack" is the hub of this high school's computer network. (Photo courtesy of Lester B. Pearson Senior High School in Calgary, Aberta, Canada.)

Can Technology Serve Education?

Technological advancement brings with it the opportunity to approach tasks in new ways, but there is no guarantee that the opportunities will be seized. Nor is there any guarantee that seized opportunities will produce beneficial results.

By some accounts, the new technology is being used to support old ways of teaching—an approach that might make technology more acceptable to teachers, but might not be the best use of the technology. By fitting new technologies into the strategies that teachers use now, teachers' concerns can be addressed, especially concerns that have to do with practicality and how to integrate technology into existing teaching methods. On the other hand, using the new technology to support old ways of teaching may do a disservice to education because innovative uses of the technology and benefits particular to the medium alone may never be revealed, understood, or discovered.

The claim that compact disc technology can help students learn more effectively is not only simplistic, but disputed by some researchers in the field of education. Unquestionably, however, it can provide vast amounts of information that can be searched, perused, and retrieved—but is that education?

The ivory tower jury is still out. It is not yet known what effects the interactive multimedia experience will have on students or the learning process. Neither researchers nor developers have reached a consensus as to the proper context for multimedia use. The attributes of a good multimedia teaching application have yet to be defined. Until a real understanding is reached, the value and use of technology for education will remain in question.

But how do you measure the value of technology in the classroom? If one class of students uses educational resources on compact disc and its standardized test scores are not significantly better than those of students in a class without access to compact discs, does that mean that the electronic resources are no good? I think not—unless, of course, you define the purpose of education as the means for improving test scores.

The point is to define what you want to accomplish and then look at the available materials and see if they work. Compact disc titles are no different from any other resource in that some are great, and some are not so great.

Joyce Sunila, a syndicated columnist and mother, wrote an article for the *Los Angeles Times* on this subject. In it she asks, "What's the purpose of education, anyway? Isn't the higher goal to fashion people capable of creative discerning thought?" That's a purpose I can support, and I've seen many multimedia programs that can help teachers and students work toward that goal.

Whether or not technology can bring about a revolution in teaching is the subject of much debate, especially now, when we are questioning the effectiveness of our educational system. Educational technology has not yet significantly influenced curricula or altered the quality of education in our society. But that doesn't mean that it can't.

As the debate rages on, and whether or not researchers can prove that learning is better with computers, the potential of the technology can't help but influence, if not reshape, our attitudes about the meaning of teaching and learning.

Chapter 3

More CD-ROMs
in the Schools

Before I talk about different types of educational CD-ROM products and describe several specific examples, it should be noted that some educators are concerned about the content of educational CDs. Their concerns are not about whether or how to teach religion, or other such issues of political correctness. Rather, they worry that the designers of the products are neither in touch with the realities of the classroom nor skilled in the art of teaching.

These types of concerns were more prevalent in the early days of CD-ROMs when titles were flashy prototypes with big production budgets. Those discs were designed to sell technology under the guise of education. Today, most if not all educational compact discs are designed with the help of educators, curriculum specialists, and even classroom teachers, who work on the design team and/or in the role of evaluator. However, that does not mean that there is no cause for concern, or that you don't have to evaluate packages carefully before you use them.

Let's get back to some product examples. First, I'll mention some titles originally geared to home consumers that are finding their way into the schools.

(In Chapter 7, I'll cover more children's products in the home market.) Then I'll talk about turnkey solutions such as the Integrated Learning Systems provided by Jostens.

The last three categories discussed in this chapter tend to overlap quite a bit. Titles that fall under the "interactive learning environments" category are frequently based on reference materials, and products targeting a particular topic are frequently used for reference as well.

Education or Edutainment?

Whether or not a software product matches adopted state and/or district curricula, many claim to be educational. Some titles are found predominantly in the schools, but many home-market titles found their way to the classroom as well. These titles include stories and games such as *Just Grandma and Me* from Brøderbund's Living Books series, Shelly Duvall's *It's a Bird's Life* (from Sanctuary Woods Multimedia Corp.), and Brøderbund's renowned *Where in the World Is Carmen Sandiego?*

Titles originally intended for the home market can be used as auxiliary classroom resources in a number of different ways. Many of the magazines devoted to educational technology and teaching feature articles with ideas for using various products. One educator who frequently writes such articles is Dr. Carol S. Holzberg. With regard to Microsoft's *Dinosaurs*, she suggests a writing activity where students select their favorite dinosaur, use the product's atlas to learn about where it lived, and copy pictures into a word-processing program to illustrate their reports. Other ideas include using art and music titles such as Microsoft's *Art Gallery* or *Musical Instruments* to augment history, geography, and social studies lessons.

As noted earlier, getting schools to use technology is not always easy. However, publishers such as EA*Kids and Knowledge Adventure are adding more and more schools to their customer bases. These are just two of the many publishers who are not only selling their products to schools but also augmenting their products with special teacher editions containing lesson plans and activities created by experienced curriculum developers. In other words, these companies are showing teachers how to tie in their products with different educational objectives.

Electronic Arts is committed to supporting education in schools as well as in the home. Senior Vice President Stewart J. Bonn acknowledges that software

Scene from *Just Grandma and Me*, one of the popular titles from Brøderbund's Living Books series. (Screen shot courtesy of Brøderbund.)

will never replace formal classroom activities. He believes that software can go a long way toward personalizing the education process, and can be used as an adjunct to traditional teaching methods, especially during the preschool through elementary school years. Greg Bestick, EA*Kids' general manager, explains, "We primarily target the home, that's our main channel. But because our products are solid in content, and educators feel good about them and the skills that they convey, they can also be used in the schools. EA*Kids products are 100-percent learning and 100-percent fun."

Distributors such as Club Kidsoft are also having success with the schools, perhaps because they not only provide one-stop shopping for products created by various publishers, but also because they provide lots of customer support. While this may sound like a sales pitch, one-stop shopping and customer support are truly important factors for the advancement of the CD-ROM revolution.

Other publishers and distributors offer other kinds of services, packages, and support, and that brings us back to Jostens.

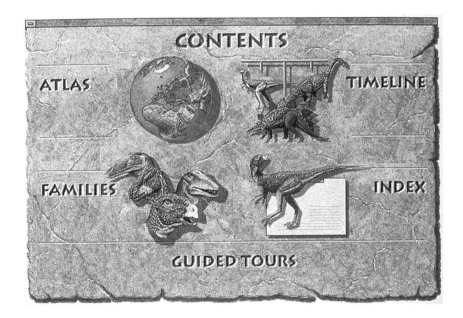

Main contents screen from Microsoft Home's *Dinosaurs*. (Screen shot courtesy of Microsoft.)

Integrated Learning Systems

Integrated Learning Systems (ILSs) are used to provide individualized instruction in math, reading, language arts, and other subjects to millions of students in thousands of schools across the United States and around the world. No longer of the dreaded drill-and-kill variety that was prevalent in the old days, ILSs are designed so that teachers can direct developmentally appropriate, well-coordinated, individualized instruction to each student. Teachers can also tailor ILSs to match the content of major textbooks as well as meet district and state objectives.

How is this done? First, the content is designed to meet adopted curriculum standards, and while these standards are different from state to state, there are many commonalities. Then, the key here is ongoing individual student assessment. You may have heard the terms computer-based training (CBT), computer-managed instruction (CMI), and interactive instruction. These terms describe educational systems where the computer handles one or more of the following tasks:

Students at work in a classroom with an Integrated Learning System network. (Photo courtesy of Jostens Learning Corporation.)

⊙ Introducing the material to be learned

⊙ Presenting practice activities or questions, and providing the appropriate feedback and tutorial material

⊙ Assessing and summarizing student responses to the material (sometimes this is a formal quiz or test administered on the computer)

⊙ Diagnosing the areas that the student needs more work in

⊙ Proscribing the necessary learning units, and controlling the program flow accordingly

⊙ Maintaining student record keeping

CBT, CBI, and interactive instruction systems usually include supplementary materials (worksheets, guides, activity directions, etc.) for both students and teachers.

A study commissioned by Jostens Learning Corporation in 1993 showed that more than half of Integrated Learning Systems were used in school com-

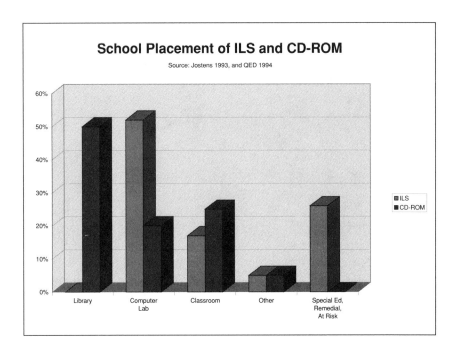

School Placement of ILS and CD-ROM

Source: Jostens 1993, and QED 1994

puter labs, and less than one-fifth were found in classrooms. The results of the Jostens study, charted above, show a much different pattern of usage than QED's report cited in Chapter 2.

The Jostens study also showed that educators cited five main benefits to using ILSs. Being able to provide individualized learning was the number-one benefit, cited by 68 percent of the respondents. Motivation was in second place, with 38 percent. Management reports were cited by 26 percent of the respondents. The ability to stimulate creativity and provide immediate feedback receiving only 20 percent and 19 percent, respectively.

The Jostens Learning product line includes a series of CD-ROM–based interactive curriculum programs for preschool through high school, research and reference products such as *Compton's Interactive Encyclopedia* and *First Connections: Golden Book Encyclopedia*, as well as student management, testing, and assessment tools.

Jostens' Teacher First product, introduced in 1994, is a presentation station—a large-screen monitor and computer mounted on a movable cart—

Scene from Jostens' *Teacher First Mathematics* program. (Screen shot courtesy of Jostens Learning Corporation.)

with special courseware designed to help teachers introduce and demonstrate instructional concepts to the entire class or small groups. The first courseware package Jostens offered, called *Teacher First Mathematics*, covers the basic concepts for each level of math study, as recommended by the National Council of Teachers of Mathematics (NCTM), and is available for kindergarten through sixth grade. Courseware for reading and language arts will be ready for the 1995 school year.

According to Rick King, Jostens' senior vice president of product development, the next generation of ILSs is likely to incorporate the use of tools for instruction. For example, students might learn how to do a research paper by using project management software (the tool), or how to organize a paper by using an outlining tool. Future ILS programs are also likely to include more opportunities for interactive student exploration.

Jostens is also looking at what is sometimes referred to as *modular markets*, or what King describes as "people looking for good instruction, not entertainment, but only in chunks." Toward that end, Jostens may take portions of its current ILS products, add a management system with only the basic features (no extra bells and whistles), and make it available to the modular marketplace.

Sharon Sanford, vice president of product development for Market Data Research (MDR), reports that, according to an MDR study, "Jostens Learning continues to be the dominant vendor of ILS products, with 53 percent of the market. The next closest competitors are Computer Curriculum Corporation with a 17 percent market share, and IBM's Writing to Read product, with 16 percent of the market."

With programs in more than 10,000 schools reaching more than four million students nationwide, Jostens earned revenues of $177 million in fiscal year 1994, making it one of the nation's largest software development companies, and the largest educational software developer in the U.S.

Interactive Learning Environments on CD-ROM

Guidelines proposed by the International Society for Technology in Education (ISTE) and approved by the National Council for Accreditation of Teacher Education cautioned that to "achieve the benefits technology makes possible, we must restructure our schools in dramatic ways," ways that will encourage students to become "active learners" instead of passive listeners.

Digital information can also be used to construct virtual realities, or "mirror worlds," as David Gelernter, a computer scientist at Yale University, calls them in his book of the same name. Walkthroughs, fly-bys, simulations (not just physical, but sociological as well), and online chemistry experiments with simulated explosions all provide new perspectives that encourage insights into our world.

Bill Gross, chairman and founder of Knowledge Adventure, advocates "learning by wandering. And wondering." A promotional brochure says that Knowledge Adventure was created "to encourage kids' instinctive curiosity about the world." The company's goal is to help kids learn "not by instruction or rote or by contests of skill, but by letting them chart their own course of discovery."

An interactive learning environment is one in which kids can become immersed and achieve a feeling of being inside or along for the ride. An interactive learning environment might also provide access to general learning tools, such as reference materials or an online notepad or word processor. It might also provide access to subject-specific tools, such as an online chemistry set (so kids could mix their own virtual vinegar and baking soda and see what happens), or a dissecting kit (so that kids could dissect a virtual frog).

Knowledge Adventure products were originally intended for the home market, but school versions are becoming popular too. Following is a description of three out of the many Knowledge Adventure titles that offer interactive movies, computer animated simulations, and extended learning modules, and that fit easily into school curricula.

The Discoverers is an interactive multimedia CD-ROM adaptation of the IMAX movie and Daniel Boorstin's best-selling book. Using the film, computer simulations, game modules, and the extended learning module, kids focus on explorers of the past and present as they learn about some of the greatest discoveries ever made.

Undersea Learning Adventure is an exploration of the undersea world and its inhabitants. It includes a reference section for older children, a series of games, a virtual reality aquarium that tests learning, and a talking storybook with tales of undersea life for those just learning to read.

3-D Body Adventure has full-screen 3-D movies that allow kids to "fly" through key organs and all around the skeleton. It includes a comprehensive reference section, and a game called the Emergency Room Game that lets kids test their knowledge of diseases and their causes as they race to save a patient.

Personally, I found this last program a little lacking in the educational department. I thoroughly enjoyed roaming around inside the 3-D organs, and looking at the organs through the 3-D glasses was terrific. But as I flew by, in, and around organs, and the sound track rattled off the names of body parts, I was unable to make any connection between what I was seeing and what I was hearing. In other words, I had fun but still don't know which part is which. And this is exactly why we need live teachers to provide contexts in which our children can make learning meaningful.

IBM's Eduquest division also believes in the value of educational interactive multimedia environments. *Illuminated Books and Manuscripts*, geared directly for the school market, is an interactive multimedia database with over 180 hours of educational resources based on the text of major literary works from five different genres (poetry, plays, letters, declarations, and oral histories).

There are no programmed lessons or tests, but through its interface design, the database fosters critical reading, thinking, and synthesizing—crucial

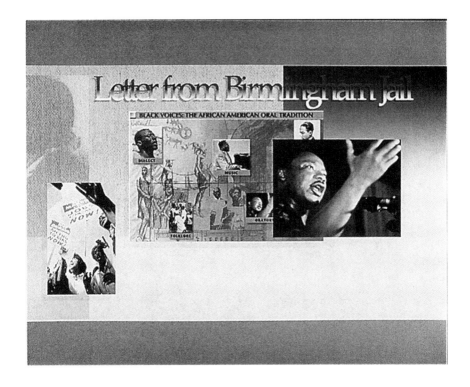

"Letter from Birmingham Jail" is one of five literary works explored in *Illuminated Books and Manuscripts*, an educational interactive program from IBM Eduquest. (Screen shot courtesy of IBM Eduquest.)

learning skills. Students can explore not only the words and methods used to create each work, but also the works' universal themes and cultural topics, as they delve into history, philosophy, and the arts. While this program is a little more educationally explicit than *3-D Body Adventure*, students using it could also benefit from the guidance of a teacher.

Several other compact disc publishers, many of whom do not specifically target children, produce educational products that could be called interactive learning environments.

Who Built America? is a disc from The Voyager Company based on a book by the same name. It covers four decades of American history, from the first centennial in 1876 to the beginning of World War I. Original source materials, hundreds of photos, archival recordings, charts, and QuickTime movies, are used to present topics such as the labor movement, the Wild West, and American imperialism.

National Geographic publishes *The Presidents: A Picture History of Our Nation*. (When this disc was first released, its title was *The Presidents: It All Started with George*.) This program uses an interactive time-line, marked in four-year segments, that corresponds to terms in office. Kids can view photo albums and video footage of each presidency as they investigate cultural, historical, scientific, artistic, musical, and literary achievements.

By virtue of its title, the *3D Atlas* from Electronic Arts should be in the next section about reference titles. However, features such as one that enables students to explore the world as they simulate flying over various geographic areas makes this CD more than a reference. Greg Bestick, general manager of EA*Kids (the edutainment division of Electronic Arts), says, "The flyovers help students visualize and put learning in context. That's what *3D Atlas* is all about: exploring diverse kinds of information in meaningful, multidisciplinary contexts."

Reference Titles

CD-ROMs don't wear out, but the data can become obsolete. That's not so bad, however, because CDs are affordable, and schools can buy updates for CD-ROM-based encyclopedias, atlases, and almanacs without having to replace entire shelves of expensive hardbound volumes. Some of the more popular titles in the reference category are described here.

Compton's Interactive Encyclopedia has the ability to play both small-screen and full-screen video. U.S. and world time-lines put events into perspective, and a click of the mouse takes you to associated articles. Other navigational and search tools include the Atlas, Idea Search, and Topic Tree.

Reviewers have decried the lack of aesthetics in *The 1995 Grolier Multimedia Encyclopedia* (some even said it was ugly!). However, they applauded the quality of its content. And while the solid, well-written articles may lack glamour, Grolier has added some new multimedia features such as Knowledge Explorer and Multimedia Maps that play narrated audio/visual presentations, each lasting several minutes.

Encarta from Microsoft is based on the *Funk & Wagnalls Encyclopedia*. With narration geared to a student audience (upper-elementary grades through

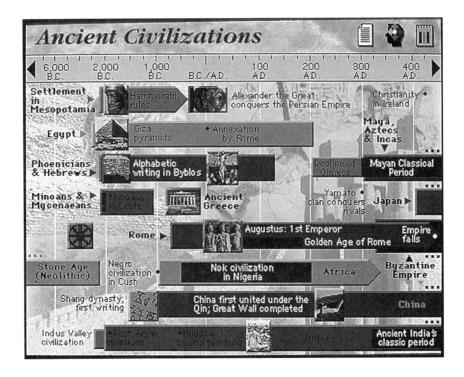

Detail of the timeline available in *The 1995 Grolier Multimedia Encyclopedia.* (Screen shot © 1995 Grolier Incorporated. All rights reserved.)

high school), this program offers outstanding graphics, animation, and video that are well-integrated with the text. The Wizard can assist with online navigation, and package materials include tips on conducting research.

Picture Atlas of the World from the National Geographic Society uses photographs, video, and indigenous music as part of a world tour. The CD includes information on population and climate, as well as discussions about economics and culture.

Time Almanac Reference Edition is a complete encyclopedia of current events and news. It includes the full text of every *Time* magazine from 1989 through January 3, 1994 and is illustrated with CNN video news clips and other photos, maps, and charts. There are personality profiles of people such as Albert Einstein and Adolf Hitler. It also has information on the U.S. Government, the economy, and environmental topics, plus data and maps covering more than

Some of the tools that allow you to search for people and places in Microsoft Home's *Encarta*. (Screen shot courtesy of Microsoft Corporation.)

200 countries. Almanac also features "NewsQuest," a quiz that challenges the user's knowledge of the news.

The 20th Century Video Almanac: Best of the Century, from The Software Toolworks, contains 100 full-motion video clips and over 2,000 articles covering major events and highlights of this century. It has four navigational tools: Timeline allows you to search for events by date; On This Day reads your computer's clock and searches for events that occurred on that same day in the past; Where in the World sorts materials by country; and The Library lets users browse through topics such as Politics, People, and Sports.

In addition to general information encyclopedias and almanacs, there are a number of specialized references such as *Mammals: A Multimedia Encyclopedia* from National Geographic Society, and the text-intensive *Books in Print* CD-ROM created by Reed Technology and Information Systems and published by R.R. Bowers.

SIRS Discoverer is a full-text CD-ROM database geared toward middle school students. The disc contains hundreds of newspaper and magazine articles selected for their educational content and categorized by subject and reading level. The program features a dictionary, a note-taking accessory, and a feature

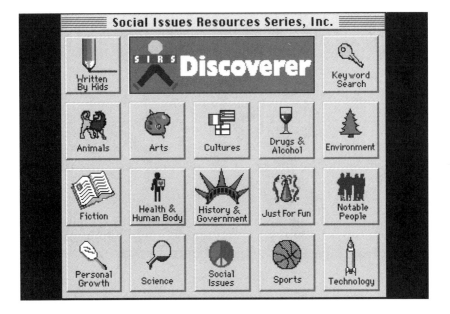

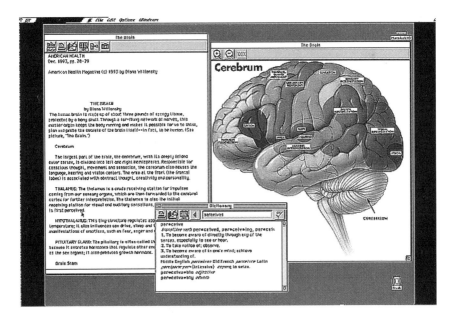

The opening screen from *SIRS Discoverer* program (top). Screen shot showing a magazine article about the brain (below), a dictionary entry for the word "perceived" used in the article, and a graphic of the cerebrum. (Screen shots courtesy of Social Issues Resources Services, Inc.)

for searching by keyword or subject tree. Like many applications targeted for school use, *Discoverer* comes with an educator's guide offering a variety of sample lesson plans, classroom and library exercises, and worksheets.

High school students will be interested in the CD-ROM versions of *Monarch Notes* from Bureau Development, Barron's *Book Note Study Guides*, and the *Shakespeare Study Guide* from World Library.

Frequently, CD-ROM resources include text from several reference books. Microsoft's *Bookshelf*, for example, includes the *American Heritage Dictionary*, *The Original Roget's Thesaurus*, the *Columbia Dictionary of Quotations*, the *Concise Columbia Encyclopedia*, *Hammond Intermediate World Atlas*, *The People's Chronology*, and *The World Almanac and Book of Facts 1994*, all on one disc. In addition to the full text, there are also 80,000 spoken pronunciations, audio clips, animation of scientific concepts, video clips of historic events, and more.

Another multiple-reference resource on a CD-ROM, one that should be of interest to educators that work with high school and college students, is *Job Power Source* from InfoBusiness Inc. This career-guidance CD-ROM is aimed at placement officers, guidance counselors, and other employment professionals. The disc contains full text from 11 best-selling career books, two hours of video training clips, interactive worksheets, evaluations, checklists, goal-setting tables, and organization and time management charts—along with a complete database of 12,740 occupational titles with descriptions and ratings based on applicant input.

Higher Education

Despite the fact that CDs cost considerably less to manufacture than hardbound books, especially books with four-color printing, it may seem strange that CD-ROM products have not yet made much of an inroad at the college level. Back in the spring of 1993, *Multimedia Week* reported, "A real market for interactive multimedia products at this curriculum level has been slow to develop, with one of the largest publishers, Heath, just releasing the first all CD-ROM title for the college market, *The Enduring Vision*, a CD-ROM version of one of its American history texts." The educational potential of CDs has never been in dispute, but concerns about the lack of an installed base have been there from the start, and from the looks of it, those concerns are still valid today.

Why should this be the case when sales of CD-ROM drives is exploding and the installed base is said to be growing at a phenomenal rate? One reason may be that there has not yet been a college text killer application to excite the market. Another reason is that, while the manufacturing costs are minimal in comparison to books, multimedia production and computer programming costs are far greater and must be laid out up front.

Furthermore, it is not enough to merely place the text and pictures on a CD and leave it at that. The real value of a CD product is not the ease with which it can be distributed, but its multimedia capabilities. A title must take advantage of the medium and add value for the consumer. Besides the content, issues such as interface design must be considered. More people with different skills must be involved, once again adding to up-front costs.

Of course, up-front costs must be paid for the development of titles for the elementary and high school market as well. So why the lack of development in the higher education market? Everybody mentions the lack of a large installed base of CD-ROM drives, but nobody I spoke with knew *the* reason. Personally, I can think of a few more factors that might play a role.

First, college level texts are usually quite specific. Each book has a narrow focus. The market is not all college students, just business majors, for example. Then, even in Business 101 at XYZ University, a required course (let's say) with perhaps a few hundred students each year, several different professors are likely to be teaching different sections of the same course—and each professor may have his or her own preferred text. Now the market for a particular title is even narrower.

A second factor for the success at earlier grade levels is the fact that many of those compact disc titles are targeted at both the home and school markets. The home market, of course, has far greater sales potential.

Yet another possible factor has to do with the depth of content and the ability to reuse the resource. A second grade teacher might use several different compact disc titles to teach a variety of subjects (such as the Wild West, or outer space). No one CD title needs to cover the entire curriculum, and the teacher can use the same resources with next year's second graders. The college textbook, on the other hand, normally is the main course reading. And while students read additional texts to gain depth or further insight, the college textbook is expected to cover the breadth of the subject being taught.

In June of 1994, the *Chronicle of Higher Education* reported that multimedia developers in higher education said their projects were being held back by difficulties in getting permission to use video clips, audio recordings, photos, and text. This too may have some bearing on the slow penetration of the college market. There is some question as to what rights colleges have under the fair-use provision of the copyright law, and many say colleges are afraid of getting sued. Meanwhile, a White House committee has released a report recommending a series of refinements in current copyright laws, including a recommendation to revise fair-use rules to include digital and online works.

This does not mean that there are no educational CD-ROM titles geared to college and university students. I recently received a press release announcing an interactive study guide to help students prepare for entrance exams. *Future Test: Admission Series*, from Future Technologies Inc. (an affiliate label of Compton's NewMedia), covers 25 different exams, including the SAT, GED, LSAT, MCAT, and CLEP.

Several college texts are available on CD-ROM, such as *Challenge of Democracy* from Houghton-Mifflin in partnership with Sony Electronic Publishing. Another example is a new version of Josef Albers' seminal work, *Interaction of Color*, released on CD-ROM by Yale University Press in association with the Josef Albers Foundation. The title includes the complete original work with notes, commentary, and color plates. It allows the user to experiment with colors to examine their appearance in different settings and combinations. Art students may record their own annotations for future reference and create their own studies with blank templates.

A number of reference titles are ideal for the college and university library. Research becomes fast and easy when students can not only search for relevant words and phrases, but also use Boolean logic to conduct searches. (Boolean logic allows you to add conditions to your searches, such as "apples *and* oranges" or "schools *not* universities.") Highlighted text linked to related information (often called *hypertext*) makes hunting down cross-references as simple as a click of the mouse or a single keystroke. These titles generally offer more data than their print counterparts but cost several hundred dollars less.

The *SIRS Researcher* CD-ROM, for example, contains thousands of articles selected from domestic and international newspapers, magazines, and government publications. Using electronic search tools, college students can find information on a variety of subjects, including topics relating to social issues; scientific developments and issues within the disciplines of earth, life, physical, medical, and applied science; and global events and issues of historic, economic, or political note.

In addition to the general encyclopedia CD-ROMs, there are many subject-specific titles, such as the *McGraw-Hill Multimedia Encyclopedia of*

Science and Technology, which includes an integrated version of the *McGraw-Hill Dictionary of Scientific and Technical Terms*.

DRI/McGraw-Hill Encyclopedia of World Economies CD-ROM is an ideal resource for colleges and universities with large business and/or world economics programs. And the *American Psychiatric Electronic Library* (from American Psychiatric Press, Inc.), which presents the full text of several years' worth of psychiatric journals and texts as well, is a must-have for students majoring in psychology.

Medical students find help from a variety of narrowly focused CD-ROM projects. *Introduction to Cardiothoracic Imaging*, from Yale University School of Medicine, won a Silver Award in the Higher Education category of the New-Media InVision Multimedia Awards 1994. *Cytovision Laser*, a CD-ROM from John Moores University Open Learning Unit in England, educates people doing cervical screenings.

In the last two chapters I have described nearly 40 educational CD titles and discussed attitudes and opinions regarding their use in the classroom. Now it's time to move from the school to the office and examine the use of disc technology in business.

Chapter 4

CD-ROMs at the Office

An advertisement for the CD-ROM Expo & Conference 1994 says it all: "CD-ROM delivers a world of information on a disc…information that can sharpen your competitive edge—save thousands of man-hours—increase productivity—slash costs—and bolster your bottom line…applications for training, sales, marketing, advertising, technical support and documentation, records management/archiving…."

Plenty of people will be surprised by this statement, or will be at least skeptical, thinking it to be nothing more than hype. The skeptics believe that CD-ROMs and multimedia applications are great for entertainment but have little business in the serious world of business. Some skeptics admit that there is a limited place for CDs in certain segments of the workplace. They concede that the MIS, computer programming, and computer support departments need CD-ROM drives because so many of their tools are now being distributed on compact discs. They might even concede that the graphics or production department could benefit from using Photo CD technology to store images. But beyond that, most people are still unaware of the many ways in which CD technology can be used in a business environment.

When I spoke with Jay Wolff, president and creative director of Big Hand Productions, he said that potential customers do not come in looking specifically for CD-i or CD-ROM applications. "They're looking for something better than their video or brochures, something better than their competition," he explained. "They say, 'I hear you guys are cool and innovative, so let me see what you have.' And their purchases are driven by this quarter's or this year's goals. So if you have to buy a CD-i player, or a CD-ROM player, to play back the most incredible presentation, and they win the deal, that's fine by them. They aren't concerned about which technology is used."

I've mentioned a few times already that the CD-ROM was first introduced as a text-storage medium. And I've heard that the business world spends about $12 billion each and every year buying information. If you stop to think about it, one of the most obvious uses for CD-ROMs in the business world is to distribute large amounts of information. So with this in mind, it really should come as no surprise that there are hundreds, if not thousands, of CD-ROM products out there offering all sorts of data. And that's just the beginning.

Not only can companies choose from a vast quantity and variety of CD-based titles, but they can use the technology to create their own business tools and applications. In this chapter I'll describe a few commercially available products and talk about novel uses for compact disc technology, such as the proposal-on-a-disc that one company created and used to land a multimillion dollar deal.

Communications

Proposals for new business; applications for government approval (especially the approval of agencies such as the FDA) with attendant background data, test results and other supporting documents; and presentations are all excellent candidates for compact disc applications—especially if multimedia is part of the content.

Portfolios and Press Kits

In a competitive job market, landing a job is no picnic. Entrepreneurs also need an edge when vying to sign new clients. Creating interactive résumés and portfolios is one way to stand out from the competition. If your work is visual, whether it's photography or fashion design, a multimedia portfolio can be not only powerful, but cost-effective as well.

Roger Black, the graphic designer behind the look of *Rolling Stone, Information Week, Town & Country, Newsweek, Esquire,* and scores of other publications, is well-known by publishers. But in these tight economic times, he found himself in need of a portfolio to show his work to the boards of directors and committees that were now making the decisions. His solution was to create an interactive CD-ROM presentation.

People are also beginning to use compact discs for distributing press kits. When unit publicists in Hollywood started using electronic press kits back in the 1980s, "electronic" meant video delivered either on tape or via satellite. Today, it means CD-ROM. The *ABC Television Fall '94 New Season Photography* and *CBS Fall Preview* discs were created to replace all the press releases and photos announcing the new fall 1994 lineup.

Annual Reports

Oracle Corporation has created a CD-ROM version of its annual report, and I expect that other companies have done the same. According to *CD-ROM World* magazine, Oracle's annual report CD was not merely a duplication of the print version. Instead, Oracle went to great lengths to position themselves as a multimedia leader. The company's annual report, produced by Mammoth Micro Productions, used technology to deliver a cross-platform disc complete with music, photographs, animation, and the requisite MPEG video clips. The report was targeted at business analysts and media people, most of whom have CDs. Oracle stockholders, the majority of whom are not likely to have CD-ROM drives, received the usual annual report booklet instead of a CD.

Putting annual report data on discs is not new. Disclosure, Standard & Poors, Silver Platter Information, and Lotus One Source all have disc-based products that contain either a summary or full-text version of the annual reports and financial data of hundreds of companies. These discs are not designed to convey a corporate image or represent any one company in any particular way. They are simply repositories of financial data.

The Oracle annual report CD was different, however. Oracle used the compact disc as a medium for actual communication and designed a multimedia annual report that represented the company and reflected its image. I suspect that, as time goes on and the installed base continues to grow, more and

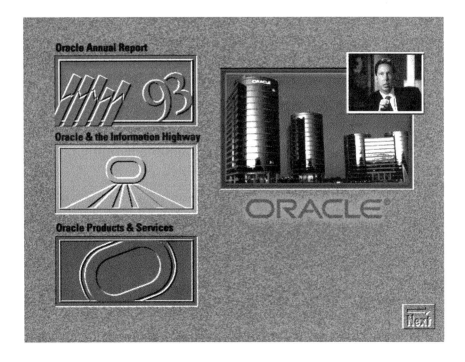

The main screen of Oracle Corporation's annual report on CD-ROM reflected an image of the company as advanced and forward-looking. (Screen shot © 1994 Oracle Corporation. Produced by Mammoth Micro Productions.)

more companies will use the power of multimedia as a communications tool. We will see more and more corporate "documents" on compact discs.

Business Proposals

Electronic Data Systems (EDS) was in the thick of a highly competitive sales pitch to Dow Jones & Company, Inc. At stake was a multimillion dollar contract to create the next generation, open publishing system for *The Wall Street Journal* worldwide. EDS pulled out all the stops, hired an outside production studio, and created an interactive CD proposal using CD-i technology. Craig Rispin, vice president of sales and marketing for Big Hand Productions, Inc., said that one of the more interesting things about the disc was that it was a hybrid product.

"Anybody could take this CD-i disc," Rispin said, "and stick it into their standard car or home CD player and still hear the entire audio presentation." EDS then provided Dow Jones with hand-held CD-i players so that senior executives from all over the company could view the CD-i proposal easily. All they had to do was hit the play button and watch a self-guided tour of the proposal that contained video clips, 3-D animation graphics, and other special effects.

Allen Chapel, EDS account manager for the project, noted, "This was a unique opportunity to capture the attention of Dow Jones management, and at the same time demonstrate EDS' commitment and understanding of multimedia technologies." The total proposal package, including the disc, won Proposal of the Year within EDS. With the cooperation of outside companies like Big Hand Productions, Inc. and Image Communications, Inc., the cost was surprisingly low, yet it helped EDS land one of the largest, most innovative editorial system contracts in newspaper history.

On-the-Road Presentations

Compact discs can play a dual role in business presentations. They can be an excellent source of prepackaged royalty-free media clips, and they are an excellent medium on which to publish your presentation when you're done putting it together.

Suppose you're ready to work on your presentation and you've mastered the necessary features of your desktop presentation program. You've even begun to work on the outline. Now what? How do you make your presentation sparkle? How do you grab your viewers' attention? All the magazines say you need to dazzle them with media. You need a multimedia blitz. You have to use sound, music, video, and animation, and show drawings and photographs. The problem is, you don't have any photos and you can't draw. You don't play an instrument either. The solution? Lots and lots of royalty-free media clip collections on compact disc.

In the next chapter I'll tell you about a few of these collections, but for the moment let's assume you've finished creating the presentation and you've printed out your overhead transparencies, or perhaps you opted for slides.

Now you're on the road giving talks at trade shows and conferences. And each audience is different. On the plane you thought about altering the presentation slightly. Because you created the presentation and chose the slides or transparencies, you are familiar with all of them. You will have plenty of time when you get to the hotel to rearrange the slides in the carousel. You hope.

The shoe doesn't fit? Too low-tech? Oh, you have a laptop and your presentation is on your hard drive. Your presentation is a whizbang multimedia marvel that takes up 100MB on your drive. Great. But what happens when your hard drive crashes and dies? Or when you get to the hall and they don't have the right LCD panel or an overhead projector? Yes, they knew you were doing a computer-based presentation, so they got a multimedia machine and hooked it up. Now it's ready to go. Okay, great! You'll just copy the files over to their hard drive. Oops! No room. Oh no, it's not even a PC. They've got a Macintosh!

At a time like this, a CD can save your day. A CD is easy to carry around and has the capacity to hold both a PC and a Macintosh version of your presentation. I do have some skeptical friends who think, given the scenario I just described, that the show planners wouldn't have a CD-ready system. Just in case they're right, you might want to carry an external CD-drive. Be sure you get one that is both Macintosh- and PC-compatible.

If the CD-based application is well-designed, you can still customize your presentation by navigating to those areas you want to cover and skipping the rest. And if it's appropriate for your business, you could press enough discs to actually give them away to conference attendees. What better way to deliver a consistent message to lots of people in lots of places? People who attend your conferences or presentations will think they got something extra—at least for now, while CDs are still somewhat of a novelty. And at $1 or $2 per disc, you can probably afford it.

Sales Presentations

Hand-held CD-i players have made presentations designed for the CD-i platform a favorite, especially among people who have to travel a great deal. Who wouldn't trade heavy sample cases and stacks of catalogs for a compact disc?

Mercedes-Benz

Big Hand Productions Inc. has worked on several sales applications, and one of its happiest customers is Mercedes-Benz. The Premiere Mercedes-Benz Information System on CD-i was billed as the first trade-show kiosk to use CD-i's MPEG-1 full-screen, digital video capabilities.

A portable Philips CD-i player. (Photo courtesy of Philips Media.)

The sales program, which was also used for in-store display and as a portable sales tool, presented information about Mercedes-Benz's Caravan line (the Caravan is a recreational vehicle), its service program, and its vehicle specifications. In addition to digital video, the sales tool offered over 300 custom graphics, 12 minutes of music with narration, and a custom-programmed interface. Big Hand Productions' Craig Rispin said that the application cost well under $150,000, much less than Mercedes-Benz was already spending for the production of custom videos alone.

Centrex

Sprint hired Spinnaker Communications, another production house experienced in CD-based applications, to create a sales program. When it was done, Sprint's LTD sales force hit the road armed with portable CD-i players and Centrex CD-i sales presentation discs in hand.

Screen from *The Premiere Mercedes-Benz Information System* CD-i application. (Photo courtesy of Big Hand Productions.)

Spinnaker took still graphics produced by an advertising agency, added motion video, soundtracks, and 2-D animations, and created an interface for accessing these items. A Sprint salesperson can interactively access information regarding over 100 benefits associated with the Centrex product. Sprint selected the CD-i platform because of the hand-held players' playback reliability and portability.

SMILE

The SMILE System is not a tool for the proverbial traveling salesman. SMILE is a CD-ROM that presents luxury homes on the worldwide market. It is sent to real estate brokers who subscribe to the service. Using a mouse or touch screen, prospective buyers select a country, region, or state from a map, and then narrow the selection by factors such as size or price. A company called System of

Multiple Colored Images for Internationally Listed Estates, Inc. teamed up with Apple to create this CD-ROM product. It shows interior and exterior color photographs, floor plans, and QuickTime movie tours of the neighborhoods where the houses are located. Information about local schools and churches is also included.

I've never seen this product up close and personal, but I have seen demonstrations on television of this system or others like it. This one is targeted for the high-priced real estate market, but I hope such systems are developed for homes in all price ranges. When you look at the volumes and volumes of MLS (Multiple Listing Service) books trashed weekly, each volume the size of a thick phone book, compact discs start to look really good. This is not to say that CDs are more ecological.

According to Jill Croft, national sales manager of the CD-ROM division at Disc Manufacturing Inc. (DMI), the problem with compact discs is that once they have been metalized, there are limited uses for recycling them. The cost to separate the various metals contained in the product (nickel, silver, and others) is prohibitive due to the minuscule amount of each metal in each disc. DMI uses a room-sized machine to shred their overruns, returns, and bad pressings of CDs. Global Plastics buys the shredded discs in quantities no less than a ton (about 107,000 discs) and sends a tractor-trailer over to pick them up.

Metatec, another major compact disc manufacturer, has found a lightweight recycling solution for their customers. In its fall 1994 newsletter, Metatec reported that their customers can ship discs for recycling directly to NE-SAR Systems in Darlington, Pennsylvania, provided that each shipment weighs no more than 50 pounds. It is unfortunate that recycling discs is not yet cost-effective unless you're a big manufacturer. Needless to say, your local recycler does not yet have the means or motivation to handle compact discs from you directly.

Marketing

Marketing departments thrive on data—lots of names, addresses, and phone numbers, coupled with demographics and other classifications. There is no shortage of compact disc titles with this type of information, and I'll describe several of them in just a moment. First, however, I want to suggest that you look at marketing from the other side of the disc, so to speak, and consider using compact discs as a medium for *delivering* your marketing messages.

Interactive Brochures

Marketers from many different industries agree that interactive brochures are well-suited for marketing products that require the consumer to make complex decisions. For example, an interactive brochure can show the design of a car from many different angles. It is easier to see the insides of an engine on a computer screen than on the showroom floor. Some interactive brochures are being sent out on floppy disks, but more and more are moving to compact discs.

The Photo CD was a natural for Mountain Travel's marketing campaign aimed at 50,000 of its best customers. The disc, developed by an outside company (Custom Process in Berkeley, California), included 224 screens, a sound track, and 197 full-screen photographs of vacation spots. The developers told *NewMedia* magazine that the Photo CD cost about $80,000. They estimated that the same application on a CD-ROM would have run as much as $250,000.

Another interactive marketing application I read about was designed to promote small-business loans. A Louisiana bank sent out a disc containing charts and animations to help explain the terminology and application process. Along with the discs, worksheets were sent to help potential applicants evaluate their financial situations. This bank reported an 8-percent response to the promotion, four times the rate of response to its standard print mailers.

Mailing Tools

A company called Mailer's Software offers a single CD-ROM or an annual subscription to a product called Mailer's *ZIP+4*. If direct mail is part of your business, this tool sounds like a dream. *ZIP+4* checks your entire ASCII fixed-length or dBASE mailing list directly. It adds the correct "plus four" extension to ZIP codes, inserts ZIP codes that are missing, adds carrier routes and delivery-point bar codes, and makes addresses conform to U.S. Postal Service requirements.

And if demographics play a role in your business, you'll also want a program like Mailer's *Geocoding*. This CD-based program uses the ZIP codes in your data to find latitude and longitude coordinates and the census tract/block group for each address. Demographic data from the Census Bureau is grouped by census tract and block groups. Once your address list is "geo-coded," you can get demographic data on your customers and create customer profiles. Then, once you know exactly who your customers are, you can search for other census tract and block groups with similar characteristics and target them as well. The latitude and longitude information is provided so you can map your customers with other mapping programs.

Of course, if you don't have your own customer list(s), many mailing list databases are available on CD-ROM. You might start with *SelectPhone* from Pro CD, Inc. Despite its name, it includes names and addresses as well as phone numbers for 8 million businesses and 72 million residences in every major city in the U.S. And yes, you can export the information from the CD to your hard drive and create your own database. The CD comes with a utility that displays selected entries on a map of the United States, not to mention an auto-dialer for placing calls quickly. The only complaint I've heard about *SelectPhone* is that it's a 4-disc set, which makes searching for data somewhat difficult. For example, suppose you're searching for data that matches a certain Standard Industrial Code (SIC) classification (*SelectPhone* covers 2,700 different codes) and you want all the listings that match nationwide. You have to search all four regions individually and then manually combine the results of the search.

ProPhone, also from Pro CD, is designed for marketing. It not only allows you to export data to mailing list programs, but it also allows you to feed phone-list data into business contact software programs such as PackRat from Polaris. Other Pro CD titles include *FreePhone*, which covers toll-free 800 numbers; *DirectPhone* for residential listings; *CanadaPhone*; and *Europages*. One drawback of these products is that Pro CD gets its information from the con-sumer and business white pages. White pages are seldom up to date, so no matter how fast Pro CD updates the discs, they still include outdated information.

PhoneDisc USA from Digital Data Associates can also be used for mar-keting. Reviewers claim that it has fewer wrong numbers, but it also has serious drawbacks if you want to use it for marketing. First, it doesn't provide as much information as some of the other products; it provides no figures on employee numbers, for example. Second, it uses only 1,700 SIC codes, less than other products. Worst of all, you can only output 50 entries per session, which is not enough for any serious marketing efforts.

Another phone disc that you might use for marketing is *American Business Phone Book* from American Business Information. Reviewers report that it has the most business entries and the most up to date information, but, like *PhoneDisc USA*, it has no employee figures, and it has no SIC codes at all. And the *American Business Phone Book* has two major restrictions. First, it is only good for one year, after which you cannot access the data. And second, even within that one year, you can only access 5,000 numbers. When you reach for that 5001, you'll find that your access has "Expired."

Perhaps your target mailing needs are more specific. If you're doing a press mailing, you might buy *Mailer's Radio & Television Database* for $190. For $149 you can buy the *Business Database*, which has the addresses of over 1.2 million businesses and organizations in the U.S. For $975, *Congressional Database* offers the name and party affiliation of each Congressional representative and demographic data for each district. This data includes the latest census and household information for each district—the population by age, gender, and race, and information on how many residents own the their homes or are renters.

Do you have any idea how many pieces of mail you waste on the deceased? Use the *Social Security Death Benefit Record* on CD-ROM to purge these records from your list.

Do you want to find everybody in the state of Texas who owns a Ford Taurus? Use the *Texas Vehicle* CD-ROM. It contains all Texas Department of Motor Vehicles registration files, complete with each registrant's name and address, vehicle make, license number, lien date and holder, and more. This one certainly raises some privacy issues, and only goes to prove that information is getting easier to obtain.

Value Added

Some discs just contain lots of raw data, column after column of information, such as company names, addresses, phone numbers, and the names of executive personnel. Other discs are designed to help you utilize this information. One such disc is called *MarketPlace Business*, from MarketPlace Information Corp. It offers information compiled by Dun & Bradstreet Corporation on 7 million U.S. companies, and is geared for businesses that sells to other businesses.

The *MarketPlace Business* program guides you through a three-step process. First, you define what type of businesses you want to target for your mailing list, perhaps starting with certain ZIP codes, states, or metropolitan areas. You can target industries using SIC codes with the disc's alphabetic index. In step 2, you examine your list, analyzing the market and making adjustments to target the markets with the greatest potential. You can delete individual entries if the total count gets too high, and this is important because—and here's the catch—you have to pay for the final list. In step 3, you print labels and reports.

Companies that buy mailing lists usually do not get the opportunity to preview the lists or customize them without paying additional charges. List sales are generally for one-time use and companies pay approximately 25 cents for each item on the list. *MarketPlace Business* users can reuse a list as often as they want for an entire year, and the cost per list item is only 10 to 15 cents, depending on whether you buy mailing or telemarketing information. The charges are handled in a fashion similar to that of a postage meter. When you buy the disc (the suggested retail price is $849), it includes 3,000 meter credits worth $300. Additional credits may be purchased in blocks of 5,000.

Advertising

I found two categories of CD-based titles that relate to advertising. The first category, represented by two products from SRDS, includes data on which you might base your advertising plans. The SRDS products relate to buying ads in magazines. They offer data such as circulation figures and ad rates, the kind of data generally found in media kits. The second category is advertisements on disc—discs that are, in and of themselves, advertisements. I've chosen TECH-ROM and the CompuServe CD to illustrate this type.

Media Research

The *SRDS Electronic Media Kit Library* is a neat idea, especially for advertising departments and media buyers. Rather than sifting through stacks of heavy press packages with sample magazines, pages of rate cards, company and reader profiles, editorial calendars and the like, all you have to do is pop the CD-ROM into the drive on your computer and look for what you need. Publications in an early 1994 version of this disc include *Advertising Age*, *America West Airlines* magazine, *Architectural Digest*, and *Automotive Executive*. And that's just the A's.

You can access a specific media kit by highlighting the publication title, SRDS classification, or parent company. Of you can perform a keyword search and let the software create a list of titles for you. For each title included you'll find reproductions of pages from the printed media kit—and, unfortunately, there's the rub. All the pages were scanned, so the quality of the reproductions is not so good. Even though you can magnify or zoom in on a page (and you have to zoom because you can't decipher the text otherwise), many of the pages are

The main screen of the *SRDS Electronic Media Kit*. Once you select either Business and Consumer, you have the choice of searching for publications by title, parent company, key word, or classification. You can then choose to view the information about one or more publications.

still hard to read. Sometimes this is the fault of the scan quality, and sometimes it's caused by the color and/or texture of the original printed page.

When you zoom in on a page, you have to scroll both horizontally and vertically to read it. The page metaphor fails, however, when the page cannot fit legibly on the screen. Also, to exit the program, you have to back out one screen at a time until you get to the first screen, where you'll find the Exit button. The graphics look great, the magazine covers are impressive, but reading the information is tough.

If the purpose of this program was to browse magazine covers, it would be great. But if you need information, this one misses the boat. It's a perfect example of a wonderful idea that, if properly designed and executed, would be well suited for the CD-ROM medium. In its present form, it's little more than

The first screen for the selected publication in the *SRDS Electronic Media Kit*. Clicking on one of the buttons at left brings up additional screens of information, most of which must be magnified to be legible.

shovelware—material from one medium (print) shoveled onto a another medium (CD-ROM) without being redesigned to suit the new medium.

There is a saving grace for this product. The design that I object to is just a front-end to a database, and if you wanted to design your own program to make use of the data, you can do so. The *SRDS Electronic Media Kit Library* uses a Microsoft Access database, so you could use Visual Basic or any number of other design or programming tools. Also, the CD is updated quarterly, so the information it presents is always relatively current.

This leads me to another important point. This particular database contains only the information from magazines that participate in the Electronic Media Kit. SRDS has other CD-based programs with far more comprehensive databases. Its *Media Planning System* (MPS) is another one of those titles designed to help you use the disc's information. MPS covers over 5,000 business and 2,500 consumer publications. The program is designed to help you find and collect data that meets your needs, perform calculations or rankings on large amounts of quantitative data, and create media budgets, schedules, and flowcharts.

Another alternative for advertising departments is the *Standard Periodical Directory* on CD-ROM. It provides data on more than 85,000 periodicals, including circulation figures, auditors, contact names, primary readership, and more. It even tells you which publications rent mailing lists.

Advertising Discs

I can describe a few examples of advertisements on compact discs. Chrysler Corporation advertises their Neon car on them. TECH-ROM Library Corporation developed the *InterActive MultiMedia Windows Shopper* disc to target potential consumers of hardware and software. Their disc includes tools for obtaining more information and connecting with a dealer/distributor. I also consider discs with demonstration versions of games, programs, and online services to be advertisements of a sort.

The *CompuServe CD*, described as a cross between an electronic magazine and a guide to the online service, is another type of advertising disc. If I were not already a CompuServe user, I would find this disc a compelling advertisement for CompuServe. Another type of advertising disc is the shopping catalog on disc, a subject I'll leave for Chapter 9.

Chrysler Corporation's Disc for the Neon

Chrysler Corporation has created a CD-ROM dedicated solely to advertising its Neon subcompact car. In addition to video clips (including a few television commercials), 450 photographs, and lots of text and graphics, the disc allows potential buyers to customize the display by selecting colors and features. They can then print out their ideal feature package and take it to their local dealer for pricing.

"We would not do this for every car," Mike Perugi, marketing plans and merchandising specialist for Chrysler's Dodge Division, told *Investors Business Daily*: "Only for vehicles that fit the demographics of the computerized generation. The Neon customer is in tune with what technology is all about."

Automotive advertising on computers is not a new concept. Ford Motor Company has been offering floppy disk catalogs to their customer since 1987. Now they, too, are working on a CD-ROM. And they're not the only ones. The next time you go to buy a car, you may be offered a compact disc instead of a glossy color catalog or videocassette.

TECH-ROM

The *InterActive MultiMedia Windows Shopper* from TECH-ROM Library Corp. is a great idea. It combines the benefits of CD-ROM storage with the communications abilities of an online bulletin board system (BBS). TECH-ROM contains hardware and software demos featuring products in 300 categories from 80 manufacturers. It's the brainstorm of a man named Terrill Epps, who believed that people (individuals as well as corporate purchasing agents) needed an easy way to get information about a variety of hardware and software products— information that included visuals as well as data about prices, levels of service, and support.

The TECH-ROM disc is more than just a database of information. You can place selected items into a spreadsheet to facilitate comparisons. Even more innovative is the inclusion of a communications program that allows you to send lists of products you're interested in to the TECH-ROM BBS. Information about your request or query is faxed to a local reseller. The reseller can then contact you with information about things like prices and delivery options. The BBS also provides an opportunity to post your comments about product needs, your complaints, etc. TECH-ROM forwards those comments to the manufacturers.

Demo and Sampler Discs

All kinds of companies are putting out demo discs. Microsoft Home has a CD sampler that was made for promotional use only. I got one free when shopping at Egghead Software one day. Many companies producing expensive CD-based titles have found it necessary to provide a demo version because consumers are unwilling to make costly purchases sight-unseen. If a demo is available, you can usually get one directly from the publisher or distributor. Some print magazines even arrive in the mail with demo discs enclosed. *CD-ROM Today*, for example, offers a combination print and disc subscription. The *CD-ROM Today* disc is not an electronic version of the magazine; rather, it is a compilation of demos.

I encourage you to request demos. All too often the ad copy and screen shots in the brochure look great, but the design turns out to be less than practical, or the tools not as useful for what you need. I'm not suggesting that the brochures lie, only that the actual utility of many of these products still leaves much to be desired. But that's to be expected; this is still a new medium, after all.

It is also worth noting that product cycles can be lengthy, usually forcing marketing and advertising personnel to work from ideas and memos long before the product is fully functional. You would also do well to take early product reviews with a grain of salt. Most magazines have a one to three month lead time. Reviewers, myself included, often have to work from beta versions of programs under review. It is not unusual for reviews to mention features that have not yet been implemented in the program, and sometimes program publishers decide to cut these features from the final product. Sometimes we get a really big surprise when a program publisher changes the whole interface design.

CompuServe CD-ROM

PC World calls the CompuServe CD-ROM disc "a cross between a digital magazine about CompuServe and an interactive, multimedia guide to the online service." The subscription costs $7.95 per disc (discs should be appearing monthly by mid-1995) and includes a $5 usage credit and the latest version of CompuServe's Information Manager for Windows, an interface program that makes navigating CompuServe a bit easier. You can preview forums and find files of interest before logging on and racking up connect-time charges. If you use the File Finder tool on the disc to locate and mark the files you want, they will be downloaded automatically when you log on. The Member Services department provides tips and techniques to help you get a handle on the vast resources available through the online service.

Just like *CompuServe* magazine, the disc includes articles and a shopping section. Hobbies, games, and other family-oriented topics are covered in the Home & Leisure department. Personal productivity from financial planning to desktop publishing can be found in the Personal Enterprise department. The Entertainment section includes news, reviews, and sneak previews of upcoming movies and recordings. The Technology & Trends department focuses on software, demos, and equipment reviews. Then there's the Shopping department tied in to the Electronic Mall, which allows you to connect and place orders directly.

Have It Your Way

I talk a lot about value-added features. It seems to be in our nature to want something for nothing. Well, maybe not for nothing, but we all certainly want more value. We comparison-shop and negotiate deals to get more for our investment. We

Shopping is just one of several departments featured on CompuServe's CD. (Screen shot courtesy of CompuServe Incorporated.)

offer premiums, incentives, all for a little added value. Multimedia messages have added value. They can communicate in multiple languages, visually as well as aurally, and with greater impact than a direct mail piece. CDs are full-color and cost less to create than a multipage, multifold, four-color mailer. And saved time is, in itself, added value.

"Have it your way" was a successful advertising slogan, and it's still what people want. When businesses buy mailing lists, for example, they can get more bang for their bucks when the list is customized, targeted, and tailored to match the demographics of the most likely customer. With CDs able to store large amounts of data, added value comes with the ability to sift and sort through the data to cull only what is most useful. Customization also plays a role in tailoring instruction to meet individual training needs.

With all of this said, I must also tell you that what sounds good, doesn't always work so well. Most of the problems I have with all the CD titles I've been looking at have to do with lack of standardized technology, poor interface design,

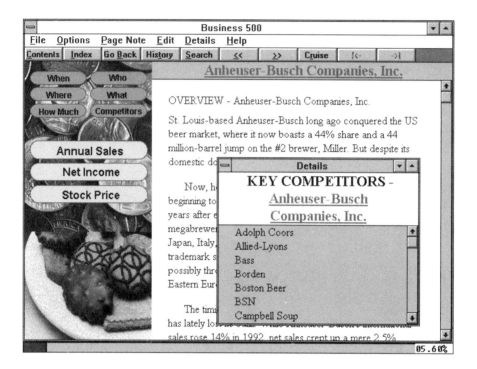

The main window from *Multimedia Business 500* after selecting "Anheuser-Busch" from a list of companies. Clicking on the Competitors button brings up the list in the foreground window. Clicking on a competitor's name brings up more information about that company.

and, most disappointing, poor use of content. There is nothing more frustrating than having technology at your fingertips, literally, and not having it do what you need it to do. Sometimes I wonder if these products are ever really field-tested by average users.

One simple example of my frustration came when I was browsing the *Multimedia Business 500* disc. This disc is one of the better ones in terms of interface and relative ease of use, and I didn't have to be familiar with SIC codes to use it effectively. I had looked up a particular company and was able to click on a button to see a list of that company's competitors. At that point, I really wanted to click again and jump right to a competitor company's information. Nope. Instead I had to do a search on the company name, then browse the window containing all the hits, and then click on the one I wanted.

Fine, but when I wanted to see another competitor, the window naming the first company's competitors was gone. I found that I could use the history feature to return to the first company's competitor listing and then do another search for the next competitor. And so on. I know I should be impressed that the data was there to be had, and that the design did have a history feature, but I wanted it to be faster and more easily accessible! Personally, I only have occasional use for the disc, but if I had to use it frequently, I think I'd begin to get annoyed.

Again, I must reiterate that these frustrations were fueled by the design of the application, not the technology itself. The technology is new, and I believe the art of its use has barely begun to evolve.

I can't end this chapter without telling you about an application that I read about. It struck me as extremely creative, but unfortunately when I tried to contact the company that made it, the number was no longer in service. I hope the disconnected number means the company was very successful and simply moved to bigger quarters at a new location. The company is Dynamic Media and the CD application that struck my fancy was *Talent Source: The CD-ROM Screen Test*, a CD aimed at replacing casting calls.

Casting offices overflow with files full of photos, resumes, and video tapes. Now all that can be replaced with a little disc that not only has photos and footage, but also an index. If the casting director is looking for someone of a specific height or weight, age or hair color, or wants a particular type, such as "rugged individualist" or "girl next door," he or she can query the database and see the photos of actors who fit the bill. If the photo looks like a possible, the director can view the actor or actress's resume, along with more photos, audio clips, and video clips. I don't see the in-person audition disappearing anytime soon, but a tool like this could go a long way toward narrowing the field.

No matter what industry you work in, narrowing the field is important. As more and more data becomes available to us, we will need better and more powerful tools with which to process that data.

In the next chapter I'll cover some more CD-based products for business use, focusing on reference, data distribution, and training.

Chapter 5

More CD-ROMs at the Office

In the last chapter I focused on CDs used in corporate communications. I discussed CD-based proposals and presentations, as well as discs used for marketing and advertising. In this chapter, I look at some reference CDs and talk about the use of the compact disc medium for storing and distributing data, and providing training.

Reference Use

There are all kinds of reference materials. There are general references (dictionaries, encyclopedias, etc.), and subject-specific references (business topics, legal tomes, medical journals, technical support manuals, etc.). Then there are data resources such as government documents and guidelines, and patent and registration information on file. But before I describe some of the sample titles in the reference category, I've got to tell you about an idea for a reference that I found particularly interesting.

In an old issue of *MacWEEK*, I saw a product announcement for a CD-ROM with the complete proceedings from the SEAM conference held in San Francisco in 1992. SEAM stands for Scientific and Engineering Applications of the Macintosh. I'm not a Macintosh user, so it wasn't so much this particular disc that enticed me as it was the idea of putting a conference on a disc. I can't tell you how many conference brochures I get each month and how many of these conferences and expositions I wish I could attend. But alas, time and money are both limited, and I always feel like I'm missing something.

These days, most conferences are recorded and you can usually buy the cassette tapes. Occasionally parts of a conference, if not the whole thing, are video taped, and you can buy a video tape or even a video disc such as the ones produced for the Technology Entertainment Design conferences. Cassettes are okay, and great for listening to in the car, but you miss the nuances that you would have caught if you had been there, and usually you can't hear the questions that were asked from the floor. Video tapes are okay too, but you can't do an electronic search to find a speech or reference a keyword of interest on a video tape.

I don't know if there are many conferences on disc. But I am intrigued by the idea and usefulness of putting conferences on disc. Now, back to basics.

General References

Basic reference books, especially those cumbersome tomes and multivolume works such as encyclopedias and dictionaries, lend themselves well to CD-ROM applications. Back in 1992, Jean Louis Gassee reviewed the disc version of the 20-volume *Oxford English Dictionary, 2nd Edition* for *MacWEEK*. After describing the hypertext links between words and definitions, and a search engine that allows you to look for words, phrases, parts of speech, etymology, definitions, quotations, and more, he concluded, "It provides one of the better proofs that our minds aren't genetically geared for sifting through mountains of data without the aid of silicon and software."

Microsoft Bookshelf is another good all-around reference, as are the electronic encyclopedias from Microsoft, Comptons, and Grolier, I described all of these in the last chapter, so I won't describe them here. As far as business use goes, not only do these titles provide solid basic reference tools, but those trivia tidbits and quotations can help spice up a speech or presentation.

Subject References

Another type of CD-based reference is the topic-specific library on disc. I cover quite a few such references in both Chapters 6 and 8, but here are some more.

Business

If you're looking for reference books on business topics, such as careers, marketing, managing, tips for success, etc., you should look at the *Business Library* CD-ROM from Allegro New Media. It offers 12 best-selling business books and a search engine, hyperlinking capabilities, and annotating capabilities. The 12 books are:

- *Business to Business Communications Handbook*
- *The Feel of Success in Selling*
- *Finance & Accounting for Nonfinancial Managers*
- *How to Get People to Do Things Your Way*
- *How to Make Big Money in Real Estate in the Tighter, Tougher 90's Market*
- *International Herald Tribune Guide to Business Travel in Europe*
- *Joyce Lain Kennedy's Career Book*
- *Meetings Rules & Procedures*
- *State of the Art Marketing Research*
- *Successful Direct Marketing Methods*
- *Successful Telemarketing*
- *Total Global Strategy: Managing for Worldwide Competitive Advantage*

In addition, *Business Library* also gives you footage from three digitized business videos: "30 Timeless Direct Marketing Principles," "From Advertising to Integrated Marketing Communications," and "New Product Development." Unfortunately, the video appears in a very small window onscreen, and the quality is not terrific. The only audio on the CD, other than the music opening, is the audio that plays with the video, and the use of graphics is limited.

This is not to say that all you see is text. The interface looks okay, but I'm just not convinced that books on disc is a concept that works well.

Computers

Need some technical support? Tech references, in my mind, are a different story altogether. A good index, a quick text description with an illuminating graphic, is

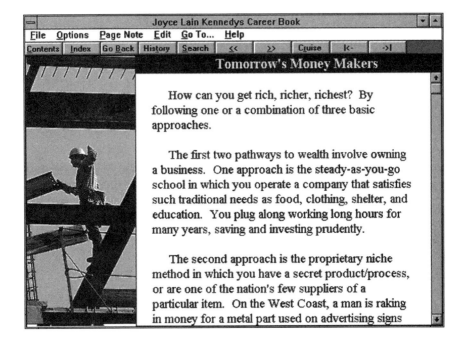

This screen shot from Allegro's *Business Library* shows the beginning of a chapter from Joyce Lain Kennedy's "Career Book." The picture on the left changes for each chapter as you scroll through the book.

all I want in a technical reference. Here it makes sense for information to be provided in little chunks. Generally, you are looking for some specific information to solve a technical problem or you need to learn how to use the features of a particular program.

Perhaps you own or work at a small company and there is no one on staff to help you figure out how to use Paradox or Quicken, for example. Or perhaps you could benefit from some tips on memory management. You don't want to go to a two-day training session—who has time?

Again, Allegro New Media has taken the library book approach with its *PC Library* CD-ROM. Allegro claims that if you need assistance with hardware, database programs, networking, productivity, spreadsheet programs, word-processing programs, or operating systems, *PC Library* can help. It offer 32 best-selling computer references, tutorials, manuals, and videos—over $800 worth of books on a $99 disc. The disc does have some excellent works, but again I question the practicality of reading books on disc.

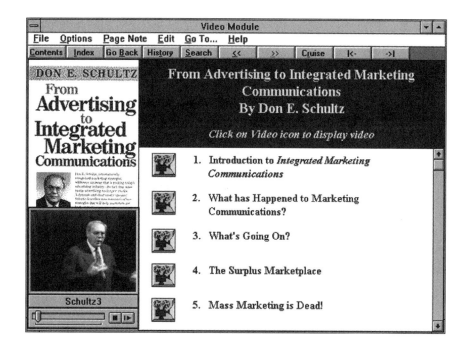

This screen shot from Allegro's *Business Library* shows the list of video clips excerpted from Don E. Schultz's "From Advertising to Integrated Marketing Communications." The video plays in the small window at the lower-left corner of your screen.

Don't get me wrong, I think the library on disc concept has its place. But that place is probably at home, where you have time to read. When it comes to technical references, I would turn to products such as Microsoft's *Knowledge Base*, Computer Library's *Support on Site for Networks*, and Datapro's *Client/Server Analyst*. These discs are available as subscriptions and contain articles, technical support materials, and question-and-answer pieces. Search engines are included so that you can find exactly what you need.

In addition to technical support discs, CD subscriptions such as *Computer Select* offer several computer industry magazine articles.

It is the nature of technologies to evolve, but evolution used to be a slow process. Today the pace of change is rapid. The idea of subscribing to technological information on disc seems to me quite practical. A book can be out of date by the time it hits the shelves. Monthly print-based magazines pile up on my desk, chairs, and coffee table until I find a few free minutes to "catch up on my reading." The cost of online services is still a bit steep, so it's not cost-effective to keep up with

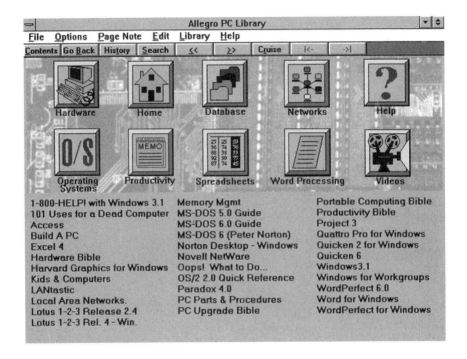

This is the main screen from Allegro's *PC Library.* If you click on one of the icons in the top half of the screen, a small window appears, listing the books for that category. Click on an entry from that list to move to the actual text from that book. Alternatively, you can click on an entry from the list in the lower half of the main screen.

technical advances online. With a subscription disc, however, I can stay up to date and easily find what I want when I need it.

Medicine

Doctors agree that in the medical field, where advancements occur daily, journals are one of the main resources for staying up to date. But there are so many journals, and they take up so much space. There is also little time to read the studies—and then, just when you find one that's of interest, it often vanishes into the pile of journals in the bookcase.

Unlike their print counterparts, journals on CD provide instant access to information. One of the many professional medical CD titles on the market is *The Annals of Internal Medicine* from Creative Multimedia. It offers medical journals licensed from the American College of Physicians. The disc(s) include all the text, color photographs, and illustrations, tables, graphs, and charts found in the original print versions.

Besides electronic searching and indexing, an added benefit of this program is its printing capability. When you want to share or discuss information with colleagues, study information further, or give articles to patients, you can print the articles. Time and budget constraints have long made collegial discussions an all-too-rare occurrence. Doctors seldom have time to confer when they're "on duty," unless it's a billable consultation. And patients often complain that doctors don't have enough time to answer questions.

Many physicians find that giving a patient an article or two about a particular problem helps allay the patient's fears. It increases understanding between the doctor and patient and helps build a rapport between them.

Law

Dozens of companies specialize in CD titles for vertical markets, and the legal profession is one of the more lucrative of such markets. Most legal research is still conducted in the library. A recent survey conducted by Lawyers Cooperative Publishing found that 77 percent of the New York state law libraries surveyed subscribe to as many as 10 CD-ROM titles. An additional 11 percent subscribe to even more CD-ROM references, sometimes as many as 75 different titles.

Costs permitting, lawyers can also use online services such as Lexis. Given the fact that much of the legal research is done using dated materials (i.e., cases and decisions that once written, remain unchanged), it is only logical to place legal materials on compact discs.

Legal Systems, for example, produces CDs with state and federal laws and published appellate court decisions. This company used imaging technology to scan each page of the legal texts. You buy the discs for a flat fee per state and pay additionally for updates.

Public Information

Public information is free—when you know how and where to find it. Free information is a prime resource for publishers, and often it's worth buying a commercial product. Let the publishers unearth and compile the information you need.

Government Issue Information

The U.S. government is an amazing source of information. Would you like to know how the spending habits of the average American family have changed over the past 20 years? What is the number of people over 65 who don't have health care? Information on such topics and the thousands more covered in government publications can be found in CD reference collections such as the SIRS Government Reporter. This database contains thousands of documents and graphics published between 1990 and 1993. The program is available as a subscription to libraries and other institutions, with regular updates each April and October.

The federal government produces more CDs than I could track. I tried calling the Government Printing Office (GPO)—there's one in every major city—but the lines were always busy. Nearly 150 titles published by various government agencies are listed in the CD-ROM Directory and are available for purchase. Lots more don't ever make it into the directory. If you'd like a free catalog listing government-published CD-ROMs, call (202) 512-6000 and ask for the *Information Dissemination Federal CD-ROMs* report. GPO titles include compact discs such as President Clinton's budget proposal, which has the full text of the main budget book, the analysis book, historical tables, and even an explanation of the system.

The government is also a CD consumer. The National Institute of Building Sciences (an independent organization, although it was created by Congress) owns a CD-ROM system known as the Construction Criteria Base. This CD contains approximately 1 million pages of data manuals including the guide specifications, regulations, manuals, and estimating and processing systems for federal construction. An article in *Government Computer News* said that the Department of Defense expects to buy 10,000 subscriptions for its own use, and that the architects and engineers who design and specify materials and products for federal buildings will be using it as their standard resource.

Patents

More and more patents are being filed as companies rush to protect what they believe are their intellectual property rights. Many programs and services exist to help companies and individuals prepare to file patents. One of the first steps is always to check out existing patents. Most if not all of the online patent search services only provide the text portions of the patents on file. Some only provide abstracts. If you want to see the entire text plus all the illustrations, graphs, and diagrams, you can contact SmartPatents. This Menlo Park, California company will provide you with a CD for $100 per patent. That's not quite as expensive as it sounds when you consider that online legal services such as Lexis charge over $100 per month, plus $46-per-hour connect time and other fees.

Some subscription services provide patent information on CD. Micro-Patent Incorporated, for example, charges $1,200 per year for its monthly abstracts of European and U.S. patents.

Information Storage and Distribution

Using compact discs to store and distribute information is cost-effective—not just for massive amounts of data, but for average-size volumes as well. Compact disc recorders (CD-R), which are used to make CDs, are not new. Cash-rich companies have been using CD-Rs for several years. Now, however, lower prices for CD-Rs are leveling the playing field. Small companies even self-employed individuals can do what before was only a dream.

If you don't want to record CDs in-house, there are all types of production houses and service bureaus to help you out. In Chapter 14 I'll talk about the issues involved in deciding whether to create and press your own discs in-house, or hire an outside production company or manufacturer. In this section, I'll try to stick to the ways in which people are using compact discs, and, as usual, I'll talk about some sample applications.

Storing Data on Disc

If you work in a field that requires the constant handling of large amounts of information, compact discs may be of use. Consider an insurance company and the piles and piles of claim forms that it must process. Or a law firm where each case requires pages and pages of depositions, affidavits, photos, and evidence reports. Both of these examples lend themselves well to electronic media, for two main reasons.

First, the data can be indexed and easily searched. When you're looking for that perfect slip of the tongue recorded at a deposition, you can find and quote it exactly, then and there. And second, the volume of actual physical material is reduced and is therefore easier to handle. You can't bring your office suite into a courtroom, but bringing in a CD or two is not a problem.

These two examples describe electronic storage of data for immediate use. But what happens when the claim is resolved or the case is over? What do you do with all that paperwork? Warehouses contain boxes and boxes of "dead files," and the price of storage space per square foot is high. Then there's the cost (in both time and money) of retrieving something from a warehouse. One way to end these storage nightmares is to use compact discs for archiving data.

Archiving data on disc can't be done overnight, though. What about all the data that is already in storage? In many cases it is best to leave it there. The cost of transferring the old data to disc may not be worthwhile. You have to ask yourself whether you'll need to access the data in the future.

Then there's the question of how to get your new data onto disc. You might assume that means hiring scores of data entry personnel. If so, think again. Scanning and imaging technology has come a long way. It can be used to quickly and efficiently digitize all types of information from a variety of formats. Another benefit of imaging is accuracy, a crucial point if the data is ever needed for legal purposes. No data entry, no typos. It must be noted, however, that the use of optical character recognition (OCR) software on scanned documents can introduce typographical errors by mistaking one character for another.

What if your documents are already digital? Great, you don't have to deal with scanning or imaging. But there's another problem: You can't read a document created with Word for Windows, for example, unless you have Word for Windows on your system or network. Products such as Adobe Acrobat solve this problem. With Adobe Acrobat, you can save files in a special format that can be shared with others via a reader program. Documents are placed on disc along with the reader program, so that anyone using the disc will be able to read the files.

That raises another issue: security. You might not want just anyone to have complete access to your files. Security is a matter to be handled by the people working with the files and designing your CDs. If the program you used to create the documents supports password protection, then you might deal with security on a document-by-document basis by giving each document a password. Or you could use the navigation program to deny access to specific files without a password. But this has no bearing on the file formats, per se.

One security benefit is inherent in CDs—you can't tamper with the data once it's on the disc. You cannot write over or erase a CD file, nor can you destroy the data by placing it too close to a magnetic field.

Distributing Data on Disc

At the beginning of this section I mentioned that compact disc recorders have become more affordable. Currently they run between $2,000 and $4,000. And the cost of blank discs runs between $10 and $20 per disc. How do these dollar-and-cent figures translate into real operating expenses? Imagine that your department in the West Coast office has new data, more than 400+ megabytes, that needs to reach the New York office by tomorrow. What are your options?

You have technically savvy people at both ends, so you could use a modem to transmit the data over the phone lines. But that could take hours and add not just to your phone bill, but also to your overtime allotment. And it would be risky. I've lost count of the number of times phone line interference caused the transfer process to abort near the end of a long modem transmission, and I had to start all over again from square one.

Your alternative? Create a "one-off" using your new speedy CD-R. When you create a single CD it is called a "one-off," and the Eastman Kodak PCD Writer 600 only takes about 10 minutes to fill an entire CD. Then call your favorite overnight courier and head home to relax.

Compact discs can be used to distribute all types of data, be it programs, images, or information. And many discs now include advertisements. With all the space available on a compact disc, vendors are putting their great advertising graphics on the their discs to reinforce the company image and promote additional products. Some vendors even join forces with cross-promotional campaigns.

In this section I'll describe a few distribution applications from the public and private sectors. These applications range from fonts and clip art to parts catalogs and service manuals.

Software and Digital Resources

Software programs, and digital resources such as fonts, clip art, and sound clips, are the most obvious examples of products being distributed via CD. More and more programs are shipping with added-value items that include "clip collections" of all types. But value-added clip collections are only a drop in the bucket compared with the plethora of CD clip collections marketed independently.

Agfa and Monotype have both made their font libraries available on CD-ROM. With a CD, you don't have to laboriously transfer font files to the hard drive from multiple diskettes. You also don't have to worry about whether your printer has enough memory to handle the fonts. The *Monotype FoneFonts* CD, a cross-platform disc, combines PostScript and TrueType fonts. It includes software that allows both Macintosh systems and PCs running Windows to access the fonts.

Another advantage of CDs is the opportunity they give vendors to include extras, such as interactive tutorials and product information, that they didn't have room for before. The *AgfaType* disc contains more than 2,000 typefaces from the Agfa and Adobe libraries, in addition to such value-added items as tutorials and typographic utilities.

Photos are always in demand for advertising, illustrating, packaging, and more. One of the issues surrounding the use of photos is that of commercial rights and royalties. More and more collections are allow you to use the images for commercial and/or advertising purposes.

For example, Digital Zone has created a Photo CD offering 50 images. The price, $599, might seem steep for only 50 images, but the product includes advertising-use rights and the right to alter or modify the images, all without any royalty obligations.

Seattle Support Group took a different approach for its *Vintage Quality Photographic Images* compact disc series. Each disc features the work of one photographer, and the photographer receives a percentage of the disc sales in lieu of commercial-use royalties.

You will find more resource collections than you would ever dream of needing—drawings, photos, cartoons, sounds, music, video, even fractals. Prices vary wildly depending on the content and which type of usage rights are included.

Just like the photo discs I described, music libraries are available for outright purchase, no royalties attached. The same is true of video clip collections. The only catch is that you have to read the purchase agreement or license. A standard license or purchase agreement has yet to be devised, so each is different.

The Paperwork Reduction Act

I always thought that the Paperwork Reduction Act was supposed to mean a reduction in paper *work*, not just a reduction in paper. But for the sake of the trees, I'll be happy with the latter. It seems that government agencies are taking the Paperwork Reduction Act to mean they should deliver their rules, regulations, and other information via compact disc.

Directives from the Department of Transportation are issued on CD. The State Department ships CDs with updated phone directories and thousands of pages of Foreign Affairs manuals to overseas posts each quarter. The General Services Administration produces the Federal IRM Regulation (FIRMR) and

Federal Acquisition Regulation (FAR) CDs, with subscriptions available through the Government Printing Office for $106 per year.

Private companies also produce compact disc titles with the same or similar data. Government Counseling Ltd. provides subscriptions to FIRMR, FAR, Office of Management and Budget circulars, and other informational CDs, to the Bureau of Prisons, the Coast Guard, the Justice Department, the Commerce Department, and others subscribers. West Publishing Company and Information Handling Services are two more companies that produce FIRMR and FAR compact disc titles.

Field Service Books and Catalogs

Cost and time are important when you are responsible for maintaining and distributing large amounts of information, but just as important is the question of whether end-users can get the information easily. Everybody talks about fitting shelves and shelves of manuals on a single disc and how much is saved in space, paper, printing, and distribution costs. The size and weight of a disc compared to the size and weight of a book lends itself to such hoopla. What is truly amazing to me, however, is how *accessible* data on a disc is—provided the disc is well designed.

Allen Bradley, one of the world's largest suppliers of factory automation products, now sends out a single compact disc with all its field service books. The printed books, all 60,000 pages, used to be four to six feet high when stacked on top of each other and weigh in at more than 630 pounds. They cost a pretty penny to ship too.

Customers of Waukesha Engine were happy with their new illustrated electronic parts catalog. This division of Dresser Industries builds industrial engines, big ones with lots and lots of parts. Searching for information about a part used to mean thumbing through volumes of printed catalogs or scrolling through microfiche. Now customers can search by serial or order numbers, look at illustrations, and review price lists and bills of materials at the same time.

Training and Consumer Education

As discussed in the last chapter, multimedia has some advantages for training. With sound, video and animations to enhance impact, and computer intelligence to manage the instruction and adapt to the needs of the trainee, multimedia can be a valuable training tool. The benefits of using multimedia for training can be summarized as follows:

- The ability to show events in real-time
- The ability to provide event simulations for purposes of practice
- Targeted instruction, which is perfect for situations where specific information is needed quickly in order to proceed with a task (often called *just-in-time training*)
- Faster training than is possible in lecture or classroom settings
- More effective training, because multi-sensory input stimulates retention
- Better use of employee time, and less time away from work
- Cost-effectiveness, since the need for costly consultants and travel expenses is eliminated
- Consistency in the presentation of information
- Self-directed learning, as users can work at their own pace and schedule sessions conveniently

Government agencies have long been in the forefront when it comes to developing training applications using new technologies. The Electronic Warfare Onboard Training system (EWOBT) and Shipboard Training Enhancement Program (STEP) used by the Navy are just two of dozens of examples of government-sponsored training applications. Instructional Systems Specialist Dennis Knott told me that 2,500 copies of STEP are distributed to the fleet every six months, and each version of the disc contains several hundred courses, covering a broad range of topics. Not only is it easy to distribute training courses on disc, but it is also easier to protect classified materials. CDs are not only durable and cost-effective, they are tamper-proof and easy to secure.

In business, one of the most sought-after benefits is time savings. Live training sessions that once took a whole morning and disrupted employees' schedules can now be administered to individuals at their convenience in a mere 30 minutes. Information delivered in seminars lasting several days to a week can now be placed on interactive training discs so that employees can access it as needed. Keeping up-to-date on new developments, as well as just-in-time training, or simply taking a refresher course, has become much easier thanks to CDs.

Custom-Built Training Programs

Spinnaker Communications and the Scientific and Commercial Systems Corporation created a CD-i training program that the Federal Emergency Management Agency (FEMA) uses to train field personnel in disaster response procedures for radiological emergencies.

The entire CD-i training disc takes about two and a half hours from beginning to end. But a good training program adapts to its users. So as to not waste their time, the FEMA program makes trainees take a "pre-test" and then guides them to certain segments of the training program based on the results of the test. Besides the pre-test, the program includes six game-like training exercises, six review sections, a "post-test," and an interactive accident scenario re-creating a radiological disaster.

On the training disc, disaster strikes when a truck carrying radioactive materials overturns in traffic and bursts into flames. When the fire fighters arrive on the scene, they notice the radioactive symbol on the side of the truck. They're not sure what to do, so they call FEMA. The trainee takes the role of the person answering the fire fighter's questions. As long as the trainee gives the correct answers, the program continues until the disaster scene is under control. If there are too many wrong answers, the trainee is sent to a review section for further instruction.

The project was massive, containing 60 animations and over 600 graphic screens. It took six months to complete but was well worth the time and money. This training disc replaced a two-day training seminar FEMA used to offer its employees. It has an added benefit, in that employees can use it as a refresher course and a means of reviewing disaster procedures.

McDonald's Service Enhancement Training is a less explosive, but no less important training application. It was created by Andersen Consulting. The purpose of this training course is to teach employees basic job skills and show them how to handle difficult situations. Video clips dramatize different scenarios, such as a customer trying to bring a dog into the restaurant.

Commercial Titles for In-House Training

Having seen the many video cassette courses teaching the ins and outs of popular computer software programs, I was not surprised to find interactive software training tutorials on CD-ROM. Personal Training Systems offers titles covering Microsoft Windows 3.1, Word 6, Excel 5, Office 4.2, and PowerPoint 4

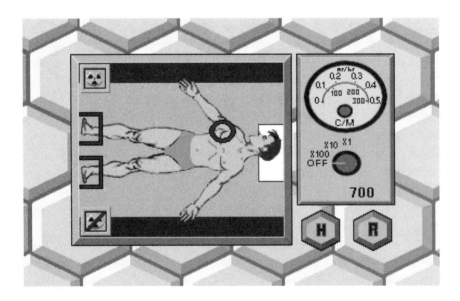

The Federal Emergency Management Agency training program. The top screen is from the Site Survey, in which you take readings in each sector of the radiation-contaminated accident area. The bottom screen is a training exercise in which you find "hot spots" on a victim of radiation exposure. (Screen shots © 1993 Spinnaker Communications.)

for IBM PCs and compatibles, and System 7 and PageMaker 5 for the Macintosh.

But software is just the first of many subjects for which I found consumer-oriented training CDs that might be of interest to businesses.

Language and Travel

If you are headed on a business trip to Japan or Mexico and need to learn about their language and customs, look into the *Berlitz Live! Japanese* and *Berlitz Live! Spanish* CD-ROMs from Sierra On-Line. In 10 chapters, with the help of an animated coach, you can build a 3,000-word vocabulary and learn about the Tokyo subway and Mexico City bus systems.

Learn to Speak Spanish, a CD from Hyperglot Software Company, Inc., bases its lessons on a business trip to Mexico City. The program, which includes video footage, allows the user to watch and hear dialog in Spanish. The disc includes vocabulary and grammar exercises, as well as information on cultural practices. If you have a microphone, you can test your Spanish pronunciation. The program plays your words back for you following a demonstration by a native speaker.

Repair

Need to teach plant mechanics how to change a boiler feed pump? *This Old Pump*, from Nolan Multimedia, is a just-in-time training program that simulates job tasks using video and 3-D graphics.

Sales and Management Skills

I don't know much about a CD titled *Sales Source 2000: Beer-Selling Basics* from Anheuser-Busch, but I read that it won a Silver Award for Training at the 1994 NewMedia InVision Multimedia Awards. I mention it only because Anheuser-Busch is a leading U.S. company and my *Multimedia Business 500* CD ranks it fourth out of the Best 100 Companies to Work For. I just thought it was interesting that this company is also using new technologies to train its employees.

People Who Lead is the title of a CD from PERC Macromedia Group, Inc. Aimed at management, the disc offers eight hours of content, including simulations, exercises, and tests. Topics covered range from how to improve employees' work habits and run effective meetings, to information on labor law, government regulations, and safety requirements.

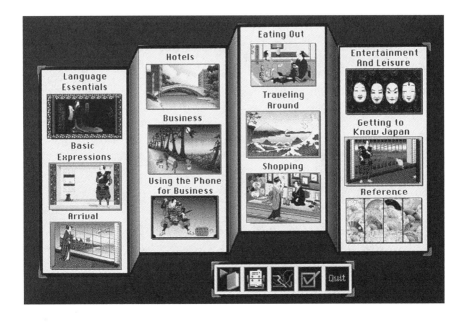

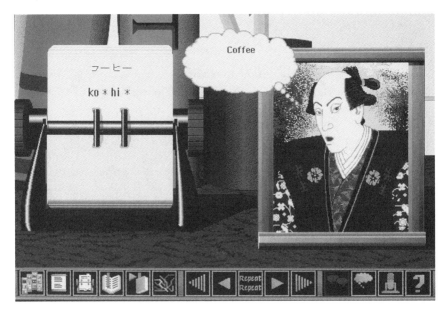

Berlitz Live! Japanese shows you everything from language essentials and basic expressions to eating out and getting to know more about Japan. (Screen shots courtesy of Sierra On-Line.)

Time Is Money

People are in a hurry. They devour fast-food and they want their information fast too. Businesses believe "time is money" and they want to increase produc-tivity and elevate the profit margin. Businesses also know that they need to make customers happy, and that means responding to customer needs quickly too.

CDs can play a role here in several ways—they can retrieve information, automate time-intensive procedures using data in electronic form, and provide just-in-time training tailored to the learner's specific needs.

Hand in hand with speed go convenience and accessibility. Today's con-sumers want what they want, when they want it. Anyone who ever placed an order with, or answered the phone at, a 24-hour mail-order house knows this. Infomercials are on late at night because the rates are lower, true. But they are also on late because that's when people are at home, and once the pitch is made, the deal can be closed then and there by phone. No trip to the store, no stop at the bank for cash, no time off from work. No potential obstacles to closing the sale.

The same principles apply to services. How many times have you been frustrated by missing a deadline for placing orders? You look up from your desk to discover it's already ten minutes past 5:00, but you dial the customer service number anyway and get that recording: "Thank you for calling Widget, Inc. Our customer service hours are 8 a.m. to 5 p.m. Please call back then. Good-bye."

CDs are there for you, containing all sorts of data, ready for use whenever you might need them. And the search capabilities and hyperlinked indexes make it easy to get to the information you need.

Up-to-the-minute coverage is also a part of both speed and accessibility. This is where you might think that CDs need not apply. After all, once the data is on the disc, it cannot be updated. And that's true. But one of the new trends in CD titles is a hybrid CD/online application. Steve Case, President of America Online, spoke about this, as I mentioned in Chapter 1. And in Chapters 7 and 8 you'll read about two of these hybrid titles for the home market.

While I did not happen to come across any similar hybrid titles for the business market, I know many researchers, myself included, who use CD-ROM discs to do the basic research, and then augment those findings with the latest information by going online. For example, you could be using the *Corporate American* CD-ROM from Dialog's OnDisc series. It presents demographic and classification information on 1 million businesses, and the disc is updated quarterly. So you do your research, and when you've narrowed down the field to a select handful of targets, you can dial up the Dialog Online service and grab the latest data on only the companies you've targeted.

In the last two chapters I have mentioned or described more than 50 business-related CD applications. In the next chapter I'll take business out of the office and into public places.

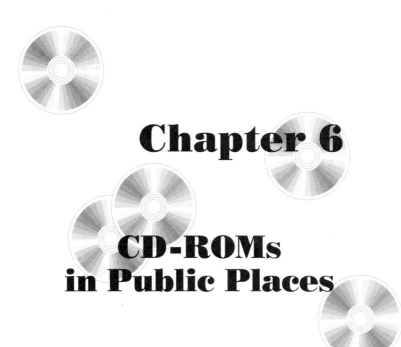

Chapter 6

CD-ROMs
in Public Places

Historically, advances in technology have altered our means of communication, and means of communication in turn have influenced new trends in information delivery and cultural attitudes in general. With each advance, it seems that more information becomes available to increasing numbers of people more quickly. The printing press brought written works out of the monasteries and churches and into the hands of the people. The telegraph wire brought news from afar faster than the pony express. Today, television networks use satellites and other electronic devices to bring events such as the Gulf War, the Los Angeles riots, and the trial of O.J. Simpson into our homes with up-to-the-minute coverage.

If you're at work or elsewhere without access to a television or radio, you can dial-up an online computer service such as CompuServe, Prodigy, or America Online to get the latest news. In fact, getting back to CD-ROMs, CNN markets a consumer CD-ROM product about the O.J. Simpson trial. The CD offers all of the available information at the time it was created, plus a dial-up component by which the user can log on to CompuServe for the latest updates.

In this chapter, I'll tell you what I've found out about the use of CD-based products in libraries, museums, and other public places. I'll cover some of the main issues, pro and con, and talk about how the integration of CD products in these locations affects both the providers and the consumers. The technology is here, but its integration will take time. Hardware and software are readily available, but budgets are tight and the benefits still unproven.

This is still a time of great experimentation, and not without some trepidation on the part of the experimenters. For example, librarians and curators worry that when the public can get its information digitally, people will no longer visit libraries or museums in person. Of course, time will tell....

In Libraries

The library has long been a major provider of information to the public. So it should be no surprise that libraries were the first CD-ROM customers. Chris Andrews, a CD publisher from way back, says that a man named Brower Murphy was the first-ever CD-ROM publisher, and that Murphy sold the first system in 1985 at the American Library Association conference. The Library Corporation claims that their BiblioFile cataloging was the first commercial application of CD-ROM technology. I suspect that BiblioFile and Murphy's system are one in the same. It was a natural sale, because libraries had long been users of microfilm, microfiche, and online retrieval services.

In the beginning, computer usage in libraries was limited to automating circulation and inventory control. We saw the electronic card catalogs and the beginning of automated information indexes. Meanwhile, the electronic representation of the content itself represented new opportunities.

New products emerged that exploited electronic storage and retrieval of the information itself, and electronic versions of frequently used reference titles began to appear. Over the last several years, publishers and online providers have been creating digital versions of classic literature and periodicals, particularly works for which it is believed there will be a long-lasting demand.

As the technology continues to evolve, and digitization becomes more reliable and cost-effective, lesser-known works and materials for which there is less demand may also find their way onto CDs. (Of course, by that time, CDs may have given way to yet another new technology.) Until then, the library as we know it today will continue to maintain, and occasionally duplicate, its collections in their present forms, including printed matter, film, microfiche, audio cassettes, video tapes, and compact discs.

In library sciences literature you can find a number of studies and research projects that relate to the use of CD-ROM discs. While it is not within the scope of this book to report on the details and outcomes of these studies, it is worth noting a few for the sake of historical perspective.

In the mid 1980s, ADONIS (Article Delivery Over Network Information System) was born as a pilot project. Partners in the project included a publishing consortium of Elsevier, Springer-Verlag, Pergamon, Blackwells, Acadata, and John Wiley. Its object was to investigate the issues involved in electronic document delivery with CD-ROM technology. In 1991, ADONIS became a for-profit company providing CD-ROMs with indexes and text for several hundred scientific and medical journals.

In 1987, Ohio State University started a project called Gateway to Information. Partnered by the Department of Education, the objective of the project was to develop a front-end to an online catalog and other information sources. The front-end would teach students to find, evaluate, and select materials that met their needs regardless of format, and to access and integrate CD-ROM-based databases.

Project Mercury began at Carnegie Mellon University in 1989. Its objective was to build a prototype electronic library and test the system with a real user population. In its first phase, the project included over a dozen databases containing citations linked to full texts on CD-ROMs.

Clifford A. Lynch, Director of the Division of Library Automation for the University of California Office of the President, wrote a 1993 article in *Serials Librarian*, titled "The Transformation of Scholarly Communication and the Role of the Library in the Age of Networked Information." In it, Lynch points out the distinction between modernization and transformation. "Modernization can be defined as the use of new technology to continue to do what you have been doing, but in a more efficient and/or cost-effective way….Transformation addresses the use of new technology to change processes in a fundamental way."

While debates continue as to exactly where we are along the modernization/transformation continuum, most agree that if a transformation has taken place, it is minimal compared to what the future will bring. In an article titled *The Library Tomorrow: a Virtual Certainty*, James LaRue, Director of the Douglas Public Library District in Castle Rock, Colorado, wrote, "I would argue that what we have achieved in our libraries to date is nothing more than an electronically assisted library, not a virtual library." There is no doubt, however, that the roles of library and librarian are changing.

Librarians

While it is true that the number of consumers with CD players and/or access to online services continues to grow exponentially, libraries will be a major provider of access to new electronic systems for some time to come. And even those of us who have access to digital data, at home or in the office, have little knowledge of the depth and breadth of information available, let alone where to find it. We will need to call on experts to direct us to available resources and to help us shape our searches.

The introduction of new resources brings with it the need to learn how to use those resources. Librarians will need new skills. They will have to become familiar with many new references in order to recommend the best resources for specific needs. They will have to teach new skills for conducting research. They will even be called upon to show others how to navigate in cyberspace.

This could turn out to be a big problem. Librarians agree that people who lack the appropriate cognitive skills, who don't understand the difference between subjects and keywords, for example, won't get much benefit from interactive research discs. People have to learn how to construct appropriate search strategies, or they'll be disappointed with the results of their searches. But as Daphne Allen, Business Administration and Economics Librarian at Portland State University Library, points out, librarians may or may not be available to provide expert help due to the budget cuts that libraries face. The central reference desk at the Portland State University library, for example, is no longer staffed. With the push to fund technology, libraries are cutting even more positions.

Library Tools

Shelf space, and the lack thereof, has always been a big headache for libraries when it comes to deciding what references and literature to buy and maintain. Now, however, when an entire encyclopedia can be put on a single disc, more shelf space can be made available. Furthermore, the cost of updating an encyclopedia by buying a disc is far less than that of buying an entire new set of hardbound volumes. CD-ROM journal collections are touted as being better than textbooks, even textbooks that are continually updated.

Other enticements include fast and comprehensive search tools that support Boolean search strategies and don't rely on subject authorities. For example, text searches allow you to find data without regard to how categories or subject references were set up by the professional indexers. All you have to do is enter a keyword, and all instances of that word become available. (Boolean search strategies use words such as *and, or,* and *not* to narrow down your search results, making it even easier to find what you're looking for.)

Hyperlinked cross-referencing is another way to bring readers' attention to associated materials. A *hyperlink* is a connection between one word, phrase, or topic, and another. Hyperlinks are indicated by some sort of visual cue, such as a button or change in text color; when you click on one of these links, the associated material appears. Multimedia features can also provide visual points of reference that enhance information presentation—a help for those who may not be familiar with the topic.

Online services and CD-ROMs are marketed to librarians—to public librarians, academic librarians, even to corporate librarians. Increasingly, these same products are being marketed to consultants and R&D specialists as well. In this section I'll give you some examples of titles that are likely to be found in public, academic, and corporate libraries.

General Reference

The first electronic source of information you're likely to find in a library is the computerized card catalog. Companies such as The Library Corporation in Inwood, West Virginia, help libraries to create these indexes, often on CD-ROM.

Lots of newspapers and magazines have been cataloged and reproduced for CD. The *Boston Globe*, *Miami Herald*, *Los Angeles Times*, and *San Francisco Chronicle* are just a few of the newspapers available on CD-ROM from Dialog's OnDisc series. Magazines from Dialog include the *Consumer Reports* disc, which offers two monthly newsletters, *Consumer Reports on Health* and the *Consumer Reports Travel Letter*.

Another staple in any library is *Books in Print*, available on CD-ROM from R.R. Bowker and marketed and distributed by Reed Technology and Information Services. And then there are the phone books and census data discs. As I mentioned in Chapters 4 and 5, quite a few CD publishers have created electronic phone books and compiled lots of government data, including census figures. *PhoneDisc* is a well-known CD, but because it shuts down after 5,000 lookups, it's not much use in a library.

Academic References

Indexes to academic literature were among the earliest CD-ROM applications. Now academic electronic references can be found for a variety of specialized topics. These reference CDs often include full text in addition to abstracts, and sometimes they offer graphics as well.

Marketed by Dialog, ERIC it is the world's largest and best-known educational database. ERIC (Educational Resources Information Center of the U.S. Department of Education) collects articles from 750 educational journals and thousands of research reports, covering a broad spectrum of educational subjects. The ERIC database on CD-ROM comprises two print indexes: *Resources in Education* (RIE) and *Current Index to Journals in Education* (CIJE).

Other education-related titles from Dialog OnDisc include *The Philosopher's Index*, which covers philosophy books and journals of philosophy and related interdisciplinary fields, and *Grants* database, which describes grants available from foundations and private, local, federal, and international funding sources.

The *McGraw-Hill Multimedia Encyclopedia of Science and Technology* looks like it would be of interest to the home market, but with a price tag of $1,300 it's more likely to make inroads in the library and school markets. Students of economics looking for industrial production and retail sales indexes, or for import/export statistics, will find these indexes and lots more in The *DRI/McGraw-Hill Encyclopedia of World Economies* on CD-ROM.

Daphne Allen reports that the most commonly used reference discs at Portland State University library include:

⊙ *US Government Census.* The print version for 1990 alone took up five rows of shelving. The compact disc version spanned approximately fifty CDs, but none of the discs are full because each contains only subject-specific information.

⊙ *Tiger Line Files.* Data provided by the U.S. Bureau of the Census.

⊙ *American Business Disc.* Unfortunately, the phone numbers are, on the average, about 27 months out of date.

⊙ *ABI Inform.* Bibliographic citations and abstracts to over 800 business journals.

⊙ *PsychLit.* This is a spin-off of the print volumes of *Psychological Abstracts.*

⊙ The *Science Citation Index*, *Social Science Citation Index*, and *Humanities Citation Index.* Each of these provides citations to leading journals and periodicals in each field.

⊙ *Compendex.* This is an engineering reference.

- *ERIC.* Covers 750 educational journals and thousands of research reports.

- *EconLit.* Citations and abstracts of worldwide economic literature.

- *Predicast.* This is for economic forecasting.

- *The Bible.* Three different versions are offered.

Professional References

A variety of professional references are also likely to be found in public and university libraries. Specialized references, however, are more likely to be found in public and private libraries devoted to one field of study. Medical and legal libraries, many of which are open to the public, as well as private corporate libraries, usually offer specialized references.

Health and Biomedicine   Creative Multimedia has a Medical Division that produces CD-ROM products for both the professional and home consumer market. Its professional journal titles include *Annals of Internal Medicine* (described in Chapter 5), *The New England Journal of Medicine*, and the *Pediatric Infectious Disease Journal*, to list just a few. It is not unusual for CD-ROM publishers to produce text-only versions of periodical literature. The medical journals on CD-ROM from Creative Multimedia, however, offer the same color photographs and illustrations, tables, graphs, and charts found in the original print version.

The American Psychiatric Electronic Library features volumes of literature, figures, photos, and information. Produced and marketed by Reed Technology and Information Services (RTIS) in conjunction with American Psychiatric Press, Inc., this disc is available at a subscription rate of $595. Also distributed by RTIS is the American Heart Association Compact Library, the AIDS Compact Library, and Physician's MEDLINE.

Science and Technology   Dialog OnDisc has more than 20 titles in the field of science and technology. Titles include *Aerospace Database*, offering NASA technical reports in addition to the standard journal articles, conference papers, and theses; *Kirk-Othmer Encyclopedia of Chemical Technology*, now with images; and *Nuclear Science Abstracts*, which covers worldwide nuclear science and technology literature from 1948 to 1976.

Law and Government   In addition to the *SIRS Researcher* and *SIRS Discoverer* CD-ROMs mentioned in Chapter 3, Social Issues Resources Series, Inc., also produces *SIRS Government Reporter*, a CD-ROM with the complete text and graphical information published by federal departments, agencies, and commissions. Besides subject and keyword searching, you can browse by department or agency. The Library Corporation publishes a CD-ROM called *The Library of Congress Records* that can be found in more than 37,000 libraries nationwide. The Library of Congress itself also produces a CD-ROM containing its records.

In fact, the U.S. government publishes a lot of CD-ROM discs. The long list of government offices and agencies that publish CDs includes Congress, the Patent and Trademark Office, the National Institute of Health, the Government Printing Office, the Navy Publishing and Printing Service Management Office, the Social Security Administration, the Law Revision Council of the House of Representatives, and the Department of the Interior.

Dialog OnDisc has three titles that pertain to law and government: *The Federal Register,* the U.S. government publication through which the public is notified of official agency actions, including regulations and legal notices; *TRADEMARKSCAN—Federal,* a complete record of active Federal trademark applications and registrations filed with the U.S. Patent and Trademark Office; and *TRADEMARKSCAN—State,* a record of trademarks registered with the Secretary of State in all U.S. states and Puerto Rico, including records for every type of commercially marketed product and service. Counterpoint Publishing Inc. also publishes a CD-ROM version of *The Federal Register.*

Business Information   Back in February of 1993, *Byte* magazine reported on a CD-ROM title published by The Office of Business Analysis, a part of the U.S. Department of Commerce. It was the *National Trade Data Bank* CD-ROM, and it contained information about international markets compiled from 15 different federal agencies.

The H.W. Wilson Company publishes the *Business Periodicals Index,* covering 350 trade and business periodicals and research journals. If you're looking for full text, the Information Access Company publishes *Business ASAP,* a CD with articles from business, trade, management, computer, and other journals.

Dun & Bradstreet publishes the *CD Credit Register.* And *American Banker, Corporate America, Merger and Acquisition Transactions,* and *U.S. Business Reporter* are just a few of the business information titles available from Dialog OnDisc.

Will CDs Replace Books?

Library use of CD-ROMs definitely has benefits. Unlike books, CDs do not yellow with age. Once accessed from a workstation connected to a network, the same CD can be used by several people at one time. And no one can steal or deface its pages. It's true that computer networks have their own hazards, not the least of which are hackers and computer viruses. But CD-ROMs have the edge. As a read-only medium, they are immune to viral infection.

There are those who think that "CD-ROM" is synonymous with "multimedia," and they often overlook the benefits that electronic searching, cross indexing, and linking of related information bring to text-intensive titles. Hundreds of text-based consumer CD-ROM titles are available today, and while I can't envision librarians starting any bonfires, it seems logical that when the pages of those hefty multivolume references have yellowed, they will be replaced by electronic versions.

As for other types of books and magazines, both fiction and nonfiction, electronic versions are likely to emerge, but not to replace their printed counterparts, not yet anyway. Perhaps not ever. Technology has replicated the data, but not the experience of reading books. Audio CDs most certainly did not replace live concerts, no more than movies replaced theater or videocassettes replaced going to the movies.

Furthermore, there are still technological hurdles to overcome. For example, today's computer monitors have limited contrast and resolution, making it hard to read text on a screen for long periods of time. When the day comes that we can put electronic information in our back pockets, or access it while riding a train—complete with quality sound and video—then maybe hard-copy versions will cease to be of use or interest. But for now, most library scientists believe that print and electronic technologies will coexist for years to come.

What we may see in the not-too-distant future, however, are CD-ROM titles that you can check out at the local library. Some libraries have already begun to experiment with CD lending policies.

According to PSU librarian Daphne Allen, checking out discs is an idea that will make many librarians very unhappy. She says that it is not uncommon for people to destroy CDs accidentally by inadvertently inserting them into the computer's 5¼" floppy disk drive. This sentiment was echoed by Pat Onsi, associate director and systems manager for the medical library at the State University of New York Health Science Center. Most librarians prefer to handle compact discs themselves. Frequently used discs would ideally be put on a local area network with a server that can hold several discs at one time. According to Allen, professors can't check out discs from the Portland State University library unless they can prove that their department has the appropriate equipment and they know how to use a CD-ROM player.

Nevertheless, if Blockbuster and Major Video Concepts think renting CD-ROM titles is a good idea, consumers may come to expect free library access to CDs. Perhaps it won't be long before CDs show up on library shelves.

Disc vs. Dial-Up

At present, the pros and cons of owning CD-ROM–based materials versus online access are fairly straightforward. Cost-effectiveness is one of the primary concerns. Libraries charge no fee for borrowing books (unless, of course, you forget to return them on time), so it seems unlikely that libraries would pass on the cost of online access to their users. With the exception of the Internet, online access to information is still fairly expensive, at least for individuals and small businesses. In the spirit of providing information free to the public, it would make sense for libraries to purchase available resources on disc—at least until prices for online services become more affordable.

A second concern is how long it takes to access information. No doubt about it, searching for data on a well-indexed CD-ROM product is much faster than thumbing through volumes of books. And accessing data from a local CD-ROM drive is still faster than accessing it online via modem. At least it is today. On the other hand, even local area network CD access, such as that found in libraries, begins to slow down when too many users attempt to access the same disc. (Of course, it should be noted that the same is true of online services.) Access speed will always be important in a society that believes "time is money." Technological advances in local area network software, data-compression algorithms, remote system protocols, to name just a few areas, will continue to increase the access speed of CD-based and online resources.

A third area of concern is multiple-user access. Whether or not many users can access a CD at once is not relevant to people working at home or at stand-alone office workstations. It is, however, a big concern for libraries, especially because many libraries cannot afford to support individual CD-ROM workstations unless they are networked. This means that the CD-ROM software products used in libraries must also be designed to support network use, and CD-ROM publishers will have to offer network licenses if their products are to be used in public places.

It does seem likely that libraries will decrease their investment in CDs as more files become available on the Internet and more people start "surfing the net." Some CDs, however, such as phone directories, will always find use in the library. And on the whole, CDs won't be replaced until the whole nation is wired for transmission, and access is affordable. That won't happen for many years.

Of course, the subject of CDs and how libraries make use of them matters little to the library goer. All library goers care about is whether the information appears when they sit down at a workstation. Whether the information is being accessed from a network of CD-ROMs or from a remote service connected by modem is of little importance.

The Role of the Library

Libraries will continue to maintain collections of information resources, whatever their format. Some will be maintained on site, other resources will be accessed from afar. Yesterday, an interlibrary loan meant waiting days, if not weeks, to receive a title borrowed from another library. Today, technology makes it possible to access information from long distances.

Where the information comes from, whether it is stored on a network of CDs located at the library and updated periodically, or whether the library workstation is connected to a database in Timbuktu, will be of little concern to the user. Barbara Von Wahlde and Nancy Schiller, in *The Virtual Library: Visions and Realities*, described the library as follows: "The library might be seen as a machine with many simultaneous users, each of whom perceives that he has the whole collection to himself, and further, through connections to other libraries access to much greater resources than are physically present."

For now, CD-ROM publishing still looks to be a boom business for the library market. Of course, by the time online access to information services becomes less expensive than purchasing CD software and hardware, and said access is fast, is easy, and is available to everyone, we'll all be connected and the definition of a library may be more along the lines of the following, as written by Lawrence E. Murr and James R. Williams in an article in *Library Hi Tech* back in 1987: "'Library' as a place, will give way to 'library' as a transparent knowledge network providing 'intelligent' services to business and education through specialized librarians and merging information technologies."

In Museums

In the world of art, masterpieces are priceless. Will museums lose revenues when people rip off electronic copies of artworks? Or even worse, will someone use Van Gogh's *Starry Night* in an advertisement for a professional escort service that specializes in celebrity look-alikes? Will the reverence and awe that famous works inspire be minimized when these works can be easily seen at any time? Will the relatively low cost of electronic rights lessen the value of the original artwork? These are some of the many concerns of museum curators and their boards of directors.

Being able to scan great works of art is more than a notion. The process of digitizing artworks, and the possibility of their ending up with inadequate resolution or inexact color, evokes nightmares. Companies such as Continuum have the technological expertise to digitize artworks, but some museums are reluctant to let these companies scan the works because, in return, the companies want to own the digital rights. The loss of these rights could mean a tremendous loss of income for the museum.

Anthony Hushion, head of information technology services for the Royal Ontario Museum, in Toronto, Canada, points out that for public institutions, the situation may be even more difficult. A public museum is a custodian acting on behalf of the public. As such, the museum itself may not own the rights in the first place. However, as advancements in scanning technology continue, the problems of dithering and inferior color reproduction should soon abate. Then it will become easier for libraries to digitize their own artifacts and use the images for a variety of purposes inside and outside the museum.

Museums always have budget problems. For years they have relied on docents—unpaid, art-loving volunteers—to give guided tours and help in other ways. Today museums are beginning to augment their resources by integrating interactive multimedia stations into their exhibits. In this section, I'll tell you how they're doing this.

Besides running out of money, museums are always running out of space. Often they send whole exhibits on tour, which is great, but it's a travesty when they have to warehouse them. However, if a museum puts its collections on CD-based applications, the works can still be available to the public when they are on the road, in restoration, or in a warehouse. Mind you, standing in front of the *Mona Lisa* is not the same as viewing her on a computer screen, but viewing a screen image could be the next best thing to not seeing her at all.

CD-ROMs as Part of the Exhibit

If you want to know the name of an artist or piece of artwork in a museum, you have to read the wall label—unless, of course, you are on a museum tour where the guide provides the information instead. Some museums even supply cassette tapes and guidebooks so you can create your own informative tour.

Today it is unusual—but it will be less so in the future—to find touch screens attached to CD players in strategic museum locations. The National Gallery in London was one of the first major institutions to enter this arena, and the National Gallery in Washington, D.C., has followed suit. Both museums created what they call the "Micro Gallery," a series of touch-screen terminals that give access to all kinds of information about the library's collection.

Similar in style to some of the interactive learning environments described in Chapter 3, the Micro Gallery allows visitors to learn more about the art world. They can get biographical information about the artists, their works, and art history.

The key to a museum is its collection, and the Royal Ontario Museum's Anthony Hushion is always looking for new and better ways to tell the story of each artifact. "It's one thing to have an arrowhead sitting in a case somewhere, maybe with a little label or plaque. But it's another thing to have an interactive display showing the building of the arrowhead and its use in a hunt."

In 1993, the Royal Ontario Museum launched a pilot multimedia exhibit called "Lights and Gemstones." Housed in the gem gallery, two Macintosh Quadra stations, each with a 20-inch monitor, support an interactive program that allows visitors to learn more about gems than they possibly could by reading labels. For example, as part of a demonstration illustrating how gems are cut, the visitor can rotate an image of a stone on the computer screen to see how it's done. One can also learn how and why diamonds sparkle by changing a diamond's shape onscreen and watching the results.

Another option for museums is to create learning centers that are separate and apart from the exhibits, but a part of the museum. In Los Angeles, the Beit Hashoah Museum of Tolerance includes a Multimedia Learning Center with 30 Quadra systems linked by an Ethernet network. The stations have access to CD-ROM drives containing 10,000 original documents. The content is enhanced with tens of thousands of photographs and hundreds of hours of video footage that, due in no small part to their volume, are stored on video laser disc.

Exhibits on Disc

There are a number of consumer discs on the market. Microsoft publishes *Art Gallery: The Collection of the National Gallery, London*, which is based on the London Micro Gallery that I mentioned earlier. Electronic Arts markets the *Electronic Library of Art* series. *Renaissance Masters I*, for example, has over a thousand images, with biographies and indexes by artist, date, school, and

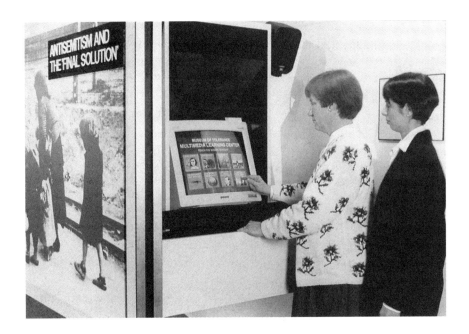

The Multimedia Learning Center at the Beit Hashoah Museum of Tolerance, housed in the Simon Wiesenthal Center in Los Angeles. (Photo courtesy of the Simon Wiesenthal Center. ©1993 Jim Mendenhall.)

subject. *National Portrait Gallery,* from Abt Books, Inc., has over 3,000 images and 200 detailed enlargements dating from the seventeenth century to the present.

The Frick Museum in New York City has taken a different approach. According to an article in *The New York Times,* the Frick has produced a CD with in-depth information about 138 of the museum's artworks. The difference is that this disc is intended for professionals and carries a price tag of $250.

In addition to serving the professional community, museums have long been interested in supporting education and the schools. Anthony Hushion notes that programs such as "Light and Gemstones" could conceivably be used in schools. Meanwhile, enterprising educators are using home-market products to enrich their classrooms, often providing virtual trips to the library when the real thing might not otherwise be available.

Is Anybody There?

Just as libraries wrestle with the fear that online systems may soon cause their customer bases to dwindle, so too do museum curators worry that people will no longer come to museums when museums can go to them. A number of museum collections on CD-ROM have become popular in the home market. While some of the more traditional curators are worried, new blood is banking on the idea that museums are reaching and informing a much wider audience than might otherwise have been interested.

The cost factor is often a major obstacle, and one solution has been for institutions to band together. In Ontario, Canada, for example, agencies belonging to the Ministry of Culture have grouped together to form the Information Technology Council. Chaired by Anthony Hushion, the council has submitted a proposal to the Provincial Ministry to create a Cultural Multimedia Center where prototyping work could be carried out. The Center could become a hub of the information highway.

But if the plan doesn't work out, Hushion and his colleagues will find alternative methods to promote and incorporate the use of technology in the arts. Who knows, museums may soon be creating interactive CD-based programs in their own in-house production studios.

In Stores and Other Commercial Venues

Kiosks are showing up all over the place. Many of them display information accessed from a computer hard drive, but quite a few are utilizing CD technologies, most notably CD-i, CD-ROM (more often CD-i than CD-ROM), Photo CD, and Video CD. Most kiosks are still experimental pilot projects launched by forward-thinking marketers who believe that interactive point-of-purchase displays will soon proliferate. And why not? The benefits are enormous.

In-store displays provide instant gratification for the hurried customer. Vendors, meanwhile, feel better about selling their goods because they need not rely on store personnel who may not be familiar with all of the company's products. Kiosks also provide a means of disseminating information about store or vendor promotions and customer services.

Because consumers like to make informed purchasing decisions, kiosk programs could be programmed to provide product comparisons, although that could get touchy in a store that carries competing products from multiple vendors. Still, if it remained fact-based.... Intelligent kiosks could take many variables into account before recommending a product. Printers attached to in-store kiosks it could even print a shopping lists with the store location of items.

In a computer-based system, a CD catalog could include an automated ordering system. And CD catalogs could do double duty as de facto training tools for employees to help them keep up with new merchandise (this would help trim the corporate training budget too). The rest of this chapter gives descriptions of a few CD-based kiosk projects, some created for in-store use, some for trade shows, and a couple that were used in company service offices.

Lee Apparel

Sitting in the middle of the boys department at Macy's in New York City is a kiosk from the Lee Apparel Company. Created by Spinnaker, this five-foot kiosk houses three CD-i players with three touch screens.

According to Spinnaker's executive producer, John Velie, the response to the kiosk has been very good. "The client wanted three things," explains Velie. "They wanted signage, information delivery about their products, and a way for customers to walk up to this thing and choose the right size jeans without having to talk to a sales clerk."

When no one is interacting with the kiosk, the three monitors spell out *L-e-e*, one letter per screen on top of cartoon-like background animations depicting the city. When touched, two of the monitors play in-store commercials, while the third monitor displays an interactive animated sequence that encourages boys to enter their height and weight so that the program may suggest appropriate pants sizes.

Department Store Gift Guide

In 1993, holiday shoppers at six Dayton's, Hudson's, and Marshall Field's stores in the mid-West got help with their gift-buying dilemmas. At a kiosk, customers could browse the electronic catalog for unique and unusual gifts by selecting one of the four prices ranges. In less than 30 seconds, the customer saw suggested gifts displayed on a television monitor and heard an accompanying audio description of each gift.

The gift guide was created as an alternative to in-store, continuous-play videotaped presentations. Not only is it interactive, so the consumer is involved, but it also saves time. Many customers won't stand around to watch a whole

One of the Holiday Gift Guide kiosks created for the department store division of the Dayton-Hudson Corporation. (Photo courtesy of Prism Studios, Inc.)

video clip, but they will spend 30 seconds to get information specific to their own needs.

Another benefit is the superior quality of the digital photographs as compared to video tape. The interactive guide was produced and distributed on Kodak Photo CD Portfolio discs. (For more information about Photo CD, see Chapter 12.) The stores also sent out copies of the disc to the homes of customers who owned Photo CD players.

Warren Harmon, senior manager of advertising photography for the department store division of the Dayton-Hudson Corporation, created both the kiosks and the discs in only thirty days. Once Mr. Harmon's boss, Creative Director Jack Nugen, endorsed the idea, they had to work with the merchant division to select the featured products and make sure that they'd be in stock. Then they had to work with the visual merchandising people. It's no small matter to take up valuable retail space, never mind during the busiest season of the year.

Mr. Harmon says that they will not be repeating the exact same project anytime soon, but he did feel that it was a successful experiment, and various departments of the Dayton-Hudson Corporation are looking into a variety of potential uses for new technologies.

Wal-Mart and Best Buys

The Preview Machine, developed by Big Hand Productions in partnership with Interactive People Systems, is an award-winning application that has the Silver Medal for Sales & Marketing (1994 Interactive CINDY Awards) as well as the Silver Medal for Interactive Advertising (1994 NewMedia InVision Awards) to its credit. This interactive, touch-screen system was originally designed to run from a personal computer with a CD-ROM drive, but the designers switched over to CD-i for full-screen, full-motion video. The PC couldn't meet the needs at that time, and CD-i cost a lot less money.

The Preview Machine was tested at Wal-Mart, where sales increased as much as five percent, and a contract was signed to put one in every Best Buy Store in the country. The system allows customers to preview songs from new recordings and scenes from new videos. Big Hand's vice president of sales and marketing, Craig Rispin, tells me that the company will add software games to the system.

Customers won't actually be able to play a game, but they will see a 30 to 60 second preview. "Retailers are asking us to not allow the kids to play the games. They want them to be enticed to buy it, not to stand there and play it. They don't want to become a free arcade." Rispin also points out, "There is not a system out there currently that addresses all three—music, video, and software games."

NoteStation from MusicWriter

Sheet music is expensive. Consumers pay several dollars for a single song, and it's often written in a key that is outside the average person's vocal range. Sheet

The Preview Machine allows you to sample tapes, CDs, and videos (top). From this screen (bottom), you can hear three different songs from Janet Jackson's album, "janet." (Photo and screen shot courtesy of Big Hand Productions.)

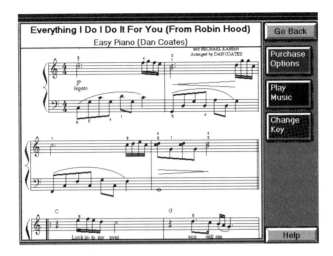

The NoteStation allows customers to view sheet music onscreen, listen to the song, change the key, and print the music. (Screen shot courtesy of MusicWriter, Inc.)

music is also an expensive proposition for retailers, not only in cost, but in terms of shelf space and inventory-management. In the long run, the solution may be point-of-sale manufacturing.

MusicWriter Inc. has introduced NoteStation, a multimedia kiosk offering more than 4,500 songs. Consumers can access their favorite song by entering the title, composer, or performing artist. The kiosk sports speakers that allow you to hear the song, and you may choose to hear it in a different key. When you're ready to buy it, the song is printed on a high-resolution laser printer.

NoteStation was tested at Attina's Music Store in Atlanta. In an interview with *Multimedia Today,* John Attina said "I can sell more music, because I've got more titles. And it's simply not possible to run out of stock on fast-selling titles, because the kiosk can always print more." The kiosk is user-friendly and each CD-ROM holds more than 20,000 songs.

UPS

UPS has been around for a long time, so they created a kiosk to provide both visitors and employees with information about UPS's history, as well as its technology and delivery network. The program has been called entertaining, and is said to be illustrated with fun facts.

The UPS interactive multimedia kiosk provides a detailed look at the company's past, present, and future to visitors of the UPS World Technology Headquarters in Mahwah, New Jersey. The award-winning touch-screen application uses video, graphics, audio, and original music to dispense information in a high-tech format about the increasingly high-tech world of package and delivery information. (Photo courtesy of United Parcel Service.)

Andrew Lunde, the research and development programmer from Floyd Design who created this kiosk, says that people are expected to use the kiosk for 15 to 20 minutes, although full exploration can take 45 minutes to an hour. It offers 23 minutes of linear video footage, and was designed to be used by anyone who might walk by.

The system uses MPEG video, high-resolution graphics, and a custom soundtrack. There are currently installations in Seattle, Atlanta, and New Jersey. Mark Hadlock, communications department manager of UPS World Technology Headquarters, spearheaded this project, and reports that, in time, kiosks will appear in other UPS locations. The original kiosk won a Gold Award at the 1994 NewMedia InVision Multimedia Awards.

The primary purpose of the compact disc in this application is to distribute over 400 megabytes of file information to multiple sites. When the disc is received by Information Services supervisors or field support personnel, all they have to do is download the new data onto the hard drive. Running off the hard drive increases application speed, but each kiosk installation has to have at least a 540MB hard drive to support it. Alternatively, they could have designed the program to run directly off the compact disc.

CD-What?

You can put a kiosk almost anywhere, and it can provide access to information 24-hours a day. Touch screens are inviting, and colorful graphics and sounds can be enticing. Multimedia can excite, entertain, and motivate viewers. Depending on the platform, kiosks can be used to provide information, market products and services, perform transactions, and even solicit information from users.

CD-i, Photo CD, or CD-ROM? There is a definite cost difference between the three. You can get a CD-i player that is capable of full-motion video and attach it to a touch screen television monitor for about $2,000. The CD-i player is also Photo CD–compatible, although a Photo CD player can not play CD-i discs. A computer setup with a CD-ROM drive and a touch-screen RGB monitor (you can't use a television monitor with the computer) is likely to cost three times as much, if not more.

On the other hand, when using CD-i or Photo CD with a television screen, you're working with video resolution that is nowhere near the quality of a computer display. Most users are used to television and don't notice the difference anyway. CD-i will let you program transactions and gather user input, but computer systems to date have been more reliable than CD-i machines when it comes to connecting peripherals such as printers or modems to the system. However, this is due mostly to the maturity of the platform. As time passes, CD-i should not have as many problems with the availability, or lack thereof, of printer drivers and the like. Of course, computers do have a greater tendency to go down, whereas CD-i players rarely freeze up or just quit functioning.

Right now many of these CD-based projects are adjuncts to existing materials. With companies already exploring digital photography, and the unlimited reusability of digital assets, digital displays in public places are likely continue to proliferate for some time to come.

Chapter 7

CD-ROMs in the Family Room

This chapter is the first of three devoted to CD-ROMs in the home. Originally I allotted one chapter for this subject, but there's just too much to cover. Even in three chapters I will barely scratch the surface. Why? Because the number of CD-ROM titles has skyrocketed and the main target market is the consumer at home.

Compact disc titles for the home come in all types. In the early days, content programs (as opposed to tools such as word processors) offered either reference data or entertainment. And entertainment meant games. While there is still a plethora of video games, many of them arcade style, other types of titles have begun to appear, and in large numbers.

First-time CD-ROM buyers frequently purchase bundles. A bundle can be an excellent way to get a cross-sampling of titles—depending on the bundle, that is. Most bundles are sold with equipment. Buy a new multimedia system and you get free CDs, or five CD titles at a reduced price. You're best off if you can pick your own titles, but sometimes the titles in the bundle all come from one publisher. Some publishers specialize in specific types of content or presentation, while others build diverse catalogs.

Microsoft Corporation is just one of many publishers with a diverse group of titles. Microsoft Home has its own logo, and the Home product line is divided into the following categories:

- **Personal Productivity.** Products to help track finances, manage mailing lists, create calendars and greeting cards, and even run a home-based business.
- **Entertainment.** Titles such as *Flight Simulator* and *Golf.*
- **Children's Creativity.** Products such as *Creative Writer* (writing and publishing software) and *Fine Artist* (a complete art product). In these titles a cartoon character named McZee greets the kids in Imaginopolis and encourages them to create.
- **Edutainment & Reference.** Titles such as *Art Gallery, Cinemania,* and *Encarta* to inform and educate your family.
- **System and Accessories.** Stuff to make your computer fun to use.

It is not easy to divide the titles I've come across into clear-cut categories. Rather than adopting the classifications of any one publisher, I've chosen to organize titles in the following groups, in keeping with the theme for the first half of this book:

- **Family Room** is the focus of this chapter. This category includes games, movies, music, art, and sports & hobbies.
- The **Home Library** (Chapter 8) covers books and magazines on CD.
- **Around the House**, my catch-all category (Chapter 9), covers how-to titles, personal productivity, adult-rated entertainment, and CDs that allow you to shop at home.

As you'll soon see, many different types of CD titles can be found in the family room, and again the categories are not clear-cut. As the compact disc evolves as a medium, categories of CD titles seem to merge. Children's "books" are becoming more interactive as developers integrate games and activities into the stories. This is also true of infotainment and edutainment titles that include one or more games related to the subject matter. The line becomes further blurred when movies or movie characters become the basis for games. When it comes to music-related titles, whole new genres are being born, part music, part game, part karaoke, and part participatory, as you'll soon see.

In this chapter and the next two, I will give you a feel for the kinds of CD-ROM titles that are available. To show the breadth of the marketplace, I will limit my descriptions to only a few titles for each genre.

Books and Activities for Young Children

Children's video games were the first interactive entertainment to infiltrate the home. But games are not the only form of leisure activity on CD-ROM. As the age range of CD-ROM users expands, the CD content becomes more diversified. Not only are more and more adults getting into the act, but more young children are too. In fact, very young children represent a substantial segment of the CD market.

"The economic power of children has grown much faster than that of any other age group in the past decade. By some measures, their annual discretionary income is greater than that of college students," says Dr. James U. McNeal, a professor of marketing at Texas A&M University. Statistics compiled by American Demographics for 1993 concur. According to American Demographics, parents give their kids as much as $14.4 billion a year to spend as they wish, and children influence household purchases amounting to more than $132 billion a year. *Time* magazine said that parents spent more than $243 million on educational software in 1993, 66 percent more than they did in 1992.

So what are these kids buying? Is it educational? Entertaining? Usually it's both. Welcome to the wide world of *edutainment*. Charlie Finnie of the market analysis firm, Volpe, Welty & Company in San Francisco, has a term for the difference between the entertainment value of video games and that of educational software. He calls it the "fun gap." In an article in *Multimedia World*, Finnie says that the consumer multimedia software market is growing because the fun gap is narrowing. He says, "The video game market is currently ten times larger than the education software market for one reason: Video games are more fun."

In Chapter 3 I talked about edutainment titles for the home market that found their way into schools. *Just Grandma and Me* from Brøderbund was one example. Other companies, however, such as Optical Data Interactive, are taking the opposite route and augmenting their successful school products with new home market titles. The Wanderoos family of products, geared for children

Some of the Wanderoos titles from Optical Data Interactive come packaged with a stuffed wanderoo. (Photo courtesy of Optical Data Interactive.)

aged 3 to 8, are based on *KinderVentures*, the first videodisc-based science program designed exclusively for use in kindergarten.

Pocket and Tails are the two adventure-loving, kangaroo-like creatures that host *The Wanderoos Go Exploring* in Trees-n-more Forest. In *The Wanderoos Go to Town*, Pocket and Tails take kids on visits to a doctor's office, a museum, and auto shop, and other places in town. "These adventures introduce children to the wonders of science and social studies while they play fun and lively games," said Robert Kersey, president of Optical Data Interactive. "We believe that parents want solid educational learning programs that are challenging, entertaining, and [that] sustain children's interest by building on their natural curiosity."

Multimedia is appealing to children who love sounds and animation. Musical backgrounds and additional features, such as word definitions and narration by choice (sometimes in foreign languages) enhance the environment. CD titles for children may be based on an old metaphor, the storybook viewed page by page, but these "point-and click-playgrounds" (a phrase coined by reviewer Bob Lindstrom) are quite popular with both children and their parents.

The Manhole: Masterpiece Edition is supposed to be a children's title, but it's one of my favorites (and I don't have any kids). I guess it appeals to children and adults the same way *Alice in Wonderland* did. *Manhole* started out as a black-and-white HyperCard adventure on a diskette. Now it's grown into a CD-ROM masterpiece for kids, with sights and sounds that please adults as well. Climb the beanstalk, explore hidden passages, a castle, and a sunken ship. Meet Molly the rhino and Rejan the elephant. And explore to your heart's content. This is one of very few CD titles that offers no specified goal, no puzzle to solve, no game to win.

Lenny's Music Toons stars Lenny. Who else? Lenny is a penguin, described as part musical genius, part big-time director, part fast-action hero. With Lenny as a guide, kids can produce their own music video, create a band, and solve puzzles. There was so much to do in Lenny's penthouse that I personally spent most of my time there. *Lenny's Music Toons* (from Paramount Interactive) is geared toward 5–11year-olds, and it won the National Parenting Publications Award for Best Software. The disc comes with an instruction guide that describes each of the areas and suggests noncomputer activities as well.

Lenny's Time Machine and *Lenny's Circus* followed the success of *Lenny's Music Toons*. *Lenny's Circus* allows children to assist the ringmaster at the circus, direct the circus acts, make music, and play booth games. Children are challenged to use a variety of skills, including deductive reasoning, memory, and visual and auditory discrimination, as they play and explore The Midway, The Big Top, The Bandstand, Clown Face Painting, and Souvenir Stand.

In *Lenny's Time Machine*, kids aged 6 to 10 join Lenny aboard his time-traveling ship. They can visit 15 destinations in historic time, including the Dinosaur Era, Ancient Egypt, and Philadelphia in 1776. The creative activities and games set in historical context were designed to help children learn what life was like in different time periods. Kids learn about famous people, events, social customs, styles of dress, music, and inventions. They can use Lenny's special "time traveling tools" to create and their own historical art, as well as add characters, artifacts, music, and sound effects.

Busytown is a CD for children aged 3 to 7. It meets guidelines set by the National Association for the Education of Young Children—guidelines that emphasize learning through play. Characters from The Busy World of Richard

This is Lenny's room. Just about everything here is interactive, from Lenny's TV to his fly-eating fish. Lenny's room is part of the *Lenny's Music Toons* disc from Paramount Interactive. (Screen shot courtesy of Paramount Interactive.)

Scarry—Huckle Cat, Lowly Worm, Mr. Frumble, and more—fight fires, build houses, and check the gas, oil, and tires on a car, among other things. The disc includes 13 original songs with sing-along lyrics.

Busytown won the gold at the 1993 Invision Awards for the Children's Enrichment Category, as well as the 1993 Parent's Choice Award from the Parent's Choice Foundation. The disc comes with a guide for parents that describes each of the 12 playgrounds, suggests extra activities, and describes the skills that children will learn—with a matrix showing which skills are practiced in which playground.

Inside the box is a card for teachers announcing the availability of the teacher's guide. The 72-page guide, available from the Computer Curriculum Corporation (a Paramount Communications Company), contains developmentally appropriate activities created by early-childhood experts that tie directly into the themes presented in the *Busytown* playgrounds.

Become a firefighter in *Busytown*, from Paramount Interactive. Save a burning house after preparing Smokey the Firefighter's truck with everything it needs for safe fire fighting. (Screen shot courtesy of Paramount Interactive.)

What Is a Belly Button? is another edutaining title. It was adapted from a popular Time-Life children's book that answers early questions youngsters have about their bodies. Baxter the Bear provides simple, accurate answers for children to such questions as "Why do I sneeze?" "Why do I have to brush my teeth?" and "Why do my friend and I have different skin colors?" This disc from IVI Publishing presents thirteen learning games and activities that reinforce the topics raised by the question-and-answer activities.

Several publishers, including Brøderbund, Simon & Schuster Interactive, and Discus, have lines of interactive storybooks. The premise is to take a children's story and add animation and/or interactivity so that kids can control their own reading environment. Perhaps the best-known line is Brøderbund's Living Books series. It includes such popular titles as *Just Grandma and Me, Arthur's Teacher Trouble, Harry and the Haunted House,* and *Tortoise and the Hare.*

What Is a Belly Button? from IVI Publishing presents visuals in a storybook design that make learning fun and easy to understand. (Screen shot courtesy of IVI Publishing.)

Living Stories is the name of the Simon & Schuster Interactive line. It includes such titles as *Alistair and the Alien Invasion*. This particular title, based on the book by Marilyn Sadler, features animation with 360-degree views of Alistair's world.

Titles from Discus include *The Tale of Peter Rabbit, Cinderella, The Night Before Christmas, Mud Puddle,* and *Thomas' Snowsuit.* These titles are easy to use but contain no animation and may not hold children's interest in the long run.

The Rabbits at Home combines multimedia CD-ROM software with hardbound books. It features Rags, Rosie, and Roly, the three children of Mr. and Mrs. Rabbit from the well-known series "Learning Together" from Brimax Books Ltd. The title is geared to children between the ages of 3 and 6. Like many of the titles for this age level, it is designed to encourage the development of reading, counting, and time-telling skills.

In *The Rabbits at Home*, the books and CD-ROM deliberately overlap at certain points. For example, parents and children may pull the books down from a bookshelf in Mr. and Mrs. Rabbit's bedroom, then read to children the same bedtime story that Mr. and Mrs. Rabbit read to Rags, Rosie, and Roly on the CD-ROM. Like the software, the books feature large, easy-to-read type, along with bright illustrations. The disc includes interactive games, puzzles, and craft projects.

When the kids are ready to start writing their own stories, turn them loose with *Creative Writer* and *Fine Artist*. Microsoft Home has released these on CD-ROM with added sounds, stickers, and more animation than before. *Creative Writer* includes "starter stories" (stories that kids can add to and complete) by children's writers and information about how these writers create their stories. The idea is to inspire children to write their own stories.

Microsoft also has forged alliances with other companies to create CDs. For example, Microsoft formed a partnership with Disney to produce *Mickey's Carnival*. Children's Television Workshop also has a deal. They will provide add-on materials for Microsoft's *Creative Writer* based on the *Ghost Writer* TV series.

Cross-marketing is also part of Microsoft's plans. McZee, the cartoon character from *Creative Writer* and *Fine Artist*, will be showing up in other creativity titles, and Microsoft is reportedly planning to license McZee's likeness.

When you add animation, sounds, and games, even a dictionary can be fun for children. A character named Zak guides children through the multimedia edition of the *Macmillan Dictionary for Children* from Simon & Schuster Interactive. The dictionary includes 12,000 words and more than 1,000 colorful illustrations. Each word is not only defined, illustrated, and pronounced, but also hot-linked to related words. Click a button to hear one of more than 400 lifelike sound effects, such as howling coyotes or the whir of a helicopter. Another button displays additional information such as word histories. The My List feature encourages children to make a list of words they want to remember, and kids can play Hangman or Words Within by themselves or with friends.

Games of One Sort or Another

We've come a long way from Pac-Man. Now we can have virtual arcades in our homes, with a multitude of titles that will engross both kids and adults. According to *The New York Times*, Americans spend more on computer video

Children can look up their own words or play learning-skills games in the *Macmillan Dictionary for Children* from Simon & Schuster Interactive. (Screen shot courtesy of Simon & Schuster Interactive.)

games than on movie tickets. *NewMedia* magazine reports that, according to Robertson Stephens & Co., the market in computer games, cartridges, and CD-ROMs alone rose from $700 million in 1987 to $4 billion in 1994, and is expected to reach $7.7 billion by 1997.

The game audience is growing, not just in number, but also in age. And with age comes more diversity and a demand for more interactivity. Plot lines and emotional character development add substance. Integrating the user into the story or game via role-playing heightens the sense of adventure and makes simulations seem even more real. The use of digitized video, often borrowed from movies, also lends realism.

Television is also playing a role. MTV Networks, a division of Viacom Incorporated, owns and operates three basic cable television programming services: MTV Music Television, VH-1, and Nickelodeon/Nick at Night. Now MTV Networks, in collaboration with Viacom New Media, has entered the multimedia

Director's Lab, from Nickelodeon and Viacom Interactive, is a multimedia toolkit for kids. (Screen shot courtesy of Viacom Inc. ©1994 Viacom Inc. All rights reserved.)

CD market. Nickelodeon's *Are You Afraid of the Dark?* and *Director's Lab* were among the first titles released. *Director's Lab* is a multimedia tool kit for kids, and *Are You Afraid of the Dark?* is an interactive fiction title.

Randy Komisar, president and CEO of LucasArts Entertainment Company, discussed the difference between movies and games during a presentation at Intermedia 94. "We watch movies, we play games. This is the crux of the difference—interactivity." But, he hastened to point out, there is interactivity and then there is interactivity. "When you incorporate linear into digital, you come up with interactive movies, but these are only stories with branching.... The viewer is still passive. The problem with video is that it's simply not interactive. By combining digital and linear video, the strengths of both are diminished."

A San Francisco–based writer named Tim Fox wrote an article for *Morph* magazine in which he described three main genres in computerized fiction:

Are You Afraid of the Dark?, from Nickelodeon and Viacom New Media, is an interactive fiction title. (Screen shot courtesy of Viacom Inc. ©1994 Viacom Inc. All rights reserved.)

- ◉ Hyperfiction, where the user/reader selects from alternative paths, thus shattering the sequence of linear narrative (Komisar's description of interactive movies fits in this category)

- ◉ Interactive stories, where the user/reader becomes a character, and in his or her assigned role makes action decisions that affect the outcome

- ◉ Virtual expedition, where there is neither linear sequence nor a specific character role to be played

This last genre, virtual expedition, is the most game-like in that something must be accomplished, a puzzle must be solved, or a destination must be reached. And virtual expedition CDs are also the least game-like in that you can't lose, character's don't die, and there are no dead-ends.

What is true interactivity? The subject is debated not only by compact disc producers, but by educators, communications specialists, and even the creators

of computer software programs. George Lucas, speaking at Intermedia, predicted that telecommunications will be combined with interactivity to create
more complicated, long-form storytelling. I wonder whether that will really be
something new, or just a revision of round-robin storytelling, this time by the
digital fireside.

Nevertheless, like any art form, the CD medium and the game genre are
evolving. Some titles may be more interactive than others, some may be more
realistic than others, and some may use video while others use animation. The
bottom line is that all of these games and entertainment CDs are big business
today.

In 1994, Lucasfilm boasted the best-selling CD-ROM game of all time,
Rebel Assault, with 400,000 units sold worldwide. Today, publishers invest
$100,000 to $200,000 in a title, expecting it to break even when they sell the
first 20,000 units. Generally, a hit game title sells more than twice as many units
as a popular reference title, with encyclopedias being the exception to the rule.

There are many different types of games, or subgenres, if you will. Action/
adventure games generally involve some violence and a mission. The game
player either wins or loses. The successful accomplishment of the mission reaps
some reward. Losing may mean death. Warner New Media's *Hell Cab*, and
IBM's *Maddog McCree*, definitely fall into the violent category. *Journeyman* from
Presto Studios, on the other hand, is not violent. This one offers a Ghandi bonus
for completing the game without violence.

Simulation titles put the user in the driver's seat, so to speak. These not
only include titles such as *Flight Simulator*, where the user is indeed in the pilot's
seat, but also *SimCity*, where your planning decisions affect a city's ability to
survive.

Interactive fiction encompasses titles such as *Voyeur*, from Philips/POV
Entertainment Group, where the choices you make are a matter of life and death.
This was the first CD-i title to use nationally recognized actors and actresses. (Cast
members in *Voyeur* include Grace Zabriskie and Robert Culp.) Producer David
Riordan classifies *Voyeur* as an interactive multimedia story as opposed to an interactive movie: "We don't consider this an interactive movie. When we can see things
like coverage and cutaways, that's when we will have a truly interactive movie."

Many considerations come into play when evaluating titles, not the least of
which are "repeat potential" and speed. Games that require skill have excellent
repeat potential until such time as your skill exceeds the challenge. Simulations
that require strategizing (such as *SimCity*) and interactive stories also have good

repeat potential, provided there are enough decision points and alternative actions.

Titles that emphasize exploration and investigation don't usually suffer from the slower response time of a CD-ROM. But titles that feature animation, graphics, and video are often made slower by the hardware. Some producers have found ways to compensate to some degree with software solutions, proprietary algorithms, disc layout, and other tricks of the trade. The only way to really tell how a title will play on your system is to try it. Sometimes the packages the games come in list minimum configuration requirements, but "minimum" is the word, and there is no guarantee that the game will play fast enough on your system.

Myst was described by *NewMedia* magazine as "perhaps the most graphically opulent and deeply developed text and visual exploration fantasy yet." In an interview in *CD-ROM Today* magazine, co-creator Robyn Miller describes *Myst* as "a goal-oriented exploration. You are dropped into the middle of a mysterious island environment and you have no idea what you're supposed to do or what your goal is. You piece together the puzzle of *Myst* by wandering around, solving puzzles, and picking up clues." The environment sports first-rate, 3-D graphics and a soundtrack befitting the mood you would be in if you were lost on an island. Robyn's co-creator is Rand Miller, his brother. Together they have created popular children's titles such as *The Manhole* and *Cosmic Osmo*. *Myst* is their first title for adults, and it retains the same feeling of exploration and wonder as the brothers' children's titles.

Some titles rely on 3-D graphics, with or without some degree of animation. Other titles incorporate video as well. *Myst* primarily uses animation and a few video segments, but not animation in the sense that it is used in children's videos—this stuff is photo-realistic. LucasArts' Randy Komisar explained the company's use of animation and video to *PC World* magazine this way: "We use real film in *Rebel Assault*—to set the mood and to cut to scenes. We use video to tell the story and animation to allow the player to interact."

Jump Raven, Lunicus, SkullCracker, and *Dust* are arcade-type action games from CyberFlix that I would not recommend for children. These games involve high-intensity arcade play in 3-D environments and use full-screen movies. In *Jump Raven*, you're the pilot of a hovercraft. You get to select your co-pilot, weapons system, and musical score, after which you set forth to recover stolen genetic material and preserve earth's wildlife. Fly the ship and kill the enemies, all to the music you select (musical choices include hip-hop and grunge). In *Lunicus*, the year is 2023 and you are fighting to free the earth from the Hive Queen while defending against heat-seeking rockets and plasma

In this future-based, arcade-style game, players interact with crew members of United Nations Moonbase Lunicus and take to the streets of Moscow, Tokyo, and Los Angeles to battle the mechanized drones holding the earth's citizens captive. (Screen shot courtesy of Paramount Interactive.)

cannons. The preview for *SkullCracker* says it's a "side-scrollin' blood-pumpin' arcade gorefest," and *Dust* is billed as "a tale of the wired west."

PC World magazine gave the CD-ROM version of *SimCity* a "thumbs-up" and rejoiced in its full-motion video that allows users to "be harassed by actors threatening you with violence if you don't deliver funding for earthquake repairs." Live characters and realistic situations, created with the use of advanced production technology, are what make this Sim series from Maxis so successful. Now you can buy add-ons such as *Great Cities* and *Natural Disasters* for *SimCity 2000*.

Technological advancements in the field of virtual reality play a big role in the development of these titles. SimGraphics developed the first real-time animation system for creating sophisticated, computer-generated character animation using a variety of input devices, such as gloves and body sensors. (I'll talk a little bit about this technology in Chapter 10.)

Then there are titles that require the consumer to use some external equipment. *NewMedia* magazine reported on a title called *Computer Athlete*. Apparently you use this disc in tandem with some type of exercise machine (bike, treadmill, stair-stepper, and so on) and an infrared sensor monitors speed and adjusts the display, be it a winding road or a ski slope.

That same *NewMedia* feature, which I should tell you dates back to January, 1994, talked about a virtual reality helmet from Sega that lets you play "in a 360-degree, 3-D, full-color stereoscopic universe." The technology is here, but the installed base for external paraphernalia is still pretty small. Virtual reality still sounds fairly futuristic to the general public.

Critical Path, from Mechadeus, is another action adventure game that was shot like a movie. Eileen Weisinger stars as Kat. She fights off the bad guys and you have to help. If you blow it, Kat dies. This is one of those titles that makes full use of state-of-the-art hardware, and 24-bit digital video doesn't look too good without the right video card to support it.

The use of video to tell a story is even more extensive in *Dracula Unleashed*, which contains 90 minutes of video. This CD, from Viacom New Media, is billed as an interactive horror movie to differentiate it from the game genre. Using a new, original story and script, more than 150 video scenes were shot using 20 or so different sets and over 40 actors.

Unlike games in which you search for clues to solve a puzzle, interactive movies allow you to select a story and follow it through to its conclusion. Along the way, you are presented with choices that alter the ensuing action. Different choices lead to different paths, and consequently different endings. The more choices, the more branches, and the greater the potential for replay.

A review in *CD-ROM Today* magazine describes *Dracula Unleashed* as "rather sedate, and not particularly action-oriented. It really is a new and different kind of gaming experience." The reviewer suggests that this genre might be more like "interactive TV in its nascent stage."

Movies and Movie Companions

A standard, double-speed CD-ROM can store up to 70 minutes of VHS quality video, and with new advances in compression and mastering/recording specifications, soon it will hold even more. The Video CD standard is still fairly new, but the fantasy of discs replacing video cassettes is becoming a reality.

When released by The Voyager Company in 1991, *A Hard Day's Night* was the first full-length movie on a CD-ROM (not counting pornographic titles). In keeping with the Voyager tradition established with video laser discs, this CD included the script and other background materials. Bob Stine, as quoted by *Upside* magazine, said, "You can't have a serious dialog by watching a movie, [but] you can start to have a serious dialogue by reading what someone says and thinking about it. It's very important that we look for different ways to nurture people who are trying to do important intellectual things in these new media, who aren't simply tying to put the latest movie or game onto a CD-ROM."

It's a Wonderful Life, from Kinesoft, is a two-disc release of the classic movie with the kind of supplementary materials that we have now come to expect with multimedia titles. In addition to the film itself, you can view the movie trailer and look at publicity photos. You can click an icon and read the text of the story on which this movie was based, as well as check out the cast and credits. From the main screen you can choose your video windows size (four choices, from thumbnail to full-screen), and access tools for searching and placing bookmarks.

In June of 1994, the Philips Media Video CD Group announced it would be releasing a library of movie titles, including *Moonstruck*, *Trading Places*, and *Wayne's World*. Also slated for release were several series, including *Star Trek*, *Naked Gun*, and *James Bond*.

The Video CD titles are compatible with all Video CD players, but when viewed on a CD-i player with a digital video cartridge, an on-screen control bar is activated. Using the control bar, the viewer can instantly tap into information about the cast, the history, photos, or—heaven help us—the availability of the merchandise.

If you like movie trivia or just need some help deciding what movies to rent this weekend, you can now turn to movie guides on CD. I've come across four so far. As you would expect, they all offer lots of video clips of famous movie scenes. This is certainly the case with Microsoft's *Cinemania*, which also includes audio clips of dialog spoken by the original actors, theme music, songs from one hundred films, and nearly a thousand movie stills. To find movies of interest, you can search by genre, actor, director, release date, Academy Award, star rating, and MPAA rating. Through the remote control panel you have access to video, dialog, reviews, credits, cast lists, and more.

This is a CD-i 220 player showing the *Star Trek VI* movie CD. Notice the control bar at the bottom of the screen. (Photo courtesy of Philips Interactive.)

Movie reviews abound on the *Cinemania* disc. It includes the complete text of Leonard Maltin's *Movie and Video Guide*, Roger Ebert's *Video Companion*, and Pauline Kael's *5001 Nights at the Movies*, as well as other sources. Then there are articles about all sorts of movie topics, plus biographies and filmographies of thousands of movie personalities, and over 2,000 photo portraits of stars and industry moguls.

MovieSelect, from Paramount Interactive, "uses advanced artificial intelligence to generate a personalized list of recommendations that are a perfect fit for your taste and mood." So it says on the box. Artificial intelligence? The instruction guide says that the program uses "fuzzy logic," which is a type of artificial intelligence. With the automatic recommendation feature, you can select from 22 different categories to define your taste or mood, and let *MovieSelect* do the rest.

Of course, you can also search for movies by finding your favorite actors and directors. You can also search for words in the movie titles. The most useful

Paramount Interactive's *MovieSelect* database features more than 44,000 titles. (Screen shot courtesy of Paramount Interactive.)

feature is that you can print out a list of movies you're interested in and take it with you to the video rental store. The disc includes summaries of movies based on the *VideoLog Select* database of rental videos used by industry professionals. Find out who directed it, who starred in it, and what other movies they were associated with.

Infobusiness has a movie companion title *Mega Movie Guide*. I haven't seen this one yet, but the promotional materials claim that it has features not found in other movie databases, including the ability to search for titles based on length, MPAA expanded rating, place of origin, black-and-white or color designation, and availability on video.

Mega Movie Guide offers over two hours of footage, consisting of two- to four-minute clips. Also on the disc is the entire listing of all major Academy Award winners and nominees since 1927–28, and a listing of the "greatest hits of the decade" for every ten-year period since the 1920s, based on a combination of critics' picks and ticket sales.

I found out about *Video Movie Guide* from Advanced Multimedia Solutions in a mail-order catalog. It appears to be rather inexpensive as CDs go—only $13.95. It covers 13,000 films and includes over 1,300 pictures of actual video box covers. *Video Movie Guide* rates the movies on a scale of five stars to turkeys, and claims to include more offbeat and obscure films than the other guides. When I looked this title up in *The CD-ROM Directory*, I found out that it's based on a book of the same name from Ballentine Books.

Music and Art Appreciation

The Voyager Company not only released the first movie on a CD-ROM, but from the beginning the company has been on the forefront of creating and producing quality music and art titles. Voyager has supported the creative arts, and its vision in using the digital medium has itself become an art form. While Voyager continues to create cutting-edge titles on its own, it has also entered into licensing agreements with other companies, most notably Microsoft. The Multimedia music series from Microsoft was actually pioneered by Voyager. Voyager is a company that everyone should keep an eye on.

Guided by Robert Winter, a Beethoven scholar, users of *Multimedia Beethoven: The Ninth Symphony* can learn about the music's form and style as they listen. The CD includes information about Beethoven's life and the times in which he lived, and includes an analysis of the Ninth Symphony. The original version of this disc, from Voyager, was created for the Macintosh using HyperCard and is credited with being the first consumer multimedia CD-ROM title.

Microsoft markets the current version of *Multimedia Beethoven: The Ninth Symphony*. It is available for both the Mac and Windows platforms. Other titles in the Multimedia music series from Microsoft include *Schubert: The Trout Quintet*, *Strauss: Three Tone Poems*, *Mozart: The Dissonant Quartet*, and *Stravinsky: The Rite of Spring*. By the time you read this book, Microsoft should be packaging music titles in multiple units for sale in bookstores.

Microsoft is not the only publisher to combine multimedia and classical music. *Vivaldi: The Four Seasons* is one of the CDs from Ebook. While it looks nothing like the Microsoft titles, it includes all the features that one expects from any multimedia exploration of a classical composition. For example, you can follow the written score while listening to the piece being performed. Most titles include textual information about the piece and about the composer's life and time. Musical themes are identified, terms are defined, and relevant musical forms and styles are explained (sometimes with an accompanying audio example).

Classical music is by no means the only genre on which multimedia and compact discs have capitalized. There are edutaining titles about all types of music. For example, *World Beat*, from Medio Multimedia, allows you to find out about native music and its history by selecting a spot on the globe. The disc contains information about 150 musical styles from 80 countries, and includes interviews with more than 40 musicians.

Most of the multimedia CDs featuring pop or rock artists, however, are of a very different sort. Musical artists interested in pushing the boundaries of performance art and exploring music as a participatory art form have turned to multimedia CDs as a medium of expression. Interactive CD-ROM titles by recording artists such as Peter Gabriel and ♀ (the artist formerly known as Prince) allow you to actually alter the composition of the music. Other titles such as *Rock Rap 'N Roll* let you create your own compositions using prerecorded clips that you piece together and record your own.

♀ *Interactive*, from the artist formerly known as Prince, is the most unusual of these titles. It falls more in the game or "virtual expedition" category than it does the music category, albeit the title is an adventure game that revolves around his music. As you wander through a mansion, gathering hidden keys and puzzling out mysteries, you uncover all sorts of information in various forms—video interviews with other rock starts, ♀'s record catalog (yes, with audio clips), and his awards. The disc contains eight music videos, four of which are full-length. You can perform karaoke and mix tunes. It's a multimedia biography, and only slightly self-aggrandizing.

Roy Kerbs reviewed the ♀ *Interactive* for *The CDROM Reporter*. He said it was "the best music CD-ROM available" and it "successfully captures the feel of being in a nightclub, at a concert, in a recording session and in a coffee house—simultaneously." Eric Brown, editor of *NewMedia*, gave this one an awesome review. He called it "one of the most sumptuous virtual worlds since *Myst*" and cited its top-notch production values.

The disc can be played on PC or Mac, and it contains a separate audio track that can be played on an audio CD player. ♀ *Interactive* is the first music CD-ROM to support MPEG, providing full-screen, full-motion video for users with MPEG decoding hardware.

While ♀ *Interactive* may be the only game-like title, the other rock music titles offer some very interesting interactions. In Peter Gabriel's *Xplora 1*, you can visit Gabriel's studio, take part in a jam session led by producer Brian Eno, play instruments from around the world, or remix a song. "It allows the audience to become artist and explorer," says Gabriel. The disc includes four music videos from Gabriel's 1992 U.S. album, family film clips, and more. It also comes with a 60-page book of photos and articles about WOMAD, Secret World Tour, and Real World Experience Park.

Jump (The David Bowie Interactive CD-ROM) takes place in several rooms, including Bowie's office and a video editing studio. The disc includes a few of Bowie's music videos, as well as video interview footage. When you get to the editing studio, you can remix audio tracks and build your own video by selecting from the available footage.

Other rock CD-ROM titles include Todd Rundgren's *TR-i (No World Order)*, Heart's *20 Years of Rock & Roll*, *Imagine: John Lennon* (the one delayed by copyright issues), and *Bob Dylan: Discovery.*

If you want to be the star, *Rock Rap 'N Roll* allows you to choose from ten different "studios," each representing a different musical style. Styles include Big Band, Rap, Latin, Soul, and Pop. Pick a song segment, set the background beat, assign instruments, add vocals and sound effects, then mix and record. You can even record your creation onto a cassette.

Another unusual CD title is *Quest for Fame: Featuring Aerosmith.* This is a virtual music simulation and you need to purchase The Virtual Guitar when you buy your first disc. The premise here is that you are transformed into a rock star. There is no tutorial. The disc will not teach you how to play guitar, but once you connect The Virtual Guitar to your PC, magic takes place. It's sort of like karaoke. No matter how bad you pick and strum, you come out sounding like a pro.

A December, 1993 article in *U.S. News and World Report* cited Fredric Paul, features editor of *Electronic Entertainment,* who predicted that dozens of rock discs would be available within a few months. When John Hawkins of Philips Interactive Media spoke at Intermedia in March of 1994, he mentioned that two months earlier the British music industry announced plans to use Video CD. Hawkins also said that Polygram, a Philips subsidiary, had issued 17 Video CD titles for U.S. release by such artists as Andrew Lloyd Webber, Sting, and Tina Turner. This brings us out of the realm of CD-ROM and into the world of CD-i.

Peter Gabriel: All About Us is a behind-the-scenes look at Gabriel's music videos. It's a Video CD from Philips, and must be played on a CD-i player with a digital video cartridge if you want to experience full interactivity. Again, only with a CD-i player can the user take advantage of the on-screen function panel. With this panel, the user can control the flow of the presentation by selecting menu options and other icons. However, the disc can also be played on one of the new set-top Video CD players, but the onscreen panel will not be available, and outside of common features such as play and pause, the presentation will be completely linear instead of interactive.

The Todd Rundgren CD, *TR-i (No World Order)*, described earlier, is also still available as a CD-i disc. Other music CD-i discs include *Pete Townshend Live*, *The Gershwin Connection* (a jazz title), and *Three Tenors* (an opera title).

When it comes to the visual arts, any discussion would naturally include photography. However, as in the world of print, the photographic CD titles are more akin to the "coffee table" genre, so I'll leave those for Chapter 8 and stick to painting and art history here.

Microsoft Home's *Art Gallery* contains the entire collection from the National Gallery in London. In addition to viewing the exquisite visuals, you can uncover quite a bit of information, including biographical data about the artists, historical information about their lives, times, and influences, and analyses of painting techniques. Terms are defined in pop-up windows, related subjects are linked, and an audio icon provides you with proper pronunciation.

Tate Gallery—Exploring Modern Art is a new title from British-based Attica Cybernetics, an affiliate of Compton's NewMedia. The disc features six multimedia galleries:

- Pop Art explores mass media and popular culture with works by Andy Warhol and Roy Lichtenstein
- Picasso explores the myth of the artist and his works
- Men and Women explores issues relating to gender and art
- Dynamism looks at the pace of modern life on art before the Great War
- Modern British Sculpture covers works from 1913 to 1972
- Hepworth deals with abstract art and the influence of landscape on her work.

Each gallery contains up to 30 works of art. An archive feature is available for each gallery to provide information on the lives of the artists, descriptions of their work, and explanations of historical and technical terms. The Information Desk option takes you on a guided audio/visual tour.

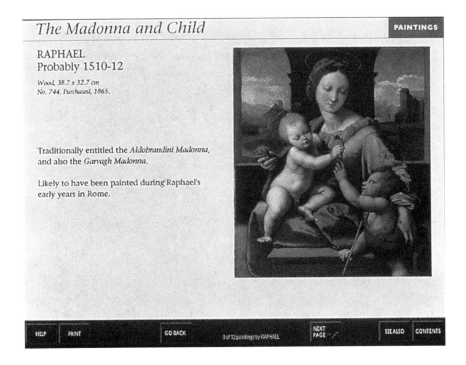

A screen from Microsoft Home's *Art Gallery*, showing *The Madonna and Child* by Raphael. (Screen shot courtesy of Microsoft Corporation.)

ZCI Publishing offers a *History through Art* series in which each title covers a historic period. Titles in this series include *Ancient Greece, Ancient Rome, The Middle Ages, The Renaissance, The Baroque, The Enlightenment, Romanticism, Pre-Modern Era,* and *The Twentieth Century.* Ebook is another of the many multimedia publishers with an art title. Theirs is called *Impressionism and Its Sources*.

Last in this section, and certainly not least, are the art titles from The Voyager Company. The company's first art titles were on 12-inch video laser-discs that you could play only on stand-alone players or play by connecting them to a Macintosh computer using a HyperCard stack. Their art-related CD-ROM titles include *Rodney's Wonder Window* and *The First Emperor of China.* Artist Rodney Greenblatt created *Wonder Window* as an interactive art exhibit for both young children and sophisticated adults. *The First Emperor* disc includes a tour of the Qin Museum.

Sports

Despite player strikes and skirmishes, the playing field for sports-related CD titles is heating up. Microsoft Home's *Complete Baseball* is one of the new breed of CD-ROM titles. It is a hybrid project that couples historical data (back into the 1800s) on the CD with new data that you can acquire via an online connection. The CD offers player and team histories, lots and lots of statistics, video clips, World Series results, a trivia game, and an almanac of baseball history. Then, for $1.25, you can dial up CompuServe and download Baseball Daily to get the scores and statistics from the previous day. Microsoft claims to have shipped an initial 100,000 copies in midsummer 1994.

Another baseball disc comes from Creative Multimedia Corp. *Total Baseball* nearly fills the CD with statistics, articles, and essays covering 120 years of baseball history. There are stats for more than 13,000 players; trading card photos of 400

Video clips show three different angles of the 75 greatest NFL plays. (Screen shot courtesy of Turner Home Entertainment.)

players; and 10 sound clips of great moments, such as Hank Aaron's record-breaking home run to beat Babe Ruth's all-time home run record.

Then there's football. *NFL's Greatest Plays* from Turner Home Entertainment contains 75 of the most outstanding plays in football history as determined by the NFL. High-quality video footage can be viewed from three different camera angles, at any speed, forward or reverse. Statistics are available for each play, and a bio of one, two, or three of the key players involved in each play are included. Diagrams of some plays can also be viewed at speed, forward, or reverse to gain insight into strategies, tactics, and execution.

And if a single sport is not enough, there's the *Sports Illustrated 1994 Multimedia Sports Almanac*. Created by StarPress Multimedia, this disc features more than 40 minutes of sports video highlights, an entire year of *Sports Illustrated* magazine, and a sports almanac with over 1,200 pages of professional and college statistics—all for under $60. Compton's New Media publishes the *Sporting News*, *Multimedia Pro Football Guide 1993*, and *1992 NFL Season* CDs, where you'll find stats, video clips, more stats, feature articles, action photos, and more video.

Early in this chapter I said that I wanted to give you a feel for the marketplace and would limit my descriptions to only a few titles for each genre. So far, in this chapter alone, I've covered more than 75 titles, and that's not even a real drop in the bucket.

A family using a 3DO interactive multiplayer system. (Photo courtesy of The 3DO Company. ©1993 Blake Sorrell.)

Chapter 8

CD-ROMs in the Home Library

Books are normally linear. They are read from front cover to back cover, with the story unfolding through text and sometimes pictures. Interactive technology opens up this format. The technology's hyperlinking capabilities match the way people think—by association. Compared to books, however, interactive technology has its drawbacks, including the size of the player devices and the fact that you can't carry them around (can't put one in your pocket yet—so much for "pocketbooks"). Besides, the equipment is still fragile.

Is the printed page better than a computer screen? So far, yes. Eyestrain, and the lack of portability of computers, might push one to favor the book. However, there are some things that books can't do. The obvious examples are sound and video. Computers also offer enhancements such as CAD programs and customized applications in which you can enter and store information. For example, with some programs you can enter the materials you need for building a deck and get back an estimate of how much the deck would cost to build.

In large reference works, you only need a limited amount of information at one time. Chunking large portions of text into screen-size bites becomes less of an obstacle. And because you only focus on the screen for a minute at a time, you're less likely to get eyestrain. References by nature are not usually linear, since you don't read them from start to finish, so hyperlinking and cross-referencing are also quite useful in reference works.

The onscreen medium is okay too for children's books, where there isn't much text on each page, pictures are crucial, and speech and animation go a long way to enhancing content. As an article in *The Wall Street Journal* points out, "It is certainly easier to do a good electronic book from material heavily laden with photos than from unadorned prose."

Search capabilities sound great, but do you really need to know how many times Heathcliff is referred to by name in *Wuthering Heights*? Again, you need to consider the practical utility of the features before you get carried away by their power. At the other end of the spectrum, however, are titles such as *I Photograph to Remember*, a photographic essay on disc by Pedro Meyer. This title is so emotionally powerful, it moved an entire convention hall to tears.

There are basically three types of electronic books: text dumps, collections of related works, and single titles enhanced with multimedia elements.

The *Project Gutenberg CD-ROM*, for example, is a collection of public-domain literature and historical documents. These titles are available as ASCII files on the Internet from Project Gutenberg at the University of Illinois, Urbana. ASCII files have the benefit of being compatible with all word-processing programs, but they come withs no formatting or visual enhancements of any sort. If you're not into surfing the Internet, you can purchase a Project Gutenberg CD from Walnut Creek CDROM.

In some instances, bad translations are offered simply because they are in the public domain. I am not saying that this is the case with the Gutenberg disc. I'm not a literary scholar, and I might not know the difference between a bad translation and a good one. What I am saying is, *caveat emptor*—let the buyer beware. Material in the public domain is free, and some people will use it to make a fast buck as this new medium evolves.

World Library produces single-disc compilations of hundreds of volumes of famous works of literature, philosophy, drama, poetry, history, and religion. These discs, intended primarily for research—as opposed to reading for pleasure—include the full text of each work, and some include the original illustrations. At the request of its customers, World Library has added various tools such as bookmarks, font options, and notepad capabilities.

Phil Hood pointed out in an April, 1994, column in *NewMedia* magazine that many CD-ROM projects could benefit greatly from the hand of an experienced copy editor, not to mention a developmental editor. He wrote, "Compared with the typical CD-ROM, the average print nonfiction book is better-researched, better-edited and more exhaustive." Surprising, perhaps, but true.

On the other hand, some books are much better as multimedia than they ever were or could be as printed books. One excellent example, is the *Dictionary of American Sign Language*. Finally, you can really see how signing gestures should be executed.

When you limit the number of titles on a disc, you have enough storage space left over to include lots of additional material that can illuminate a subject—personal letters, home photos, and videos, for example. Researchers call this kind of thing "primary source data" because it is untainted by the interpretations of others. The more data, the more informed the viewer. The data provided and the presentation of this data is what makes the difference.

Fiction and Poetry

The *Library of the Future, Third Edition*, from World Library, is a comprehensive collection with the complete text of more than 3,500 literary titles, including novels, essays, poems, short stories, plays, and religious and historical documents. Twenty minutes of video clips are also included. You'll find works by Milton, Shakespeare, Hawthorne, Steinbeck, Kipling, Austen, Dostoevsky, Thoreau, Tolstoy, Hans Christian Andersen, Joseph Conrad, Jack London, Edgar Allan Poe, and Oscar Wilde, to name just a few.

William Hustwit, CEO of World Library, points out, "The cost of acquiring hardcover copies of each text would be more than $15,000—and that doesn't include any of the benefits of the software." World Library's Instant Access search and retrieval software lets users locate a reference in the disc's more than 100 million words or phrases in a matter or seconds. The company's Instant Access software also lets you do "proximity searches"—that is, search for and retrieve text found within a certain distance of a second reference. You can search in a single text, in the works of a single author, in a category (religion, history, or poetry), in a time period or country, or in any combination of the above.

Other titles from World Library include *Great Poetry Classics*. This one contains more than a thousand poems, sonnets, and psalms from Shakespeare,

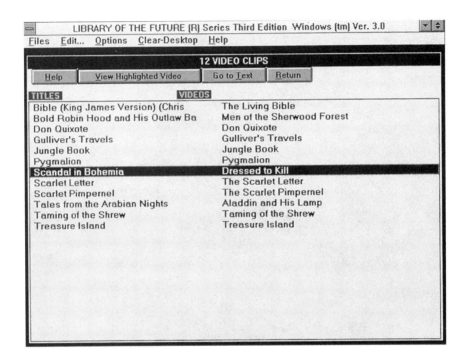

Twelve video clips are available on the *Library of the Future* disk. (Screen shot courtesy of World Library.)

Keats, Lord Byron, William Blake, Geoffrey Chaucer, Elizabeth Barrett Browning, Emily Dickinson, T.S. Eliot, Ralph Waldo Emerson, Robert Frost, and William Butler Yates. Epic poems by Virgil and Homer are also on this disc.

While I'm on the subject of poetry, I want to mention a CD titled *Poetry in Motion* from The Voyager Company. Not often do we get to see and hear writers perform their literary works. *Poetry in Motion* brings you the poets themselves reading their own works on video, where, as a reviewer for *CD-ROM World* so eloquently put it, you can "hear the intonations and see emotion well up in the poets' eyes."

Another major publisher of literary CD-ROMs is Bureau Development. Its *Great Literature Plus* disc covers 180 authors from Aesop to Wordsworth, and includes brief biographies, as well as narrative sound and music clips, illustrations, and animation. A reviewer for *CD-ROM World* magazine felt that *Great Literature Plus* has a better interface than the *Library of the Future*. The reviewer said that *Great Literature Plus* has excellent navigational tools and easy-to-understand icons, but complained that the screen redraws are slower.

Twain's World, also from Bureau Development, is billed as an authoritative reference guide for students and scholars, and a must-have for every home collection. It contains the complete works of Samuel Clemens: 10,000 pages of books, short stories, essays, speeches, transcripts of talks and lectures, and personal letters.

The disc includes music, animation, photos, and a dash of video to create a multimedia portrait of Mark Twain, his work, his life, and his times. The work is well integrated, with a time line for historical context, and hyperlinks to take you to related illustrations, narration, video clips, and sound clips.

Some fiction discs focus on just one literary work. This is the case with Westwind Media's interactive presentation of *The Fall of the House of Usher*, by Edgar Allan Poe. In addition to the narration, animations, graphics, and musical interludes, the disc offers a biography on Poe, an overview of the genre, an examination of Poe's compositional style, and an interpretation of the story. You can enter an interactive, 3-D maze too, look up words in the glossary, and explore the paintings in the Art Gallery. Westwind Media is an affiliate label of Compton's NewMedia.

In Chapter 7 I mentioned several storybooks for young children. There are also books for older children, such as *The Secret Garden* and *Black Beauty*. Produced by Sound Source Interactive, both of these titles incorporate film clips from the movies.

I suppose comic books would qualify for placement on the fiction shelf. Some comic books on CD look a lot like their paper counterparts—artistically, that is—and the dialog still appears in little bubbles, but multimedia brings the comic strips to life. One of the early entries into this field was *CD-ROMIX*, from Davidson & Associates. This CD employed the technique of lighting each frame individually and in proper sequence for a linear presentation.

Virgin's approach to comics is more interactive. In titles such as *Beneath a Steel Sky*, the user gets to portray and control the hero. Voices for the characters were recorded by members of the Royal Shakespeare Company, and all action takes place in a "virtual theater."

If mere interaction is not enough, *Comic Creator!* from Putnam let's you create the strip, select a cast from fifteen available characters (nine heroes and six villains), choose from a hundred backgrounds, and select a plot line. Or, you can leave the menu altogether and create your own story.

Nonfiction

Biography is one of the most popular forms of nonfiction. A feature article by Shelley Cryan in *CD-ROM World* predicts that the CD-ROM will revolutionize the art of the autobiography. Publishers are notorious for telling their authors to cut back, but in this medium they'll be begging authors for more. Autobiographies and biographies on CD can include all the notes, letters, and source material, not to mention those horrendous home videos that even best friends and family didn't want to see.

In the previous chapter, I mentioned several CD titles featuring the life and works of various musical artists, and a moment ago I mentioned *Twain's World*, a title that explores the life and works of a literary artist. Biographies of Hollywood stars seem to fly off the bookstore shelves, so it's no surprise that the genre has migrated to compact disc as well. Starwave Corporation is producing a line of career retrospective titles, beginning with Clint Eastwood. And as you might expect, the biographical disc will use film clips, audio, photos, and behind-the-scenes footage, with Eastwood himself as your guide.

H.R. Haldeman is a celebrity of another sort. *The Haldeman Diaries: Inside the Nixon White House, The Complete Multimedia Edition* contains the full text of *The Haldeman Diaries*, a book published by G.P. Putnam's Sons, and a lot more. In addition to the 2,200 pages of unedited text in the book version, the CD includes 60 minutes of home movies shot by Haldeman, 900 photographs, 30 minutes of Haldeman's actual dictated diary entries, and an additional 2,000 pages of text. The home movies are not just of Haldeman's family, but of state visits, trips to Camp David, and meetings and special events at the White House.

Rick Fisher, director of product development at the PC division of Sony ImageSoft, feels that the CD-ROM title has a distinct advantage over the written book. "Not only does the multimedia CD-ROM version have authentic movie sequences, but it contains the unedited journal text—twice as much as in the book; hundreds of photographs; narration by Dwight Chapin, the Appointment Secretary to President Nixon; most of Nixon's appointment logs; and major news stories that appeared during the Nixon presidency."

This is more than biographical. It's historical. But beyond categories, and beyond this particular segment of history, what is really important here is that the CD-ROM medium allows for the presentation of more unedited primary source information.

The Voyager Company, pioneer that it is, has some interesting titles that are biographical in nature. *The Complete Maus*, by Art Spiegelman, is based on his graphic comic-book novel detailing his father's experiences in the Holocaust. Unlike the book, the CD medium provides a framework for including preliminary artwork, documents, and video, plus behind-the-scenes information on the creation of the project.

Then there's Voyager's First Person series. The first three discs profile three very different author/philosophers: Donald Norman, author of *The Psychology of Everyday Things*; Stephen Jay Gould, author of *On Evolution*; and Marvin Minsky, author of *The Society of Mind*. Once again we have the benefit of hearing from the authors themselves. For example, on command, Minsky himself pops up onscreen to elaborate on his theories of human cognition, and, if you choose, he'll even escort you around his living room. Ben Calica, a reviewer for *NewMedia* magazine, was interested in the content and found Minsky's video clip explanations engaging.

Unfortunately, Mr. Calica was turned off by the interface, and said he'd prefer to read the book. He didn't give it a "thumbs down," however. He just said the interface needs work. He felt that the interface was poor, the timeline unattractive, and he complained about "tiny, seemingly pointless graphics in the upper-left corner of each screen containing a minuscule amount of animation."

Of course, you might not have the same opinion about the design and presentation of information in *The Society of Mind*. Please forgive me if I become redundant, but this is a new medium. Those of us who get to see lots and lots of compact disc titles tend to become highly critical. And criticism serves an important purpose. But I often feel that I am losing sight of the fact that today's compact discs may be no more than the equivalent of cave paintings when we look back on them from some distant point in the future.

Meanwhile, average consumers are oohing and aahing over the power of the compact disc. John Q. Public not only has more information at his fingertips, but much of that information is first-person, primary source data. And multimedia brings the written word to life with sounds and sights.

One of Medio Multimedia's stated company goals is "to fulfill consumers' curiosity about topics they have previously been unable to explore." To this end, the company has developed a concept it calls Interactive Documentary that "offers people an opportunity to explore topics at their own pace and see and hear information at the level of detail they desire." The approach involves providing a narrative overview of the subject, and then allowing users to solicit further information by clicking on an image, a video clip, an animation, or a still photo during the narration.

Call it what you will, but that's a pretty good description of most non-fiction interactive multimedia titles. In addition to *Medio Magazine*, which I'll tell you about when we get to the magazine section of this chapter, other Medio titles include the critically acclaimed *JFK Assassination: A Visual Investigation*; *Jets!*, an exploration of jet-powered aircraft, their pilots, and designers; and *World Beat*, an exploration of musical styles from around the world.

There are scores of compact disc titles about all sorts of nonfiction subjects. If you're interested in astronomy, for example, there's *Redshift*, from Maris Multimedia Ltd. in London. A review in *Byte* magazine called this disc "a planetarium-cum-sky chart-cum-sky atlas-cum-dictionary." With a view of the night sky, you can click on a star to find out its name (proper name, Bayer name, Flamsteed name) and other pertinent data. Another click of the button displays an overlay of the constellations. Menus provide photos of the planets, their moons, and other deep-sky objects. Jump from the photo gallery to related entries in the Penguin *Dictionary of Astronomy*, or browse the movie gallery and watch events such as the Lunar Excursion Module touching down on the moon. Photos from NASA's Voyager spacecraft were used to create 3-D planetary images, and the program supports features that allow you to zoom in, out, and all around.

History is also a popular nonfiction genre, and there are a number of titles on the market. *Who Built America?*, from Voyager, uses documents, songs, oral histories, images, and videos to bring history to life. Not only does the title benefit from the use of multiple media, but the presentation of history is enhanced by more source information, so people can draw their own conclusions. To my mind, this title is another good example of a subject that benefits from the multimedia compact disc medium. *Who Built America?* was originally a book of two volumes, and is also part of Voyager's "expanded books" line.

American Journey 1896-1945 is another history title, this one created by Ibis Communications and distributed by Compton's NewMedia. In addition to the expected photographs, maps, charts and graphs, *American Journey* features a narrated timeline, detailed photo essays of key historical events, and video clips, including Japanese footage of the attack on Pearl Harbor.

Government documents also become history, and as I mentioned in Chapter 5, there are thousands of compact discs containing all sorts of esoteric government data. Along more commercial lines, there are titles such as *The Clinton Health Security Plan* from Allegro New Media. This disc attempts to provide a balanced presentation of the president's healthcare package by including not only the entire text of the plan, but also the White House commentary and interpretations by the American Bar Association, the U.S. Chamber of Congress, the U.S. House of Representatives Republican Conference, the Health Insurance Association of America, and others. Pictures, tables, and charts are used to explain the implications—what it means and what it costs. Video clips include President Clinton's address to Congress, and interviews with industry experts.

The economy, the unemployment rate, and job-hunting are also much-discussed topics. Infobusiness Inc. produced the *Job Power Source* CD-ROM based on eleven books about career planning by Ron and Caryl Krannisch, the U.S. Bureau of Labor Statistics' *1991 Occupational Outlook Handbook*, and a presentation on interviewing strategies and behavior by communications specialist Pat Sladey. The disc includes information about salaries, educational and training requirements, career growth prospects, more than two hundred examples of resumes and job search letters, and tips on interviewing and negotiating salaries and benefits.

A review in the *San Jose Mercury News* found much to be lacking in this title. The review said that a lot of the information was outdated and that the advice on interviewing, though the best as far as content goes, was poorly edited and not well integrated with the rest of the content. Nevertheless, any information when taken in context might prove useful. This disc is aimed at individual job seekers, and a professional version containing additional information is available for use by college career planning and placement offices, high school guidance counselors, employment counselors, and other job professionals.

Reference

The line between nonfiction and reference is a blurry one, as might be the case with some of the historical and subject-specific CDs I described before. But medical information, even at the consumer level, and works containing religious texts and interpretations, always end up on my reference shelf.

I came across quite a few compact discs that deal with religion. For example, *The New Family Bible*, from the Time Warner Interactive Group, presents the 39 books of the Old Testament with pictures and spoken narration, and 40 explanatory stories. Half the stories are text and half are narrated sequences of still pictures, each several minutes long. A review in the *San Jose Mercury*

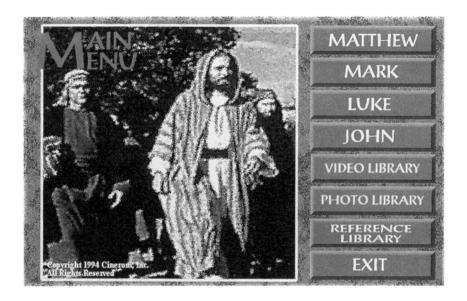

Main menu from *The Gospels: A Multimedia Guide to the Bible.* (Screen shot courtesy of Cinerom, Inc.)

News pointed out a few shortcomings, including "overly technical footnotes" and the fact that the pictures "portray both Egyptian and Israelites as white Europeans."

Another religious title comes from Cinerom. *The Gospels: A Multimedia Guide to the Bible* offers the entire text of the King James Version of the Bible, two hours of full-motion video and audio, plus nearly a hundred illustrations. You can find any verse instantly, browse through the Image Library, and print passages.

The video comes from *The Living Bible* motion picture. Movie segments can be viewed in twenty-, forty-, or sixty-minute segments, and you're not supposed to stop in midstream—a requirement I might find annoying in an interactive title. To view an image, you click on a title/description in the Image Finder's alphabetical listing, or select the Images button on the menu screen for each of the Gospels. Other buttons on the Gospel menu screens include Video, Audio, Maps, and Verse Finder.

Multimedia Family Bible from Candlelight Publishing is illustrated with paintings from the great masters and features 44 fully narrated Bible stories intended to both entertain and teach children. You can do full-text searches, or look through 500 study topics from the Bible Study Guide that are hyperlinked to related biblical verses. The disc also contains maps and photos of the Holy Land and Mediterranean region.

The First Electronic Jewish Bookshelf from ScanRom Publications features two volumes of *The Jewish Book of Why,* containing questions and answers on a variety of Judaic topics. *The Book of Jewish Knowledge* (an encyclopedia), *A Treasury of Jewish Folklore*, and *This Is the Torah* are just a few of the other books on this disc. In addition to all the text, the disc contains hundreds of photographs and more than an hour of Jewish music.

Bibles and Religion from Chestnut Shareware claims to cover Judaism and Christianity. It presents multiple versions of the New Testament, Old Testament, and portions of the Talmud. Included among its features are a cross-reference tool to find words and phrases, and Greek and Hebrew Bible dictionaries to find original translations. Most Significant Bits also produces a religious shareware CD titled *Straight from Heaven.* In addition to multiple versions of the Bible, the disc also contains Judaic and Islamic programs, a concordance, educational Bible games, Bible studies, the Gospels, and a collection of religious clip art images.

With healthcare a major issue in our times, it is no surprise to find a very large number of heathcare CD-ROM titles. These titles provide all sorts of information about medicines, symptoms, and diseases. It's not a good idea to become your own doctor and diagnose your own ailments, but it is always a good idea to be informed. Many doctors can't or won't take the time to explain things to their patients fully. And those who do often use vocabulary that sounds like Greek.

Most of the medical CDs for the consumer market include lots of photos and diagrams, features especially useful for identifying pills and understanding procedures, as well as definitions and pronunciation guides for medical terms. Some even include animation or video clips to illustrate various medical procedures. And some of the titles I mention in this section provide tools that allow you to personalize your use of the CD, such as the Personal Profile feature in *Mayo Clinic Family Pharmacist*.

The *Family Pharmacist* CD is subtitled "your ultimate guide to medication, early detection, and first aid." The coverage is extensive, including descriptions and interactions for more than 7,600 prescription and over-the-counter drugs. Fifty minutes of sound and narration, plus 68 video and

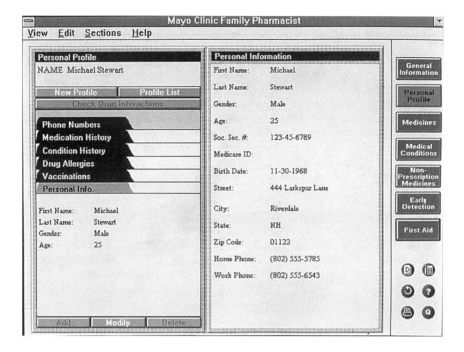

Mayo Clinic Family Pharmacist allows consumers to create and maintain their own health records. (Screen shot courtesy of IVI Publishing.)

animation clips, show first aid techniques and detection procedures for illnesses such as breast cancer. You can take notes, look up terms in the online dictionary, and search for drugs by name.

This is much more than a reference title, because it allows you to record, save, and print personal medical profiles for your entire family—interactivity of a useful sort. You can keep track of drug allergies, dates of vaccinations, medications, and histories of any illnesses. Then you can use the profile to check new prescriptions for side effects and potential negative interactions with other drugs. In today's age of specialization, this is really useful.

Ever wonder what those pills in your medicine chest are for? The label is no longer legible, or perhaps you put them into a smaller bottle for traveling and forget to unpack them. This disc offers 1,600 photographs of medications; you can locate a particular medication by entering its characteristics, such as color, size, and shape.

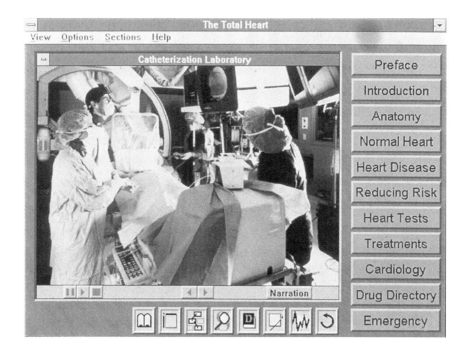

Mayo Clinic Total Heart allows patients to research procedures on catheterization and a host of other heart-related topics. (Screen shot courtesy of IVI Publishing.)

If you want to learn about the functions, conditions and treatments of the heart, check out the *Mayo Clinic Total Heart* disc. Audio lets you hear the heart as if through a stethoscope. Illustrations and 3-D video animation show you what various medical conditions look like and how different procedures are carried out. Topics are broken into nine sections: anatomy, normal heart, heart disease, reducing risks, heart tests, treatments, cardiology, drug directory, and emergencies. Features include a search engine to let you find specific words or phrases, a dictionary tool to provide definitions of unfamiliar terms, and a notes feature to keep track of your own thoughts.

The *Mayo Clinic Family Health Book*, based on the 1,378-page, best-selling book, uses 90 minutes of sound and narration, 45 videos and animations, and 500 color illustrations to cover topics in seven categories: anatomy, lifestyles, first aid/safety, keeping fit, disease/disorders, skin disorders, and modern care. In addition to information on more than a thousand diseases and disorders, it

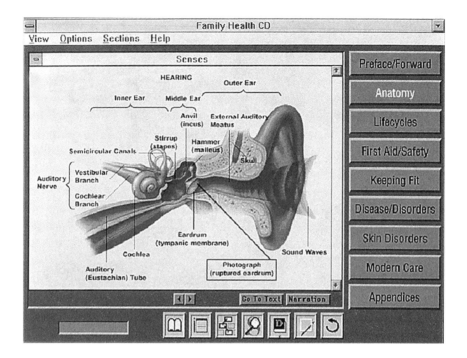

Mayo Clinic Family Health Book allows users to educate themselves about the workings of different parts of the anatomy, such as the inner ear. (Screen shot courtesy of IVI Publishing.)

discusses nutrition, exercise, and stress management as well. Like all the Mayo Clinic titles, this one features an online dictionary, keyword searching, and the ability to print out text entries.

The Mayo Clinic and ESPN Sports Health & Fitness CD is a guide to working out, sports, and nutrition. Designed to assist both the fitness buff and amateur athlete in structuring a healthy lifestyle, it includes sporting event footage from ESPN—live footage of athletes, commentators, and televised events ranging from aerobics and running to team sports such as basketball, football, and soccer. A Personal Trainer segment features a personalized exercise program that provides feedback and a journal to monitor weight loss/gain, food intake, and weight training.

Contrary to how it may appear, the Mayo Clinic series from IVI Publishing represents only a part of the market for health-related CDs. Great Bear

Technology publishes the *HealthSoft Complete Guide to Symptoms, Illness & Surgery*, with illustrations of more than a hundred surgical procedures. You can search for symptoms and read about the possible diagnoses. To find out about common treatments and medicines, you click on the Red Cross icon. And if you don't know about a suggested drug, you can look it up in Great Bear Technology's *HealthSoft Complete Guide to Prescription & Non-Prescription Drugs*.

Another major publisher of medical CD titles is the Creative Multimedia Corporation. Its *Family Doctor* disc, based on the works of Dr. Allan Bruckheim, covers the anatomy of the human body with video explaining each of the five systems. Users can access to three different levels of information, depending on how much detail they want.

The *New Prescription Drug Reference Guide* explains how drugs work, with lists of side effects and contraindications, plus photos for easy identification. A wide range of topics, from common medical conditions and illnesses to surgical procedures and patient-physician relationships, are addressed in the Question and Answer section. And if you need more information, the Resources list points you to various associations and health update booklets. The disc also sports a glossary of more than 100 medical terms and 300-plus illustrations of anatomical features, systems, and medical procedures. There is also a First Aid section with animation.

Creative Multimedia is also the publisher of *Dr. Ruth's Encyclopedia of Sex*. This disc is an excellent example of using a familiar personality to deliver information and reusing media assets. The screen interface is designed to look like Dr. Ruth's office. Users can click on the radio to hear excerpts from Dr. Ruth's radio talk show. Clicking on the telephone provides the answers to commonly asked questions. The disc also uses photos, video, and charts to cover a variety of topics, including contraceptives and AIDS.

Coffee Table Books

At the beginning of this chapter I mentioned a CD titled *I Photograph to Remember*. This is a remarkable photo essay with personal narration by the photographer Pedro Meyer. Knowing that both of his parents were dying of cancer, Mr. Meyer chose to record the last three years of their lives on camera. The disc contains one hundred black-and-white photographs with spoken narration.

Unlike the majority of multimedia CD titles currently on the market, this one was not motivated by a desire to create a commercial hit. Rather, it is a work of art that forged new ground in a new medium. No home videos, no animation, nothing to detract from the simple elegance of the photographer's eye at one with the son's heart. Pedro Meyer is a renowned photographer whose works hang in the permanent collections of over twenty of the world's finest museums.

Another acclaimed photographer, Rick Smolen, has been using the CD to create a very different type of art form. His first CD title, *From Alice to Ocean*, chronicles Robyn Davidson's 1,700 mile trek across the Australian outback accompanied by four camels, her dog, and Smolen himself, who was on assignment for *National Geographic*. The journey took six months, and afterward Davidson wrote *Tracks*, which became a best-seller. During the journey, Smolen shot 500 rolls of film. *National Geographic* used 32 images, and 142 of the remaining photos were used for the CD-ROM, along with maps, video clips, and narration by both Smolen and Davidson.

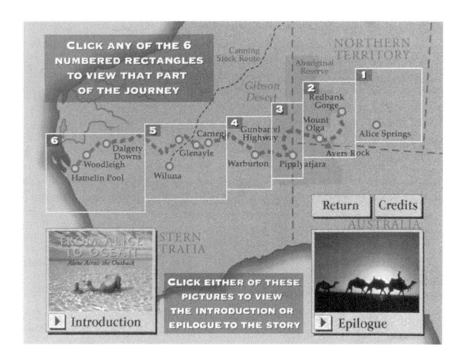

From this screen in the interactive, CD-ROM version of *From Alice to Ocean*, users can view the introduction or epilogue, or track a selected segment of the journey from Alice Springs to Hamelin Pool. (Screen shot courtesy of Against All Odds Productions.)

The final result was a large-format book bundled with a Photo CD or CD-ROM. The book is beautiful and the quality of the photos on the Photo CD is beyond excellent. The CD-ROM, however, has the most to offer. The disc is interactive, and you can travel along with them, narrative style, or navigate on your own by clicking on a particular area of the map. You can pause the story to digress to information about kangaroos or aboriginal culture, or stop for some photo tips from Smolen.

A Passage to Vietnam is another CD created by Rick Smolen. This one is a spin-off of the "Day in the Life" photojournalism series that made Smolen famous. Rick took 60 photographers on a photo expedition of Vietnam. Together they shot in excess of 200,000 pictures with electronic cameras. Only 200 made it into their book, but more made it into their CD-ROM.

When a film reel appears at the bottom of a screen in *Passage to Vietnam*, it means that a video clip is available for viewing. In this still image, brown rice lines the side of the road; when you call up the video, you can actually see and hear why this custom is practiced. This CD-ROM contains over 45 minutes of video clips of Vietnam. (Screen shot courtesy of Against All Odds Productions.)

The World of U.S. Manga Corps is a very different kind of CD. *PC Sources* magazine likened this disc to a digitized coffee table book containing more than 1,000 images by famous Japanese Manga artists. *Manga* is the Japanese equivalent of a comic book. Unlike comics in America, which are mostly for kids, Manga is a wildly popular art form. Japanese comics depict topics of all sorts, including erotica (some images are definitely adult-only viewing). The Japanese consider Manga drawings to be serious works of art.

Magazines

Back in December of 1992, *Multimedia Business Report* said that *Newsweek* would become the first general-interest magazine to publish a quarterly CD-ROM edition. Subscriptions would be marketed by *Newsweek*, while The Software Toolworks in Novato, California, would sell a retail version. That same month, *Digital Media* reported that the disc would be compatible with Sony's portable MMCD player, which ostensibly adheres to the CD-ROM XA standard, and would be ported to IBM-compatible PC platform by early 1993.

In August of 1994, almost two years later, an article in *Upside* magazine reported that *Newsweek Interactive* is a quarterly, and that *Newsweek* recently launched its third disc, featuring *The Secret Life of Animals* as one of the two main stories. This feature was originally a popular cover story for the magazine, and the content was redesigned and expanded for interactive use.

The *Newsweek* CDs are not meant to be a substitute for the printed magazine. Each issue will cover no more than three or four subjects, and the disc will contain other data, such as stories from *The Washington Post* and radio interviews from Associated Press Radio Network's *Newsweek on the Air* program.

Medio Magazine is a new, monthly compact disc news magazine with more than 10,000 articles covering news, entertainment, and sports stories culled from a variety of news sources, plus photos, audio and video clips, and stock quotes. The stock quotes and other updates are obtained by dialing into *Medio Magazine*'s online Internet hookup at no additional charge.

In addition to news, entertainment, and sports, *Medio Magazine* has five other sections. The Scene section covers travel, culture, health, and earth issues. The Finance section covers money matters with stock quotes, expert advice by a financial columnist, and an investment viewer allowing users to track stock history. Kidstuff contains some games and simple articles. Reference leads to a world atlas and the *CIA World Fact Book*. The Science and Technology section is still under development, and News at a Glance displays a photo gallery. All this for $60 a year.

Sounds great? Well it is and it isn't. When you install *Medio Magazine* on your system, you have to sit through a sales presentation about all of Medio's other CD titles (you can leave them room until the installation is complete). When I finally launched the magazine, I was treated to more narration—audio that I desperately wanted to be able to turn off. No such luck. Granted, the audio was for my benefit. The guy (it was a man's voice) wanted to tell me about all the neat things in the issue, but I just wanted to be left alone to explore in peace. These are the moments when you realize that some things are not as interactive as you might want them to be.

The disc could also have benefited from more cross-indexing and hyperlinks to related material. The only links I noticed were geographical. Whenever a country was mentioned, there was a link to a map and a corresponding entry in the *World Fact Book*. Not bad, but not enough. These are not complaints against *Medio Magazine* alone. The magazine is not the only CD with too much audio and not enough internal connections.

Perhaps I shouldn't be so critical. After all, it is still a new medium, so perhaps I should be patient while it evolves. *Medio Magazine* definitely has a lot of content (it could take me a month or more to read everything that's on this disc), and the quality of the pictures is excellent. The magazine promises to deliver "All the world on a CD-ROM," and judging from the amount and variety of content, they might just do that.

These are just two of what I imagine will turn out to be many CD-ROM–based news and entertainment magazines—the proverbial tip of the iceberg. CD-ROM magazines will proliferate, as will magazines about CD-ROMs and other digital media. Ziff-Davis Publishing is working on a new publication called *Interactive Week* that should be available by the time you read this book. At first, the new venture will appear in paper format only, but the electronic version will not be far behind.

Then there are specialty magazines that focus on a single topic or audience. *Money in the 90s* is the title of a disc from Laser Resources, Inc., that contains all the issues of *Money* magazine from January, 1990 through the 1994 Forecast issue. The disc is indexed by subject and by issue, and supports full-text searches. Back issues of *PC Magazine* are available on the *Computer Select* disc.

Computer Select, which includes the text from several computer publications, can be used as a comprehensive research tool. This one is strictly search and retrieve—it has no jazzy interface to speak of, and only recently added graphics capabilities. These are little more than archival discs for back issues of printed magazines. They are useful for research, but not all that interesting—especially when there are sizzling discs to be explored.

Everybody reads *Playboy* magazine for the interviews, right? Now you can put that supposition to the test. The *Playboy Interview* compact disc contains 352 interviews. Interviewees on the CD include Marlon Brando, Johnny Carson, Jimmy Carter, Bob Dylan, Leona Helmsley, David Letterman, Martin Luther King Jr., Malcolm X, Yoko Ono, Dr. Ruth, Susan Sarandon, Barbra Streisand, and Ted Turner, to name a very few.

The interface is simple and the disc is not overloaded with glitz in the way of multimedia features. In addition to the interview text and black-and-white photos, the disc includes 25 audio clips taken from the original interview tapes. What you get here that you can't easily get by reading the magazine is the ability to compare and contrast the thoughts, quotes, and opinions of a variety of

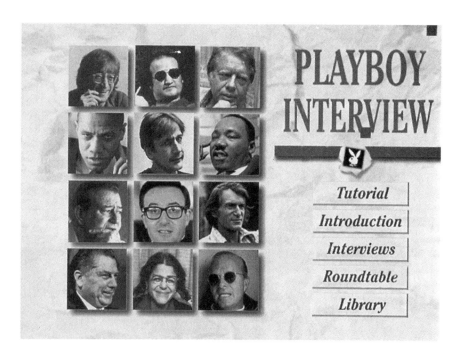

Main screen from the *Playboy Interview* CD-ROM. (Screen shot courtesy of the IBM Multimedia Publishing Studio.)

people. For example, twenty topics are the focus of the section referred to as the "Roundtable." Here, you can read a selection of quotes from several of the interviewees about a particular topic.

Another hot title is *The People v. O.J. Simpson: An Interactive Companion to the O.J. Simpson Trial*. While this does not qualify as a magazine per se, it is definitely a news-driven release. Produced by Turner Home Entertainment, CNN, and Intellimedia Sports Inc., this is another one of those hybrid combinations between a CD-ROM and online supplements. Purchasers will be able to tap in to a special CompuServe forum for late-breaking news on the Simpson case.

Stuart Snyder, executive vice president and general manager of Turner Home Entertainment, referred to the CD as "the industry's first instant publishing interactive product for consumers." The disc contains testimony, expert opinions and interpretations, and more than an hour of video. Audio selections

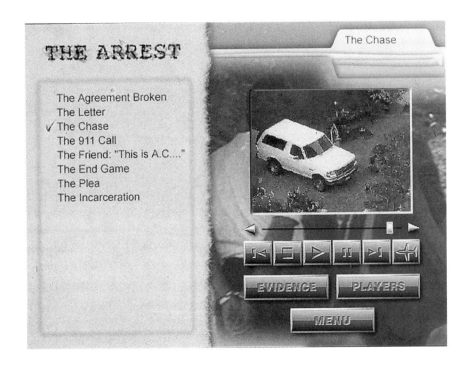

The Chase screen, part of The Arrest section in *The People v. O.J. Simpson: An Interactive Companion to the O.J. Simpson Trial*. (Screen shot courtesy of Turner Home Entertainment. © CNN Interactive.)

include interviews and sworn testimony. The Simpson disc is divided into ten sections: The Murder, The Victims, The Evidence, The Players, The Suspect, The Arrest, The Legal Debate, The Timeline, The People v. O.J. Simpson, and The Court of Public Opinion.

Because computer-oriented compact disc magazines tend to lean heavily toward a sales focus, I tend to classify them as a breed unto themselves. Why only read about state-of-the-art multimedia when you can learn about it and experience it at the same time? I recently received a direct mail piece promoting *NautilusCD* from Metatec, and that's what the brochure asked. It makes sense, and if the screen shots in the brochure are any indication, it looks like it delivers.

The contents screen of this CD magazine lists five departments (Desktop Media, Entertainment, Education, Industry Watch, and ComputerWare) and two services (Subscriber Guide and Article Listing). You select a department and the screen shows you the sections within the department. For example, the ComputerWare section has half a dozen buttons leading you to sections such as Software Demos and Tools & Technical. The Entertainment section, on the other hand, is devoted to fun. There you might find a children's tale with video, music, and narration; a music video showcasing a new recording; or the newest Tetris-like game.

All sorts of icons launch photos or videos, or lead you to more detailed information. In addition to the software tools, product demos, and reviews, *NautilusCD* has magazine-like feature pieces. Topics covered in various issues include home finance on your computer, sound on your PC, the best educational software for children, and digital pictures on your PC.

There's a terrific product out for kids and their parents. *Club Kidsoft* is more than a magazine and more than a CD-ROM. It's a cool club for kids aged 4 to 12, and the best source for parents to learn about and shop for quality, kid-tested, parent-approved software for IBM-compatible and Macintosh computers. Membership yields a quarterly large-format printed magazine, a CD-ROM disc, and a product catalog for the parents.

Like any other club, the focus is on participation. Member-submitted editorial information, artwork, and reviews can be found in the CD and the accompanying magazine. The CD features the club room, a place where members can go and check out stories from other members, learn about upcoming contests, see art that was submitted by other members (some of which is animated and set to music), watch a TV show called "Club News" that is anchored by 11-year-olds, and listen to audio tracks on the CD that are about club members and what they think about and talk about with regard to software. And then there's the purchase component. Kids can try out the software product demos, and parents can download them from the CD.

Identifying kids as the real end-users of *Club Kidsoft*, Karen Schultz, vice president of marketing, says, "*Club Kidsoft* is the only multimedia magazine written for kids, and by kids, focusing on quality software and the productive use of computers. Today's kids are very interested in interactive software programming, and parents are very interested in having them use it, if it's good. By building an identity, brand recognition if you will, *Club Kidsoft* is endeavoring to be the brand that parents feel comfortable seeing their kids get online with."

As mentioned in Chapter 1, *Club Kidsoft* is not concerned with delivery methods—today CD-ROM, tomorrow broadband. The focus is on creating an identity. "*Kidsoft* is simply a specialized identity, a network, much like the way HBO, Showtime, A&E, ESPN, CNN are specialized identities deployed over an analog distribution system, which is called cable," explains founder Rick Devine. "What consumers buy is not the system (cables, satellites dishes, etc.), what they buy is the network identity and its ability to deliver specialized programming to the consumer."

And like a network identity, *Club Kidsoft* delivers on a promise much the way Disney does with its selection of appropriate television programming on The Disney Channel. "The promise from Disney is that you can expect to see high-quality family programming material that is nonviolent" says Devine. "The promise from *Kidsoft* is that you'll find software that's engaging and exciting for kids, that's got educational value, and that's not violent."

To deliver on this promise, *Club Kidsoft* has a panel of advisors trained in educational pedagogy. The company has its own internal testing and review process that includes taking the product into schools. It also has its own lab where kids can be observed using the product. If success is any indication, *Club Kidsoft* must be keeping its promises. Membership climbed to nearly 50,000 in their first eight months.

There are two other CD-ROM–based magazines that focus on computer software and digital media: the disc that now ships with *CD-ROM Today* magazine and the recently announced *Interactive Entertainment* CD.

On May 26, 1994, *The New York Times* quoted the Pulitzer Prize winner E. Annie Prouix as saying that the information highway is "for bulletin boards on esoteric subjects, reference works, lists and news—timely, utilitarian information, efficiently pulled through the wires. Nobody is going to sit down and read a novel on a twitchy little screen. Ever." Not even a magazine? Given the sheer number of CD-based titles being sold, I have to wonder if she's wrong.

Chapter 9

CD-ROMs Around the House

This is the last chapter I'll spend touring titles aimed at the consumer at home. It amazes me that I haven't yet put even the smallest of dents into the stack of press releases and promos that have been flooding my home since the start of this book. Even you are probably beginning to be bombarded by direct mail pieces hawking the latest and greatest CD releases. More than a few of the titles described in the previous chapters were brought to my attention by junk mail and by mail-order catalogs not related to computers. These too have begun to carry compact disc titles.

"Around the house" is my catch-all category. It includes discs of the "how-to" variety (be it home repair, cooking, or gardening), personal productivity titles with a focus on finance, travel, genealogy, adult entertainment, and home shopping.

How-to "Books"

The migration from book to disc was a natural for the how-to genre. To learn how to do new things, first you watch, then you imitate. When it comes to cooking, apprenticeships have long been the tried-and-true method of learning, whether the instructor is a parent or a famous chef. There are zillions of cookbooks at your local bookstore, and at least half a zillion cooking shows on television. With interactive compact discs about cooking, you get something that is greater than the sum of its parts.

The same is true for home repair and improvement. CAD (computer-aided design) software, and 3-D drawing and rendering packages are not new. But when you add multimedia animation, video, and sound, you end up with a cross between your favorite building or repair manual and a television segment from *Home Again*, *This Old House*, or *New Yankee Workshop*. In fact, as you'll see in a moment, the folks at Hometime actually have their own CD.

Once you master the basics, you can innovate, or even create your own methods and masterpieces. In the meantime, compact disc titles can provide you with both an instructor and an assistant. You can only learn so much from text and static images. So, in addition to descriptions, illustrations and photos, there are generally video segments showing a pro at work. Usually, the pros share a tip or two while they're at it.

Some of the CD titles have additional features that can help you determine—in the case of carpentry, for example—costs and materials. This is what I meant by having an assistant. The only downside to these how-to discs is that you're not likely to have a computer screen in the garage or on your kitchen counter. But the CDs usually make up for this difficulty by allowing you to print out lists and instructions that you can carry with you.

Food and Wine

Better Homes and Gardens Healthy Cooking, *The Lifestyles of the Rich & Famous Cookbook*, and *Wines of the World* were among the food and wine CD titles I found at my local Egghead Software store. Multimedia is the perfect medium for cooking instruction. My friends will attest to the fact that I often ask questions about cooking. What does it mean to "fold-in the egg whites"? What should something look like when it reaches the proper consistency? And when it comes to wondering how a certain procedure should be done, I'm more prone to say "show me." Now I can watch video clips and not embarrass myself in front of my friends anymore. If a picture paints a thousand words, then video clips must convey at least a million.

Reviewers, who have seen even more titles than I, say that *Healthy Cooking* is the most comprehensive cooking CD title. It contains more than 400 recipes, with 80 videos covering various aspects of food preparation, and lots and lots of color photos. Nutritional and caloric information is available, and you can select recipes from an index of categories or from a general index that you can sort alphabetically, by calorie count, or by the amount of time needed for preparation. Each recipe, of course, includes a color photo.

Most of these cooking titles contain a feature that allows you to specify various ingredients (perhaps what you happen to have on hand) and find one or more recipes you can make with those ingredients. Another common feature is the ability to print out recipes and shopping lists—a handy feature for those of us who don't have computers in our kitchens or Newtons (hand-held computers, also known as Personal Digital Assistants) in our pockets.

"Champagne wishes and caviar dreams" might be Robin Leach's favorite repast, but, luckily, *The Lifestyles of the Rich & Famous Cookbook* contains more practical fare. The main screen displays four categories: Extravagant Affairs, Casual Entertaining, Relaxing at Home, and Favorite Recipes. Leach introduces each category, and the selections are based on a featured event or celebrity profile. There are celebrity photos galore, as well as the requisite shots of some of the dishes. The disc does contain some video and sound clips. In addition to the list of ingredients and preparation instructions, you will find occasional notes to assist you in locating unusual ingredients.

Wines of the World lets you browse through wine lists, searching by type, vintage, producer, price, quality, value, and more. Learn about the wine, its quality, and the region in which it grows. You can also learn how to properly open, decant, and serve wine by watching video clips. This is a comprehensive title covering 20,000 different wines.

In various mail-order catalogs, I've noticed several more cooking titles, usually from smaller publishers who haven't yet been able to break into stores. A company called Most Significant Bits has a shareware disc called *Cookbook Heaven* that contains 20,000 recipes, cookbooks, diet and health applications. Those who are super health-conscious may want to look at Magic Multimedia's *Magic Chef* cooking disc. It contains over 27,000 international, low-fat, and no-fat recipes, not to mention some special dishes for diabetics and vegetarians. If 20–30,000 recipes are not enough, you can feast forever with *Cookbook USA* from J&D Distributing. This disc weighs in with over a million recipes, 35,000 for meat dishes alone, and 500 specifically for large crowds.

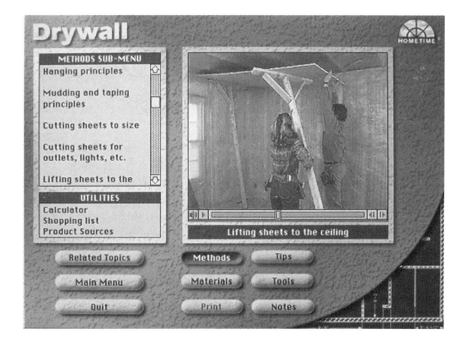

Learning about drywall from the *Hometime Weekend Home Projects* CD. A how-to video shows you the basic principles of installing drywall. The Utilities section gives you information on the materials you'll need. (Screen shot courtesy of IVI Publishing.)

Home and Garden

Hometime Weekend Home Projects, from IVI Publishing, is based on the popular PBS television series, and includes sixty minutes of how-to video. This disc offers help with ceramic tile, plumbing, wallpapering, flooring, painting, building a deck, and more. Each topic includes video, text, and graphics to provide expert advice, clear instructions and demonstrations, not to mention helpful hints and shortcuts.

With 12 subject areas and 60 projects to choose from, users can view instructional videos or click on the Materials, Tips, Tools, Notebook, or Utilities sections. Useful features include special calculators to figure out the precise amount of materials needed for a project and a shopping list that you can print out. Another print feature lets you record your own thoughts and reminders. The Product Sources directory lists key manufacturers and associations.

The *Complete House* CD takes a different approach. It provides lots of information on American residential architecture geared to people who are building or remodeling or are just interested in home design. Photos, plans, and drawings, as well as text and audio segments, are used to explain and illustrate. Using the CAD/FP Floor Planner software, you can create your own customized floor plans—including doors and door swings, walls, stoves, sinks, and beds—and envision and design your new home.

Recently, a nonprofit CD-ROM project was launched to share information from an environmental feasibility study and show how changes were made to the White House to make it more energy-efficient and environmentally sound. The idea was for the changes made at the White House to serve as a model for government agencies wanting to renovate their buildings.

Greening of the White House presents both problems and solutions. You can use a map to explore the ecological renovations to different parts of the house and grounds. Or you can walk through 3-D renderings of various rooms. Video clips play back comments from the feasibility study team members discussing the measures they took to improve the house. The content is designed to be accessible to a wide audience ranging from middle school students, to home owners, to architects and designers.

Books That Work is a popular CD series. *Designing and Building Your Own Deck* includes illustrations, animation, sound, and text, plus a CAD program so you can learn what you need to know and then design and estimate costs for your own deck. The *Home Survival Toolkit*, a do-it-yourself, home-repair guide, includes several interactive advertisements for companies such as Black & Decker that sell tools and construction materials. In fact, this disc won the Gold in the advertisement category at the 1994 NewMedia InVision Multimedia Awards.

I saw *3D Landscape* in a store. It, too, is part of the Books That Work series, and it looks like it has some nifty features. In addition to the how-to guide that explains basic principles and techniques, the Growth Over Time feature allows you to see your landscape as it matures. Shadow Caster lets you see where shadows fall at any time of the day, and Slope helps plan hillside landscapes. The Plants and Materials Estimator calculates costs, and you can always see a 3-D view from a variety of angles.

There are lots of other titles dealing with homes and landscapes. *Better Homes & Gardens Complete Guide to Gardening* contains a comprehensive plant database, instructional videos, and tips from experts. Chestnut Shareware claims that its *Gardening: A Handbook for the Home Gardener* is a truly complete guide to gardening. It offers advice on garden planning, layout, landscaping, pest control, herbology, and planting. Games and clip art are included.

Philips Media also has some gardening titles for the CD-i platform. *Gardening By Choice: Flowers and Foliage* helps you evaluate climate when planning your garden; *Gardening By Choice: Fruits and Vegetables* provides tips and techniques for growing an edible garden; and *Urban Gardener (Growing Pains and How to Avoid Them)* discusses climate, soil types, and plant preferences for potted plants, gardens, and even lawns.

Personal Productivity

As I mentioned at the beginning of Chapter 7, Personal Productivity is the classification Microsoft gave to its line of products that help you to track finances, manage mailing lists, create calendars and greeting cards, and even run a home-based business. Most of the programs that fit this description, whether or not they are made by Microsoft, are available on floppy disks. Their recent availability on CD is more a matter of convenience and cost (it's cheaper for a publisher to make CDs than floppies). There is usually some added value to the disc, generally in the form of clip art or font collections.

In this section, I skip over software programs repackaged for compact disc and focus instead on a few financial management CDs titles. I also include travel planning in my definition of personal productivity.

Finance

In today's economy, finance is foremost on a lot of peoples minds. The *Charles J. Givens Money Guide*, from Friendly Software Corp., contains 131 full-motion video clips and 800 answers to commonly asked financial questions. If you want information and advice on how to spend, borrow, or manage money, or you need to learn how to organize and maintain your financial records, the answers are here. The disc also contains worksheets, a calculator, and custom tools.

Using *Jonathan Pond's Personal Financial Planner* from Vertigo Development Group, you can build a personalized financial plan. Topics include organizing records, accumulating wealth, and future planning. The disc includes some quizzes so you can check your understanding of financial topics before you put your money on the line. You can also take the "wealth test" to assess your financial situation.

Perhaps all you really need is some help with your taxes. While wandering around the Internet one day, I came across something called the *CD-ROM Report Electronic Edition #1*. In it, I read a review by Tony Thomas about *Tax Info '93*. This disc apparently contains every tax form and schedule you could ever need, as well as a software program that allows you to fill in the forms and print them out. Thomas suggested, however, that the disc would benefit if the text from various IRS handbooks was included.

I don't know whether *Tax Info '94* will heed the call, but you can always turn to the *Turbo Tax Deluxe* CD that contains several references and tools in addition to the popular Turbo Tax software for both Federal and State returns. The disc includes *Your Income Tax*, the popular reference by J.K. Lasser; *Turbo Tax Planner*, for multiyear tax forecasting and analyses; an interactive guide to tips and strategies called *Turbo Tax Savings Guide*; online IRS instructions and taxpayer information publications; and Marshall Loeb's *Video Tax Guide*.

Travel

Now that your finances are properly managed and your tax returns under control, it's time to take that extra money and travel. Whether you're planning a short or long trip, going near or far, by car or plane, there are lots of CDs out there just waiting to make travel planning easier and more complete.

If you're traveling by car, you can use the *AAA Trip Planner*, developed for Comptons by GeoSystems. It integrates GeoSystems' GeoLocate routing and mapping engine with the American Automobile Association's travel information database. Or you can plan your route with *Map 'n' Go* from DeLorme Mapping. Set your preferences and then indicate where you're leaving from and where you're going. *Map 'n' Go* will calculate the distance, tell you the best route, and tell you how long it should take to drive there. The program also points out restaurants, hotels and campgrounds, and locations of interest along the way. Once you get in the car (probably without your computer), you can take along the 128-page *North America Atlas* that comes with the CD.

If you want information about the sites, you can check out *AmericaAlive GUIDisc* from CD Technology Inc.'s MediAlive Division. *GUIDisc* provides information about the states and their national parks, tourist attractions, and major cities. In addition to text and photos, you'll see maps showing cities and interstate routes, and QuickTime movies. Depending on which state you're interested in, this CD has some drawbacks. Most of the video clips and photographs were supplied by travel and tourism bureaus, so the states with small promotional budgets are underrepresented.

If you want to seek out specific types of attractions, such as museums or festivals, or tailor the search for activities suitable for children, use the *Everywhere USA Travel Guide* from Deep River. It offers travel information covering every state and region in the nation. Whether you're traveling for business or pleasure, you can find parks, theaters, historic sites, baseball teams, and more for any destination.

Perhaps white-water rafting is more your style. If you're in search of excitement, or want to plan your vacation around a specific activity, you can find locations worldwide with the help of *Adventures: A Complete Multimedia Resource for Worldwide Adventure Travel Experiences*. This disc offers in-depth descriptions of over a thousand travel opportunities.

From leisurely walking tours to kayaking rough rapids, you can search by type of activity, country or state, time of year, level of difficulty, and appropriateness for children. For example, you can find out where to take the children horseback riding in April. Deep River has included 45 minutes of video segments, thousands of color photos, plus descriptions of each activity, tour information, prices, and instructions for making arrangements.

A multimedia gourmet guide to the country's best restaurants, wineries, and micro-breweries is the perfect resource for planning a gourmet trip. Again, Deep River can help you out, this time with its *Great Restaurants, Wineries & Breweries* CD, which covers 1,400 of the country's outstanding makers of fine food, wine, and beer.

The disc includes more than four thousand photographs and menus, with details on house specialties, operating hours, prices, and dress codes. Descriptions and illustrations give an idea of ambiance and entrees. Also included are hundreds of recipes from great chefs across the country. Winery and brewery descriptions include information about the best vintages and ales, as well as details about tours.

Genealogy

The Family Tree Maker Deluxe CD-ROM Edition is a wonderful tool for anyone interested in cataloging family history. In addition to creating text-based family trees, a new scrapbook feature has been added to allow users to incorporate graphics (including scanned documents and Photo CD images), as well as audio and video clips.

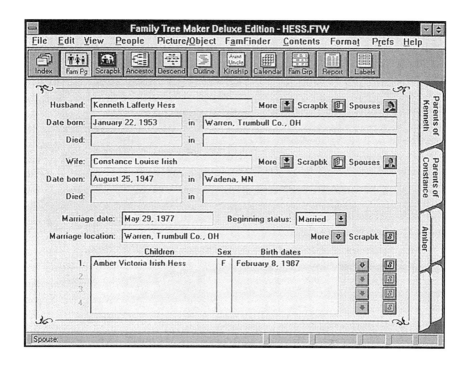

In the *Family Tree Maker*, every individual has a Family Page showing their parents. Other buttons allow you to display scrapbook entries, tree diagrams, kinship lists, and more. (Screen shot courtesy of Banner Blue Software.)

Banner Blue Software makes good use of the compact disc medium with lots of value-added tools and data. The FamilyFinder Index lists 100 million deceased people who appear in state and federal records, and directs you to specific resources where you can find more information. The disc also includes a step-by-step genealogy guide for people who want to know how to start finding their ancestors.

Adult Entertainment

Have you noticed that all the publishing houses, movie studios, and entertainment conglomerates have created subsidiaries, sister companies, and imprints with the word "interactive" somewhere in their corporate names?

Compact disc titles based on other mediums also tend to incorporate the interactive moniker. So it should come as no surprise to find a double-disc CD titled *Penthouse Interactive.*

In 1993, an onslaught of erotic CDs arrived at conventions such as Comdex and Macworld, causing some convention coordinators to ban such displays at future shows or place them all in special exhibit areas.

I've not seen the *Penthouse Interactive* disc, nor have I seen *New Wave Hookers, Nightwatch Interactive,* or *The Mark of Zara* Photo CD, all of which are advertised by StarWare. Judging from the advertisements, it looks like most of these discs are either photo compilations or digital movies of the stag variety. Others, however, appear to be interactive.

The adult-rated interactive games I've seen advertised all appear to be aimed at heterosexual men. In *Man Enough*, an adult CD game from Time Warner Interactive, the male player has to date five beautiful women, and only when he passes all of their tests will he be allowed to go on to the dream date with Jeri.

Midnight Stranger is an R-rated urban thriller with nudity and violence that could lead to sex or murder. The player controls his mood by using a color bar. Whether he is friendly/green or aggressive/red, or somewhere in between, his mood dictates how he interacts with the characters.

The advertisement for *Scissors N Stones* features a provocative photo and describes the product as an interactive game on CD-ROM where the player steps inside the depths of an arena inhabited by beautiful women. It's clearly marked for mature audiences only.

Not all of the adult entertainment CDs are pornographic, however. *CD-Romance: The Multimedia Meeting Place*, for example, is a dating database on a disc. Dating on-disc is the next evolutionary phase of video dating services. This CD is designed so that subscribers can interactively scan for prospective dates with similar backgrounds, interests, and expectations.

Another disc I saw advertised is called *Plumbers Don't Wear Ties*. The copy says it's an interactive romantic comedy from United Pixtures (no, that's not a typo) and warns that it's not suitable for children under the age of 13. It appears to be a full-length, interactive movie. *The Venus Swimsuit Issue*, from Magic Multimedia, also carries a parental advisory.

I can't tell much from the recent advertisements because most magazines no longer accept graphically explicit advertisements for erotic titles. They will, however, continue to run text ads, so if this is what you're interested in, you can still find it.

Home Shopping

You can find almost anything in a mail-order catalog. Mail-order catalogs date way back. In recent years, television infomercials have become prevalent, each with an 800 number manned 24-hours a day. Now you don't have to look at static pictures or watch video from afar. CDs are interactive and hands-on. My mail box is always full of printed catalogs, but they're expensive to produce—about $5 each. When compared to a cost of about $1 per CD, it's no wonder that CD catalogs are growing in popularity. And with the growing installed base of CD players, we might be seeing more CD catalogs soon. So far, the majority of CD-based shopping catalogs sell software, but a few pilot projects are testing the waters for marketing all kinds of merchandise.

Software

In the world of computer software, the ability to try before you buy is a big asset. Software catalogs on CD contain demo versions of programs, a feature especially good for selecting children's software, but equally useful for adults. For a nominal fee, you can buy a CD that offers demos of many different titles. Such discs may also include shareware products. Then there are demos that are free, demos that come with other packages, and demos in some of the CD-based magazines. Many consumers won't buy a CD title sight-unseen. Without a way for consumers to sample a product before purchasing it, many would-be sales never take place.

Once you decide you want to purchase a program, you just call up and finalize the transaction. In most cases, you'll get a password over the phone so that you can unlock the files of the program you want. In other cases, the product is shipped to you. Some discs have guided tours, and some allow you to search for products by title, type, publisher, or price. The disc from Club Kidsoft, for example, allows you to search for age-appropriate titles.

Some catalog and demo discs insist on running off your hard drive; others will run solely off the CD-ROM drive until you make a purchase. Of those that mess with your drives, some warn you exactly what files are being installed and exactly where they'll be placed. This is a blessing if the files are going to reside in your Macintosh System Folder or Windows System directory and you want to remove them later. Some demos that run off the hard drive warn you that files will be copied and give you the opportunity to bail out. Then there are the obnoxious ones that blithely do as they like and tell you nothing.

Making the purchase can be as easy as phoning in and getting the access key from the person on the other end of the line. In many cases, you have to download one or more files. Tales of being kept on hold and having to wait for long periods of time are not too unusual. Deborah Branscum wrote an article for *Macworld* in which she described not only being kept on hold, but also being told to keep her mouse moving so that the system would not crash while her unlocking program was being delivered. All told, she was on the phone for seventeen and a half minutes. Even without time delays, you have to consider whether there are hidden costs in this delivery method. Were there any connect-time charges, for example, or did you have to make a long distance call?

Soon, I expect, discs will come with the necessary software to place orders for you—as long as you have a modem. You might be spared an aggravating experience, but chances are you'll still rack up some costs on the phone connection, you'll still have to give more information than you'd like to, and you'll also run the added risk of "them" being able to access your hard drive without your knowledge. Maybe that's my paranoia speaking, but the possibilities of someone getting inside your hard disk do exist.

Another pet peeve of mine is being coerced into giving the seller all kinds of information, demographics plus. Inevitably, this adds to my junk mail quota, since companies not only keep me up to date on their new product developments by sending me advertisements, but they also sell my name, address, and other data to anyone who will pay. I don't have this problem when I shop retail and pay cash.

Generally, all the documentation you need is online as part of the program. Sometimes, however, comprehensive online help isn't there and you want the printed manuals (or you want the printed manuals anyway). You can usually order them, if they exist. Another snafu can arise when you have downloaded the program, but the manuals haven't arrived yet. Not that you can't learn by trial and error (it's usually the best way), but sometimes you can't install the program unless you have the proper registration or serial number handy.

The number of choices is an issue for some. Where a retail store is limited by shelf space, and a CD-ROM is limited by disc space, the number of products stocked by a major mail-order house is far greater in number. On the downside, however, you get more choices but no demos.

There can be drawbacks to demos. When a developer creates a demo version of a program, the bells and whistles are prominent and any weaknesses are often hidden or tucked away where no one can seem them. Some "demos," however, are not actually separate demo applications, but full-blown versions of the program with some type of limitation. For example, you might be able to create something, but not save it. Another type of "demo" is a full-blown program that can be used for a limited time period only. When your time is up, the program either locks up or is disabled in some way. If you call to purchase the program, you are then given the magic code to make it work again. These types of demos are usually known as "test-drives." Frequently, the discs and manuals are mailed to you after you get the magic code.

If you want reviews, you still have to look to the magazines and then play with demos, because CDs generally don't include reviews or comparisons. Retail stores may be able to offer some advice, but this seems less and less true as the stores get bigger, the list of titles gets longer, and the number of staff diminishes. I know of one exception, and that's *SuperStore*, a CD full of demos from TestDrive Corp. The *SuperStore* disc contains applications from all the big players (Microsoft, Borland, WordPerfect, and Time Warner). It also includes reviews and data sheets. You can test-drive a program up to five times. After that you have to buy it.

Who puts out these software catalog discs? There are two types of catalog or demo disc publishers: the publisher of the original software and the distributor. Companies such as Time Warner Interactive and Microsoft have pressed sampler discs of their original software. *CD Premier* from Time Warner contains excerpts from Time Warner's popular releases, including games such as *Hell Cab*, and historical titles such as *Seven Days in August* (about the Berlin Wall) and *Clinton: Portrait of Victory*. The last Microsoft Home sampler I saw covered 42 products. Samplers are more like interactive presentations; they seldom, if ever, allow you to actually test-drive a product.

Compilation demo or catalog discs are often produced by distributors, such as Ingram Micro and The Mac Zone. Frequently these discs contain entire products that remain encrypted until you unlock them with a code key. Ingram Micro's *CD Access* disc contains over 150 Mac and Windows programs. *Instant Access* is the title of The Mac Zone CD, and it includes descriptions and demos of around 200 products. The programs are actually contained on the disc, so once you decide to buy you can order by phone and get the code to unlock your new title right away.

If the product you buy is normally covered by a money-back guarantee and you want to "return" it, you have to sign a form swearing that you are removing the software from your hard drive. It's sort of an honor system, and so far it hasn't caused any real problems. But, then again, when I called The Mac Zone, customer support told me that the volume of customers ordering from *Instant Access* discs was fairly low.

Egghead Software and *InfoWorld* magazine are co-sponsoring a new CD catalog. The *Multimedia Know-it-All* series provides photos, reviews, technical information, and prices for software and hardware products. Hardware categories include accessories, communication, input devices, monitors, networking, printers, scanners, sound, and video cards. The catalog is produced quarterly by Interactive Catalog Corporation and is available as a single issue or by subscription.

General Merchandise

Whether they're selling software or general merchandise, the potential for greater sales, coupled with low manufacturing costs, makes catalog CDs an effective marketing tool for publishers and distributors. Add to that the revenue that can be derived from the sale of disc advertising space, and the opportunities really become enticing. CD-based magazine and catalog producers charge vendors by the megabyte. According to *NewMedia* magazine, advertisers such as AT&T, Lincoln-Mercury, and IBM are already paying $1,000 for each megabyte of advertising data on discs such as *Newsweek Interactive*.

Apple Computer, General Motors, Redgate Communications, and 18 catalog companies have been experimenting with interactive home shopping by distributing multiple catalogs on a single CD-ROM. Customers can call one toll-free telephone number to order merchandise. The pilot disc contained over 3,000 products from 18 companies, including L.L. Bean, Land's End, Williams-Sonoma, Pottery Barn, and Tiffany & Co. Video and audio clips were used to enhance the standard text and picture format. A lifestyle section was added to showcase similar products from different catalogues.

To showcase groups of related items, other "departments" were also added, including For the Home, Just for Kids, and For Someone Special. Additional features include the Gift Registry that allows you to record birthdays and other dates for gift giving and be reminded as the dates come up. The Personal Valet lets you search for specific items. The CD includes expert advice on fashion, decorating, and other subjects.

I hope you'll forgive me if I have sounded like a cross between a high school cheerleader and a used-car salesman in these last three chapters. I do have a background in entertainment publicity, but my goal was not to hype any particular product or even to promote the compact disc as a medium. Rather, my intention was to show the amazing variety of content that is already available on a medium that is still relatively new. There really is "something for everyone."

Chapter 10

Hurrying toward Tomorrow

If we knew where we were going tomorrow, we'd be there already. Trite but true, at least as far as any long-range predictions go. However, there are a few things that we do know about the future. We expect certain trends to continue, and there are new developments that are just now coming to light. Everybody with whom I spoke had an opinion, and I'll share their thoughts, comments, educated guesses, and predictions with you throughout this chapter.

You can be sure that CD-ROM drives will get faster and their capacity grow to hold more data. Work in these areas is already in progress. More, faster, better—this is the American way. You can also be sure that the prices of the various drives will continue to drop. This has already been the case, not only with compact disc technology, but with new technologies of all types. The laws of supply and demand haven't changed.

It's also a safe bet that technology is going to continue its march right into our living rooms. It may take the form of a single set-top box, or various components added to our entertainment centers, but whatever its form, technology will have a major impact on both our work and leisure time. New set-top boxes, options, and enhancements will continue to come from Sony, Sega, Nintendo, Panasonic, Philips, and other manufacturers.

As these set-top machines offer more and more capabilities, they could end up replacing home computers. Opinion about this is still divided. At the Intermedia 94 conference, Craig Mundy of Microsoft referred to the TV and the PC as "the two central appliances of the future," distinguishing between what he called "interaction at ten feet and interaction at two feet." He also predicted that these two appliances would be networked in the future. It was no surprise when, at the end of 1994, Microsoft made public its intentions of developing an operating system for set-top boxes.

The installed base of compact disc users is growing, and evidence of their pervasive use is cropping up in new and unusual places. Even television commercials are beginning to use increasingly familiar computer interface features such as pull-down menus and buttons to make the products they advertise seem current. And CD titles and accessories are now showing up in mainstream consumer shopping catalogs. For example, Book of the Month Club selections now include compact disc titles. So far there are just two, *The Complete Maus* and *Poetry in Motion*, but I expect the numbers will increase. Accessories for sale in some of these catalogs include artful mouse pads and travel cases or albums for storing discs.

The American Express Holiday 1994 catalog didn't take the plunge entirely. It doesn't include CD titles as stand-alone items, but it does display CDs prominently in the photos and mention titles in the copy for Compaq and Acer multimedia computer systems. The Compaq ad shows Compton's *MultiMedia Encyclopedia* on the screen and a disc on the desk. The copy lists preinstalled multimedia software, including the encyclopedia, *U.S. Presidents* from National Geographic, *The Animals*, *National Parks*, and Microsoft's *Golf* CD. The photo of the Acer system shows Microsoft's *Encarta* on the screen, and the CD-ROM drive bay is open to display the disc itself. *Encarta, Sound Collection, Cinemania*, and *Golf* (all from Microsoft) are the CD titles included with this system.

Unlike the American Express shopping catalog, other catalogs are clearly marketing compact disc titles alone. The Rand McNally 1994 Holiday Catalog, which offers maps, posters, T-shirts, books, videos, coffee mugs, and the like, also offers five CD titles: *Street Atlas USA, Global Explorer, Europe Alive, America Alive*, and *Asia Alive*. Even The Metropolitan Museum of Art is in the act. The museum's Presents for Children catalog includes five CD titles: *My First Incredible, Amazing Dictionary*; *Incredible Cross-Sections–Stowaway!*; *Big Anthony's Mixed-up Magic*; *Anno's Learning Games*; and *The Way Things Work* (based on the book of the same title).

Despite the growth of the CD industry, some people believe that CDs are just a flash in the pan. They assume that the compact disc is a transitionary medium that will be viable for only a short time until the implementation of broadband technology. Once broadband is implemented, interactive two-way connectivity delivered over the cable or phone lines will become a real alternative, and people will abandon the CD. Even without broadband, some think that because CDs are a read-only medium, CD-based titles will automatically have a short shelf life. Personally, I think CDs will be around for quite some time. I also think that we'll see lots more enhanced hybrid CDs with added online components, similar to Microsoft's *Baseball* and Turner Home Entertainment's *The People v. O.J. Simpson.*

Upside magazine doesn't seem to have any doubts about the future of the compact disc. An article in the August, 1994, issues reads, "With 10 million multimedia CD-capable game machines and computers expected in U.S. homes by the end of the year, the multimedia CD—whether Sega CD, Phillips CD-i, 3DO CD, or Macintosh- or IBM-compatible CD-ROM—is the only moneymaking interactive multimedia technology in town for the foreseeable future." Of course, the magazine didn't exactly define "foreseeable future."

So What Took So Long?

Early proponents of compact disc technology, those who were on board back in the mid-to-late 1980s, thought the medium would take hold much faster. Many were surprised, if not perplexed, when after a few years no real momentum seemed to take hold. A June, 1991, front-page story in *Billboard* magazine predicted that it would take ten years for optical discs to become the chief medium of home entertainment and information.

Even though the *Billboard* prediction was based on new advances in digital data compression announced at that year's Consumer Electronics Show, the magazine may not have been too far off the mark. *Billboard* also predicted that CD platforms would bring computers into the home "as an integral but invisible part of the entertainment system. This could represent the start of the optical disc's evolution to a complete multimedia audio/video/computer centerpiece."

So what's taking so long? EA*Kids' general manager Greg Bestick says, "I think it took so long because of the cost of the hardware, which was above the magic $500 price point. That's the magic number for consumers. And when it got down there, it started to take off in a big way. And the second reason, I think, is that there [weren't] enough compelling reasons to buy things. In the last few years publishers have published reasonably high-quality experiences that take advantage of the CD-ROM. In the early days a lot of what was put on CD was shovelware. But the market will sort that out now because there [are] enough other high-quality experiences that people are going to be able to tell the difference."

Bestick described the evolution of CD benefits as follows. First there was the ability to store large amounts of data relatively cheaply. The next thing that made CDs attractive was "the ability to navigate through large bodies of information, sort of construct your own personalized web of that data. And then, the next sort of evolution of that is the ability to store and create and display multiple media in one platform, in one delivery system."

Electronic Arts publishes on all platforms, but when Bestick was asked if there were benefits to other platforms that he would favor over the CD, he answered, "No, CD-ROM is our publishing media of choice because it's got a lower cost of goods than cartridges. The installed base is growing extremely rapidly, and you can put more information on it so you can deliver a more high-quality CD experience."

Rick King, senior vice president of product development at Jostens, thinks we're in the phase of the technological revolution where the CD is king. But Mike van der Kieft, Blockbuster's director of business development and manager of new media markets, doesn't think we're there yet. When asked whether there is a future for CD-ROMs, his answer was an emphatic yes, with a caveat: "I think there are some hurdles, and I think the biggest hurdle right now is the ease of use at the consumer level. I keep using the phrase that it's got to be 'VCR-easy,' at least as easy as the Play part of a VCR. And it's not there yet in the market."

Van der Kieft's comments were based largely on his experience with Blockbuster's pilot CD rental program discussed in Chapter 1. "We experienced significant difficulty trying to support the PC platform," he explained. "The Mac platform is pretty much plug and play, but when you get into the PC arena it's extremely difficult in a rental channel because there're so many different configurations of the PC out there, and the consumer generally really doesn't know what their configuration is when they come into the store."

Van der Kieft added that the problem is made worse by the fact that the publishers aren't always precise in telling the consumer what hardware configuration is required to run the title. "They get the title home and it doesn't work. I think that's an industry-wide problem, and until they can overcome the

problems of bringing up a title on a PC they'll never reach a mass market level."
It should be noted here that Windows 95, the new PC operating system from
Microsoft, is expected to address this problem.

Another problem that Blockbuster encountered during its rental program
was confusion in the player marketplace. "The set-top arena is a morass right
now," said van der Kieft. "There are so many different standards out there that
the public is totally confused. They don't understand what's different about a
3DO versus a Philips, unless they really look into it. Then they hear that Sony's
coming out with one, and NEC is coming out with one, and wonder why they
should buy anything at this time."

Whose Box Will Be on Top?

Will consumers have a single "megabox" attached to their TV sets, to be connected to cable, phone lines, or other delivery systems, that also will serve as a
games machine and audio/video recording and playback device? Or will the
setup more closely resemble an audio component system with a set of interlinked
but different components? How will the set-top home entertainment devices
interact with cable and telephony? How many "standards" can the home entertainment and services market support? These questions were asked in an April,
1993, issue of *Consumer Multimedia Report* and have yet to be answered.

Back in February of 1993 I read the following paragraph in a *MacUser*
article by Jon Zilber: "Problem is, you want it all in one box. You don't want to
buy a CD player for your stereo system (and a second one for your car), a Photo
CD player, a CD-ROM for your PowerBook, and a CD add-on for your Sega or
Nintendo. And don't forget you'd like to be able to play full-sized videodiscs too
and play back on your TV, which is controlled through your Mac. So far you
need six optical drives, and we haven't even gotten to the writeable drive you
need for storing those massive digital-video files you'll be creating in your home
multimedia-editing suite."

I don't think anyone would argue against the idea that we do want it all—
all the formats, all the application types (games, photo, interactive multimedia,
movies, etc.), fast speeds, and the ability to connect with others—integrated into
a single, small, portable, easy-to-use machine. The convergence of the consumer
electronics, computer, and communications industries is nothing new. For
example, we've been making inroads in the areas of video-conferencing and cel-

lular communications for quite some time now. What is new is that the focus and interest is now on the mass market, driven by home-based entertainment.

When asked about CD-ROM versus CD-i or other CD-based platforms, Eric Brown, editor of *NewMedia* magazine, said, "I think that probably in terms of all those game players, the ones that focus more on hot graphics, like Nintendo's Ultra, Sega Saturn, and 3DO, those sorts of things are going to do better than ones focusing on infotainment. Generally people who do [infotainment] are going to have a PC at least for a while. I don't see huge growth in that area unless, of course, they somehow get double as a set-top box for interactive TV."

As Michael Nadeau, author of *The BYTE Guide to CD-ROM*, points out in a *CD-ROM World* article (October, 1994), Sega is the only company that has penetrated the home market successfully with a CD-ROM-based device to be connected to your television. Nadeau bets that CD-ROMs will replace videotapes. The discs are certainly more durable than tape, and manufacturing costs are lower. Cutting-edge technologists are working on cramming more data on each disc, and new video formats are being defined.

Whether the Sega machine will win out as the home device remains to be seen. Atari and Nintendo gained home entry with their game players, but they were not CD platforms. Philips tried to market its CD-i player some years ago and was not successful. Now they have renewed their efforts with an aggressive advertising campaign to promote CD-i. The market is now more receptive, but now there is also competition, not only from Sega but from 3DO as well.

In the spring of 1994, *Advanstar Interactive Multimedia Report* suggested that by the fall of 1995 consumers would have a choice of half a dozen or so different multimedia players, all costing $500 or less. Nintendo is banking on a 64-bit player called Project Reality, with a new cartridge from Silicon Graphics that purportedly has an access time 2 million times faster than that of a CD-ROM. Of course, cartridges don't have the storage capacity of a CD, though this new one can hold approximately one-sixth the capacity of a CD-ROM.

Sega had a two-part plan. In 1994, it added the 32X, a 32-bit plug-in component, to its Genesis cartridge player, and slated the release of its CD + cartridge Saturn player for 1995. 3DO, CD-i, and the Amiga CD32 are all CD platforms currently battling for market share. Advanstar believes that the battle won't truly begin until both the Sega Saturn and Nintendo's Project Reality are on the street.

But wait. While these battles are being fought, the technology of the disc itself is evolving on two main fronts. Speed and capacity, faster and more, are the twin focal points for compact disc improvements.

Please Sir, May I Have Some More?

Speed, or the lack thereof, is probably the single largest deterrent to putting all games on CD-ROM. CDs are less expensive to press (you can press CDs domestically for $1 each), and the manufacturing turnaround time is shorter for CDs (about 1 week). Nevertheless, without adequate speed, these savings are irrelevant and game makers will opt for the higher production costs and four- to six-week turnaround time of the faster, cartridge-based systems.

Even for those who are not creating game titles, speed is still a problem. The original single-speed CD drives can't handle the transfer rates required for today's multimedia applications. The slower drives are capable of 30-frame-per-second video when using video compression standards such as MPEG-1 or DVI, but already there is a desire for 60-frame-per-second, full-screen digital video, which requires MPEG-2, or TrueMotion, and really needs the quad-speed drives.

The use of triple-speed drives is rapidly increasing, but you can expect quadruple-speed drives to become standard very soon. Probably the only thing hindering quad-speed's immediate acceptance is the higher price and the fact that few titles have yet to take advantage of the faster speed. This is the classic chicken or the egg situation. Developers don't want to create products for a market that doesn't yet exist, and market acceptance of the new players is naturally slower because there isn't much you can play on them.

Meanwhile, drive manufacturers are investigating ways to enhance speed. They are taking two approaches. One is for the laser head to move faster, so work is underway to develop lighter heads. The second, an approach that would boost speed even more, is for the discs to spin faster. A faster spin rate could increase speed to approximately 900K per second (Kps), six times faster than the current 150 Kps rate.

Increasing disc capacity is slightly more complicated, but, again, solutions are sought on two separate fronts. The first approach is data compression, where software is designed to compress the data. The second approach is a hardware solution that alters the way the data is placed in the disc.

EWB & Associates has developed a data storage compression technology for CDs called capaCD (pronounced similarly to "capacity"). EWB claims that CD-ROM publishers can triple the normal capacity of a CD-ROM disc with their capaCD technology. As with any compression software, the actual compression rate depends on the type of data being compressed. EWB claims that the compression rates range from 1.5 to 10. The company says that the system is compatible with existing CD-ROM drives, so there are no additional hardware or software requirements.

How does EWB's data storage compression technology work? It adds a layer of storage called "the virtual medium layer." Because it works independently of the disc's file system, capaCD technology will always be compatible with whatever the CD-ROM file system standards are, today or tomorrow. And the compression is not supposed to lower performance in drives with at least a 300 Kps transfer rate on dual-speed drives.

Other companies have developed their own proprietary compression algorithms to pack data onto a compact disc. For example, *Digital Media* reported in December, 1991, that ICOM Simulations Inc. (now Viacom New Media) had developed a proprietary compression scheme that was compatible with six different hardware platforms. By using this technology for its *Sherlock Holmes Consulting Detective* title, ICOM was able to release individual discs for each platform, thereby increasing the title's sales potential without incurring additional development time and costs. But efforts such as these pale in comparison to the new developments in optical disc technology.

Toward the end of 1992, *PC Magazine* reported that Sony had developed a technology called "blue-beam CD-ROM laser" that could triple the capacity of a standard CD-ROM disc. The wavelength of a blue beam is shorter than that of a red beam, so the blue beam can read smaller data structures than are currently used on discs using red-beam lasers. Using blue-beam technology, an audio CD would be able to hold three and a half hours of music (the current limit is 74 minutes) and a CD-ROM would be able to contain 1.7GB (billion bytes) of data, more than 2½ times the 650MB we have now.

In addition to placing the tracks closer together (pitch), the width of each track (pit density) is also narrower, bringing the capacity up to approximately 2.7GB. Other enhancements to the specifications, such as error correction, bring the total capacity up to 3GB. When you use MPEG 2 compression, you can get two or more hours of TV quality video. Laserdisc-quality video would require 6GB, according to JVC's estimates.

At the time of its late-1992 article, *PC Magazine* predicted that products would not begin to use blue-beam technology for at least five years. Current predictions suggest that we will see the use of blue-beam technology by 1996, spurred in part by the desire for higher-quality video that takes up lots of space. Of course, by then we'll be developing something new.

On May 15, 1994, the *New York Times* reported that IBM had demonstrated an optical disk technology that enables CDs to hold about 6.5 billion bytes of data. This feat was accomplished by layering the disc and storing information on up to ten individual layers. Laser beams were focused on the disc such that they read each layer individually. The article speculated that, by combining multilayering with blue laser technology, it might be possible to create a palm-sized CD that could store the equivalent of several thousand 200-page books.

So what are we waiting for? According to Craig R. Rispin, vice president of sales and marketing at Big Hand Productions, "The laser has to be more accurate in order to read these new CDs. But double-speed, multi-session CD-ROM drives, which is the majority of CD-ROM drives out there, do fall into the category that can read these higher-density disks. So, for reasons of compatibility, both Philips and Sony are kind of holding back the technology for the consumer who bought a single-speed, non-multi-session CD-ROM drive two years ago." Rispin also pointed out that the situation changed in late 1994 when, after some prodding from other companies, Philips and Sony submitted their own suggestions for a new standard to the ISO (International Organization for Standardization) Committee.

It will take some time, but the birth of the HDCD ("high-density CD") is inevitable. "It's just a standards issue, not a technology issue," concluded Rispin. "It's not like you have to have a new pressing plant to make new CDs. You use exactly the same pressing plant, you just put the tracks closer together, so you can still get the same costs. It will still only be about a dollar a CD to manufacture, but then you'll get 3GB of information." I have heard other reports that concur with Rispin's assessment that no modifications are needed for pressing the new high-density CDs. However, some questions have been raised as to whether the blue lasers will be suitable for mastering or whether ultraviolet lasers, which are narrow, might be required.

Dr. Alex Scherer is working in the field of nanotechnology at the California Institute of Technology. His research deals with microfabrication to improve the performance of optoelectronic devices, all of which has something to do with enhancing the size and threshold power reduction of vertical cavity surface emitting lasers. Still sound like Greek? To me too. But what it boils down to is that researchers continue to push the envelop of laser-based technologies, striving for smaller beams, smaller components, smaller everything in order to achieve greater speeds and capacities.

Other cutting-edge developments include holographic storage products from companies such as Tamarack Storage Devices. As always, cutting-edge technology is expensive, and Tamarack's MultiStor is no exception. MultiStor is a device that automatically loads data from 30 individual 2½" disks containing a Du Pont photopolymer material. The device will initially cost $6,000, but the price is expected to drop to $3,500 when demand increases. Each 1GB disk costs $5.

In an article titled "The Keys to the Future" that was part of "The Information Revolution 1994" special issue of *Business Week*, Robert D. Hof and Neil Gross wrote, "Researchers continue to push the optoelectronic envelope. By recording information as holograms or using so-called blue lasers with shorter wavelengths to read more tiny 'spots' on a disk, scientists may create devices with unheard-of storage capacity. Scientists now predict they'll be able to pack perhaps 18 trillion bits of data on a single 12-inch platter. With new lasers and optical switches, they're pumping data over fiber at 10GB per second and figure on hitting 100...."

Who? What? Why?

In Chapter 8, I mentioned the Phil Hood columns in *NewMedia* magazine that said, "the average print, non-fiction book is better-researched, better-edited, and more exhaustive" than a typical CD-ROM. Hood argues that the only industry that currently has the necessary skills for publishing information is the print-media industry.

The titles produced by developers today still feature more flash than flesh, more style than substance. The focus is still on multimedia as a thing unto itself. Companies are producing and selling multimedia, but as CDs become more commonplace, their allure as a sexy, new technology will begin to fade, and perhaps then we can begin to focus on multimedia as a tool and find ways in which it can be practically applied.

Many products on the market really don't use multimedia effectively. The design may seem cumbersome, the interface difficult to comprehend. Or maybe what seemed like a good idea just didn't hold up under practical application. It's still too early in the game to define *the* criteria that constitute a good interface or design. And while there are a few rules of thumb and commonsense approaches (discussed in Chapter 13), there are no formal standards as yet. The development of such standards will probably come about *ipso facto*. In our age of infinite spin-offs and copycat applications, the common features across the most successful products will become the assumed standards—until something new comes along.

Creative communicators who are unfettered by the past and impervious to the fast bucks that can initially be reaped by producing shovelware will find ways to use the CD medium as a tool to entertain and inform. The CD as storage medium attitude will eventually fall by the wayside.

"You still have to deliver an eloquent design, good content, solid, engaging and interactive experience. There is an aesthetic to this and there is a craft. And the craft has to be mastered, just like in movies, or writing a novel or a play," says Greg Bestick, EA*Kids' general manager.

Data Integrity

Information at your fingertips is the vision of a world online. The problem is that the information is not always accurate. The warning that you shouldn't always believe everything you read must now be applied to a new medium—the CD. With each new medium there is an initial perception of its reliability, truth, and accuracy. We trust in it. People are more aware that not everything they read is true, but many still forget that seeing is not believing. Not only can images be altered (especially easy in a digital world), but the image itself may have been cropped. The picture taken of you smiling at the devil is not the same as the version where the devil is cut out of the frame. No alteration, it's just not the whole story. Then there is the effect brought about by the mere inclusion or exclusion of information. And least manipulative, but equally offensive, is the simple mistake, whether it be a typo or an inaccurate fact. A number of reviewers have made these complaints.

"As the information becomes easier to reach, then we must make an all-out effort to ensure that the information is accurate." So says Charles Petzold in an article in *Windows Sources* magazine. This is an interesting premise, but one might ask whether those who deliver information should be held responsible for its accuracy. What if the deliverer is not the creator or provider of the information? Should accuracy be the burden of the deliverers as well as the information providers?

It may not be earthshaking that in Microsoft's *Cinemania* CD the synopsis for *Casablanca* mixes up the name of a character with that of an actor, and quotes the following line from the ending: "Major Veidt's been shot. Round up the usual suspects." The character's name was Major Strasser, and the role was played by Conrad Veidt. In this case, Microsoft was the information deliverer, and it used existing material from Baseline's *Motion Picture Guide*. So the data provided by the *Guide* was inaccurate, but the error was perpetuated by

Microsoft. Errors will appear more often as information is "recycled" and used for many different purposes.

Some say it's the responsibility of the consumer to analyze, question, and even verify information before accepting its truth or veracity. But even if you try to verify your information you may err. You could check a second source that was derived from the same inaccurate source you are trying to verify. And worse, there may be no indication as to where the information came from. When all information is truly available and instantly accessible, then I might argue that the primary source (i.e., the original source) is always available for verification, and because it is easily accessible to one and all, the responsibility for verifying information lies with the consumer. However, this is not yet the case, and may never be. *Caveat emptor.* Or if not let the buyer beware, then at least let the buyer be aware.

Talk to My Agent

It's one thing for a user to seek and find information, and another for an information deliverer to convey unrequested data. A CD may indeed contain the information you seek, but you may be deterred from your quest if you must wade through masses of unsolicited data to get to it. Whether we talk about advertisers or proselytizers, the opportunity to address a captive audience is too good to pass up. And for developers, the cash that can be derived from selling that opportunity is also too good to resist. Besides, it will offset the production costs of the disc.

The only true line of defense is to send in the troops, in this case your agent(s). The technology for agents is still developing. At the lowest end, an agent is more like a filter that weeds out the extra stuff and presents only that which you need. It may simply be a script or routine in which you specify your preferences and interests. You send it out and it executes on its own, preferably while you are doing something else if the process is lengthy.

For example, a powerful searching tool is truly valuable on a reference CD. Just imagine a CD full of information, with many menus. To find what you are looking for you select a menu option and up comes a submenu. You click on a submenu option, and up comes yet another submenu. You could end up having to move through a dozen or so menus before you get to what you are looking for. A good search tool allows you to specify what you are looking for right at the beginning. It retrieves the pertinent data without taking you through all the menus.

Many of the online services have features that allow you to specify a topic of interest. When a news item becomes available that matches your criteria (maybe keywords), a copy is automatically placed in your electronic mailbox or some other designated area. In either example, it's a lot like having an assistant who will do the grunt work for you.

Ideally, after an assistant gets to know you, he or she acquires some insights into what information might be useful and interesting to you. You hope the assistant is also enterprising enough to go out and get information for you without your instruction. This is the behavior to which agents aspire. A good agent is an example of true artificial intelligence—it has the ability to learn from experience and act accordingly. And as strange and unbelievable as it may seem, technology is already getting close to being "intelligent."

Make a CD

So far, the boom in the sales of CD drives has been driven by decreasing costs. Now the possibilities afforded us by the capability to make our own discs is spurring that growth. Interest in CD recorders is heightening and the prices for these drives is dropping. According to the "CD-ROM & CD-R U.S. Market Update" report from Auger Visions Inc., the number of CD-ROM recordable drives in the United States will jump from approximately 30,000 in 1994 to nearly 200,000 in 1997. *Windows Magazine* reported that Bill Frank, author of the Auger Visions report, believes that "CDs will replace hard copy, tape, optical disks and microfiche."

New products and enhancements continue to evolve on all fronts. In late 1994, Sony announced a new recordable, double-speed CD drive that is not only affordable (it's expected to have a street price of only $1,500), but fits into a drive bay slot in your desktop PC. 3M Software Media and CD-ROM Services introduced a new scratch-resistant, CD-recordable media and anti-static CD-R technology. The CD recordable disc with Scotchshield surface protection resists scratches and abrasions and provides greater disc durability.

End users are now becoming the creators. Paul LeBlanc, Director of Technology for the College Division New Media Group at Houghton-Mifflin, sees great potential for CDs as tools. "It's a wonderful viable medium for teachers who want to create their own instructional software titles, which is not what most people think about when they think about CD-ROMs," said LeBlanc. "But the fact is that there is a proliferation of increasingly easy-to-use authoring and mastering systems that are becoming more affordable. A lot of teachers can assemble materials in a way they've never been able to before, and CD-ROMs give them source capacity to do that easily." LeBlanc did add, however, that there are still some obstacles. For example, most faculty don't own the resources they would like to put on a CD-ROM, and the copyright and intellectual property issues are not insignificant.

In the business world, people have been experimenting with electronic newspapers and magazines, complete with great graphics and color. It's still a drag to spend 45 minutes using a 2,400-baud modem to download such a magazine from an online service, but these applications are great for compact discs.

Archiving data is another prevalent business use of CDs. The catch is, will the person retrieving data from the disc later on have all of the programs on his or her machine that were used to create the documents? One solution to this dilemma is to use a product such as Adobe Acrobat. You can create documents using whatever software you want. When you're done, you use Adobe to translate the document into the Adobe format so that anyone with the Adobe Reader can read the document regardless of what programs you used to create it originally. The Adobe Reader can be distributed without cost, so you can always include it on the CD just to be safe. And an added side benefit is that the Adobe Reader only allows you to read a document, not alter it.

A lot of neat, new tools have been developed to help CD makers create very sophisticated products. SimGraphics has developed the first real-time animation system for use in creating sophisticated, computer-generated character animation. The animation system uses a variety of input devices such as gloves and body sensors. This is a godsend to game-makers and other CD-ROM creators who want to enhance the realism of their products. The Vactor Animation System supports:

- **Real-time motion capture:** The tracking and acquisition, in real time, of human movements, usually by means of exoskeletal, magnetic, or video-based devices.

- **Real-time motion analysis:** Translating the captured motion data into usable 3-D positioning data.

- **Real-time rendering:** Calculating and rendering imagery at up to 30 frames per second.

- **Real-time gesture recognition:** For face tracking and kinemorphics, reducing the amount of effort required to create lifelike "organic" characters.

This is the technology that was used in the SimCity title that I talked about in Chapter 7, and more and more developers are using virtual reality equipment to increase the realism of their products. Vactor also offers complete integration with the major, traditional frame-by-frame animation packages.

The Marketplace

Mergers and leveraging assets is the name of the game in this new marketplace. And this includes cross-promotional campaigns that involve licensing and merchandising, as well as publishing, broadcasting, and movie showings. Conglomerates have the most potential. Take Turner Home Entertainment, for example. Much of its CD-ROM title *NFL's Greatest Plays* was gathered by the TNT cable network for a feature-length documentary special highlighting the history, development, and great achievements of the NFL and the game of football. Turner Publishing will produce a commemorative book honoring the 75 greatest football players of all time. And then there's the merchandising deals for apparel, sports equipment, toys and games, stationery products, and packaged goods. TV airing, distribution of the books, and licensed properties will be coordinated to hit during the opening of the 1994–95 NFL 75th Anniversary season. Advertisements for the CD-ROM will begin airing during the television broadcast of TNT's *NFL 75th Anniversary Special.*

Movie and game companies are joining together to create movies based on game characters and games based on movie characters. For example, MGM and Sega are teaming up to make video games, movies, and television programs for several Sega platforms. The CD games will feature real actors whose recorded actions respond to players' commands. The collaboration will work both ways: some games will be based on upcoming MGM movie releases, and some movies and television programs will be based on popular games.

In addition to the featured appearance of familiar fictitious characters and celebrities, movie actors are playing roles in interactive games. Movie production companies are spawning interactive multimedia subsidiaries. Even record companies and recording artists are getting into the act.

The merger and leveraging strategy is not only employed by movie and game companies. Aris Entertainment, for example, has joined with Capital Cities/ABC Multimedia Group to develop and market clip media CD-ROM titles based on the maps and illustrations used by ABC News in all of its programming.

Phil Hood, editor of *NewMedia* magazine, refers to information as "the intellectual DNA of the human race" and believes that the "traditional publishers, not game companies or movie studios, have the ultimate repurposing treasure trove."

Distribution

The key is customization.

The biggest problem in retail distribution is space, or the lack thereof. In the audio CD market, for example, well over 100,000 audio CDs are available, but there is room for only about 15,000 in a typical Blockbuster store. So Blockbuster, in a joint venture with IBM, has created a system whereby customers can make their own customized audio CDs on site, while they wait. The news reports say that the system can manufacture a CD, including a color brochure to fit inside the case, in about ten minutes. Of course, until the record companies sign on, the shelf remains bare. Meanwhile, Blockbuster and IBM are working on a similar system to make high-speed video recordings on demand.

"That's going to ensure inventory to meet any demand situation there is," explained Mike van der Kieft, Blockbuster's director of business development and manager of new media markets. "And it's going to impact the B-title market because a lot of your B titles move when the A titles aren't available. When you go into a store and want to get *Mortal Kombat*, but it's not on the shelf, you pick the game next to it instead. But if *Mortal Kombat's* always in stock, you're never going to pick the one next to it."

"Anything that you can move around digitally and record, we can handle at the store level," said van der Kieft. It's only a short step from there to on-site pressing of digital CDs containing software and interactive entertainment.

Now that it has become economical, several small companies and service providers are taking advantage of the opportunity to create single CDs or small quantities of CDs for their clients. In some cases it's a matter of giving the client what it wants, no more, no less. In other cases, certain types of information gain currency when published on demand. The more rapidly data changes, the more beneficial is the ability to press on demand.

The SAS Institute and Donnelley Marketing Information Services (DMIS) are two such companies that began investigating the production of CDs for their clients. In early 1993, as cited in a *Byte* magazine article at that time, the SAS Institute, a creator of statistical software programs, began producing custom CD-ROMs with only those components required by the client. Meanwhile, DMIS was exploring ways to provide specialized discs for clients who wanted to merge their own data with data provided by Donnelley. At the time, the concern voiced by software development directory Mike Herman was one of cost. But as the prices continue to drop, you can expect more options for customization.

CD storage technology can also help with point-of-sale manufacturing. For example, music stores selling sheet music have discovered the benefits of on-site production, such as that afforded by the NoteStation kiosk described in Chapter 6. In this case, what is being manufactured is printed sheet music, while the CD is used as a resource. The disc contains the data allowing the customer to hear a song in different keys and print out a customized copy. Vendor and customer response to this type of application has been great, so I expect that we'll see more and more variations on this theme.

Is Broadband around the Corner?

"Today, access equals purchase. Tomorrow access will equal access," says Rick Devine, founder of Club Kidsoft, describing a model where you won't need to go to the store to buy your interactive media on a platter, cartridge, or floppy disk, and stick it in a machine to start it up. You'll be able to order it online through a specialized identity. You'll pay as you go, you'll pay for usage, and you'll pay online.

In some ways, tomorrow is already here. For about $50 per month, telephone companies can currently wire you up for ISDN, which is capable of single-speed CD-ROM data transfers. Avram Miller, VP for business development at Intel, talks of higher bandwidths on the order of 1.54MB per second within the next couple of years. This speed would support good-quality, two-way video-conferencing. It would also support instant accessibility of multimedia databases and interactive applications connected to Pentium machines.

It really is a matter of how aggressively the cable and telephone companies move. Some seers predict that a number of millions of homes might be enabled by 1996. "Enabled" doesn't mean "accepted," however. Whether there is anything on that broadband that customers will be willing to pay for is usually a function of what the industry calls a "killer app." What is on the broadband that they'll want to pay x dollars a month to have? Perceived value is the key. The public at large is usually willing to shell out the bucks for the good of the children, so companies like Club Kidsoft that endeavor to produce the killer app may lead the way.

Imagine, if you will, your favorite CD-ROM application, perhaps Microsoft's *Baseball,* with an online component. You lovingly remove it from its box, insert it into the CD-ROM drive bay, click on the appropriate drive icon or open a folder/window, and click on the launch icon to start up the program. To obtain the current stats, you turn on your modem, make sure the kids aren't tying up the phone line, and dial up the current stats. It may not be all that difficult, but there are certainly a lot of steps involved—and I didn't even describe the first-time installation process.

Now imagine being able to log onto a service as easily as turning on a television and selecting a channel. The day will come when sports fans will be able to watch a game and, as it happens (i.e., in real time), make viewing choices akin to those of today's live broadcast directors. For example, sports fans will be able to request instant replays, or slow motion, or reverse or freeze-frame action. You will also be able to request an immediate analysis of a play, or peruse history, stats, and biographical information.

Work must still be done before video server technology reaches the caliber that customers require. Meanwhile, businesses investing in just-in-time training applications will be the first to reap the interim benefits. As the quantity of available courseware increases the burden on CD-ROM jukeboxes and servers, interest in video server technology will intensify. So, as is the case with many other hardware and software developments, businesses are likely to be the first testing grounds.

That day is not quite here yet, but when it comes all you'll have to do is call your local cable operator, get a cable modem installed, and subscribe to the service(s) you want. And you won't have to buy another bookshelf to store your growing CD collection. Whatever you want will be available to you, whenever you want. Meanwhile, you will see more and more CD titles, such as *NFL's Greatest Plays*, that allow you the same control, only not in real time.

Whether this service will connect to your television or your computer, or some other device, is not yet known. Some people think the personal computer has a leg up because of its sophisticated communication capabilities. It's much further along than player-only devices such as Sega and 3DO, which are really single-purpose computers. Also, since this is supposed to be an interactive medium (not a passive medium you just sit back and watch), your device will need to have computer-like capabilities for saving files. And who knows? You might want to print something out, so it should also be able to deal with different external peripherals. For example, it could be a PC that's attached to a digital display that's also used as a TV. The same broadband wire might also deliver analog or digital signals to you. You might watch TV programming on it, and then you might switch your computer on and gain access to these interactive networks. Then you might unplug it and take it to work and hook it up to a display there. The whole world's going digital. The whole world is going to bits.

Considering the advent of broadband technology and its impact on CD-ROMs, Paul LeBlanc, the director of technology for the College Division New Media Group at Houghton-Mifflin, said, "It seems to me it has been argued that the CD-ROM is a transitional technology—that's probably right, but that transition may go on for a long time." Blockbuster's van der Kieft believes that "it's a question of how soon [broadband] becomes an economic reality in the home. I honestly believe that it's going to take quite a while before the cost is down to a point where it makes sense to subscribe in the home."

Hearst New Media & Technology Group is poised to enter the age of interactive television. In an August, 1994, article in *Upside* magazine, the head of the group, Alfred Sikes, is quoted as saying, "For the foreseeable future, CD-ROM will generate most of our cash flow. That could be the next three years or more."

NewMedia editor Eric Brown thinks that "in a few years [broadband] will begin, but it's going to be much longer before everybody is so wired, or even a majority of people are so wired, into interactive services that will match CD-ROM [capabilities]." However, Brown also points out that broadband may actually be slower than CDs at first. "When they finally start to implement those services," says Brown, "it's going to be slower than CD-ROM because in the next year or two CD-ROM is going to double, triple, or quadruple in speed and size, and in capacity. And at that time the cable modems are going to be equivalent to about a double-speed CD-ROM, and even worse for video because that will take longer to unload over your lines.... All of this gives CD-ROM a longer life span."

Actually, Brown and others agree that even when "you can order anything you want at any time and have instantaneous access just as fast as a CD-ROM, even still, you're going to want to have some storage medium and ways of passing data around that's not networked. You just look at it today, paperbacks are a huge business...."

When asked if broadband will kill the CD, Josten's senior vice president of product development, Rick King, agreed with Brown. "Home people will still want to buy it, have it, hold it," said King. But he added that it could affect distribution. "More, I think, for the home than for the school. If I want to access something from home and I've got a computer, it's probably going to be cheaper to access many of these things over some networks through the cable or telco situation. At a school, where I may have 60 or 100 or 200 workstations, it's not as effective...not so much in terms of speed, but more in terms of cost. The notion would be that for a certain number of stations, and a certain volume of usage, each local spot would need some kind of server to stage a lot of the material. Also the license fees would seem to be better bought at the school."

Will Privacy Be Compromised?

Houghton-Mifflin's Paul LeBlanc talks about the social aspects. "The other major thing is the movement from the PC as personal desktop instrument to becoming a social instrument. Access and connectivity are required in order for interactions with others to become the cornerstone of one's interaction with software. You won't interact only with the software, but you'll interact with the software and with others."

Once you're connected, however, the issue of privacy arises. When you're connected, how much do you want others to know about you? When it comes to CD-ROMs bought in a store and paid for with cash, you remain anonymous. When you pay by credit card, both the store and your credit bureau have a record of your purchases. The store knows exactly which titles you purchased and the lender knows where you shop. When you order CDs by mail, both the store and credit bureau learn your address and either your bank information (from your check) or your credit card number. When you order by phone from trained order takers, you probably divulge a lot of information about yourself during the conversation.

What happens when you buy a CD that has a dial-up component with an online service? You'll never know what they may know about you. Not only must you register by filling in all sorts of information, but once you're online, these services can access your computer without your being aware of it. I'm not trying to scare you—and, yes, I do participate in several online services without much fear of intrusion upon my privacy. However, I am concerned about whether my privacy will be violated in the future.

An article in a Computer Press Association newsletter reported on a meeting with a guest speaker from the IRS. She said that the IRS already has access to all the information it needs in order to generate our individual income tax forms. She suggested that perhaps the IRS should just calculate our taxes for us, debit our bank accounts, and send us a statement. That's pretty scary.

Here Today, Gone Tomorrow?

When I asked *NewMedia* editor Eric Brown to comment on the transient nature of technology, he said, "I think that there are a lot of technologies that people thought would go away quickly that kind of took hold, and then once they took hold it was hard to get rid of them. They're all flawed. Take the videotape, for example. I think that the CD will replace the videotape whether that's a CD-ROM or a Video CD. But even so, videotape is going to be around well into the next century. I think CD-ROM is going to be around even longer. There's always going to be a need for portable storage."

"Ultimately, it's society, not technology alone, that will determine how the Information Revolution will play out," wrote John W. Verity in his introduction to *Business Week*'s special "Information Revolution 1994" issue. Technological tools are shaped more by the social than the physical sciences. "Just think," Verity continued, "the mass-produced automobile was a godsend for people isolated on farms. But who could foresee how its overuse would eventually choke cities with traffic and smog and create a debilitating dependence on oil?"

It seems likely that someday all information will be easily accessible, and we'll use some sort of miniature computer or set-top box that will be as universal, and as transparent, as a television. We'll all be part of a giant network, and data representation will be increasingly realistic. But speculation about the impact that this revolution will have on our lifestyles and the ways in which we conduct business is still guesswork.

Chapter 11

Becoming a CD-ROM User

Some of us don't have a choice but to become CD users. Computer programmers and developers must have a CD player because much of what they need is now distributed only on CD, especially those prized SDKs (software development kits). Authors like myself who write about new software programs need CD drives because that's how publishers distribute the beta test versions of their software. And many software publishers are pressing more discs for commercial distribution because it is cost-effective. In fact, most are happily anticipating the day when they can stop duplicating diskettes. End users who have a choice usually opt for the disc version because it contains extra goodies.

As you saw in the first nine chapters of this book, a tremendous amount of content is available on disc. So much is available, you're likely to find at least a few titles that are of interest to you. But beyond interest, and even beyond usefulness, there are a few other considerations. If you list the pros and cons of the medium itself, they may seem to weigh down on the minus side, but then again, this is just the beginning of a new age as far as the CD-ROM is concerned.

On the pro side, there is no question that these little discs can cram a lot of data in a small space. And that makes the content generally more affordable than would be the case if the same data were offered in a different medium. The discs are also eminently transportable—they are lightweight, compact, and not too fragile. Of course, the disc player may not be so easy to transport, but that too is changing rapidly. Earlier I mentioned the portable, hand-held CD-i players, and more and more laptop computers have internal CD-ROM drives.

Then there's the downside. If you start using lots of discs, you'll soon experience the take-it-out and put-it-in syndrome you thought was over when dual diskette systems became the norm and your hard drive got bigger. Also, reading data from a CD is slower than running it off a hard drive. As Phil Hood said in his January, 1994 editorial in *NewMedia*, "Three hundred kilobytes per second, the transfer rate of a double-speed CD-ROM drive, is equivalent to riding a trolley, not a sports car." But he also pointed out ongoing CD-ROM improvements in speed (double, triple, and quad rates), caching software, and the lag time it takes content developers to take advantage of the new improvements.

Back on the plus side, you can install large programs from one disc instead of feeding your computer 10 or 20 diskettes, one at a time. But another common complaint is the difficulty of the installation itself. Most often these complaints have to do with installing the hardware, but complaints about installing the software also abound.

Consumers tend to be wary of new technology, especially if the technology is evolving rapidly. Should you wait for the next model with new enhancements? Should you wait until things become more standardized? Should you wait for the price to drop? Should you wait to see if this technology is even here to stay? Assuming that there is content out there that is interesting or useful to you, I would answer no, no, just a bit, and no.

Many believe that CD-ROMs will eventually be replaced by TV or computer-based interactive networks. It's probably true. Technological advancements won't stand still. But it will take awhile, and consensus is that CDs will be around for quite some time, even after interactive networks become common. Thus far, CDs are the most flexible storage and delivery medium for all types of applications and all types of data. But having spoken in favor of the medium doesn't mean that I support all content.

On July 6, 1994, the *Wall Street Journal* reported "a backlash of dissatisfaction with products that consumers are finding slow, boring, and full of bugs."

The article suggested that some programs are averaging a 20-percent return rate, and cited an industry observer who believed that individuals were dissatisfied with as much as 50 percent of the CD software they bought.

That sounds somewhat excessive, but I do know for a fact that there is a lot of shovelware out there. The content of some shovelware may have some value to you as a data resource, and if you are able to access what you want, go for it. But for the most part, it is best to evaluate discs and shop wisely.

Evaluating CDs

When you're shopping for CDs, there are a number of things to consider. In this section I'll pass along some general suggestions as well as some thoughts specific to different types of content titles. I'll tell you about my evaluation "factors" and suggest you consider such things as potential for repeated use, age-appropriateness, return on investment, license limitations, and bang for your buck.

Evaluate the practicalities and don't be swayed by a single element. For example, a travel aid intended to help you plan trips is only useful if it works. The fact that it has breathtaking photos won't help you find the information you need about climate, travel routes, or hotel accommodations. Also beware of superficial applications that look good on the surface but do not offer enough depth. A glitzy interface doesn't represent depth of content—more often it conceals a lack of depth.

Michael Desmond, in his July, 1994, *PC World* article titled "How to Avoid a Multimedia Mugging," suggested additional precautions. He said to back up your system regularly in case the installation of a new CD alters something else on your system, check with colleagues in online multimedia forums to find out about the problems experienced by others, and look for titles with an uninstall feature or else invest in a good third-party uninstall program. I think that you should also check out magazine reviews in publications such as *NewMedia*, *CD-ROM Today*, *Byte*, *PC World*, and *Macworld*, to name just a few.

Factoring the Odds

When I consider buying a CD title, I run through my factor list. The *Hassle Factor* covers a multitude of sins, including hardware nightmares, communication fiascoes, and software debacles. On the hardware side, first you have to successfully install the CD drive. That's the most obvious part. But let's assume that's been done. Think you're all set? Maybe. Maybe not.

You pop in a CD, install the software (a nightmare of its own perhaps), and start it up. Uh oh, something must be wrong. Nothing happens, or your system hangs, or you can't hear anything, or the sound is too loud, or, or, or. I don't want to scare you away from CDs. I think they're great. But if you are not yet computer-savvy, you might want to have an expert friend or tech-support guru around to help out.

Just to give you an idea, I'll tell you about two glitches I experienced. First, my speakers don't have individual sound control; they just plug in to the back of my sound card. Consequently, I have no control when my CDs are too loud or when the sound levels vary by segment. The variations in volume might be accounted for by the fact that some discs use conventional CD audio while others use digitized audio. Some use both, and these are the ones whose sound varies the most.

A second glitch has to do with computer memory. I installed a disc that said it was PC/Windows-compatible. When I tried to run it, it said I didn't have enough memory. Can't be, I thought. I have 16MB of RAM on my system. Then I realized that the program was really running in DOS, not Windows, and it was only recognizing the amount of memory allocated for DOS. Instead of truly running under Windows, the program was closing Windows, running the disc application in DOS, and, when done, restarting Windows for me. Cute.

Communication problems usually have something to do with drivers, the software in your system that "drives" various components, such as your CD player, printer, and other peripherals. If a driver is not communicating properly with your system, the component it is driving won't work correctly.

Then there were the discs that crashed my system or wiped out my color palette. Problems like these are usually caused by software. But I really believe that time will correct sound, memory, and software problems. Of course, if you're using a set-top player, you probably won't have these kinds of problems anyway.

Besides my Hassle Factor, there's my *Newsworthy Factor*. Is the data on the disc current? Newsworthiness is generally not an issue with games and other types of leisure titles, but it might be crucial in other types of applications. If you need current data and the information on a CD is outdated, you might want to search for more recent sources online.

To CD or not to CD, perchance to go online. This is not a simple rumination. I tried to come up with an equation, something that would help me to decide when the CD option is better than going online. Something like:

$$\frac{\textit{frequency of update} \times \textit{need for currency}}{\textit{frequency of access} \times \textit{online costs}}$$

Unfortunately, I couldn't come up with any meaningful results. It's a highly individual situation, involving more factors than can fit in one equation.

The *frequency of update* variable refers to how often the information is updated. Online services update different databases with varying degrees of regularity. Some are updated daily, some weekly, monthly, quarterly, and so on. If the online service is updated quarterly, let's say, and you can get a CD subscription that is also updated quarterly, there is no advantage either way. Also, if you are seeking static information, perhaps historical, the *need for currency* variable is not an issue, and you'll multiply *frequency of update* by 0 in the above equation.

Here's another subtle consideration. I just suggested that a CD subscription that is updated quarterly is as good as an online database updated quarterly. But what I didn't consider was when the update took place, and what date range was covered. An online database may be updated during the first week of April to contain all the data through March 31st of that same year. A CD you receive in early April, however, may only contain new data through December of the previous year, or perhaps through February (no one has said that everyone must begin the first quarter on January 1st). In other words, the period covered is as important as the frequency of the update.

The *frequency of access* variable in my equation refers to how often you'll use the resource. If the answer is daily and for long periods of time, then online searching might be too costly and outweigh the benefits of currency. I call this the *Wallet Factor.* Cost may seem fairly straightforward, but there are other considerations.

Let's say that you need one specific piece of current information daily. Getting this information requires a quick and simple search, so you think. You assign the task to an employee. Now you have to consider the expertise of individual users. I have seen beginners rack up huge online charges just because they were navigating through the wrong databases or forgot to narrow the search and therefore ended up with far more data than needed. Difficulty of use and familiarity with equipment and resources are part of the *Thrash Factor.* If this same employee were using a CD, you'd end up losing some work-hour dollars, but you wouldn't have the expense of a huge online service bill.

Is there really such a thing as too much data? Often the answer is yes, but sometimes you find things that are useful even though you weren't looking for them. I call this the *Serendipity Factor,* and it is what I am most afraid of losing. As technology evolves, tools become more sophisticated. Meanwhile, people are constantly on the lookout for ways in which to save more time so they can use what time they have to maximum benefit. Put these two trends together and you can end up with a society that smells only the coffee and misses out on the roses.

For example, if you had a disc with search tools so sophisticated they would only retrieve exactly what you were looking for, you might miss out on information that would have expanded, or even altered, your viewpoint. On the other hand, technology is not to blame for causing this loss, people are. Our sample disc, let's say, provides an opportunity for more data to be included in searches. It would then up to the user to access and utilize those opportunities. But that's another subject for another book.

Considering the Purpose

When it comes to choosing games for players of any age, look for those that have the greatest potential for repeated use. If it is a game with a specified goal for winning, then it should have increasing levels of difficulty. If it is an explorational title, it should have lots of depth so that you won't discover all there is in the first sitting. If the title is more along the lines of an interactive movie, then it should have enough interactive choice points to vary the story and its outcome more than once or twice.

Repeated use is also an important factor in selecting discs for children. Look for stories that will hold children's interest (not preach to them), that are age-appropriate, and that have lots of interactivity. Products that encourage kids to create stories and pictures, or that come with suggestions for activities are also a plus. See the sidebar, "Guidelines for Parents," for suggestions from the Computer Learning Foundation.

Educational titles are not just for kids, and more and more businesses are looking closely at using multimedia for job training. Stewart Alsop, editor of *InfoWorld,* thinks that the corporate world is slow to embrace multimedia. He says that IS managers often don't feel that the equipment (CD-ROM drives, sound boards, etc.) is worth the investment. As a result, he thinks that corporations are taking the "personal" out of personal computing.

Guidelines for Parents

The Computer Learning Foundation is a California-based, international, nonprofit organization dedicated to increasing the understanding and efficient use of technology, particularly among children. The Foundation prepared some guidelines for parents on selecting educational software for children.

⊙ **Children should be able to use the software independently after receiving basic instruction**. This means that the program must provide on-screen menus and age-appropriate instructions. For nonreaders, all menus and instructions must use pictures, graphics, and verbal statements that are easily understood. For children aged 10 and above, manuals should be written at a level they can quickly comprehend and implement.

⊙ **The program's subject area should be enjoyable and motivating, or children will not use the software on their own**. In using software for remediation at home, the motivational qualities of the program assume even greater importance.

⊙ **The software should be fun and entertaining as well as a learning experience**. The best motivational programs use high-quality graphics, sound, and animation appropriately integrated into the learning game. In addition, a child should be able to escape from a given activity, and select a different option at any time, without having to turn off the computer.

⊙ **For young children (ages 2 to 7) the best products are open-ended and exploratory in nature**. The pace and direction of learning should be within the control of the child. The software should include a variety of activities or options a child can select to ensure that he or she will want to use the program over an extended period of time.

⊙ **Skill and subject areas addressed should be appropriate to the child's interests**. Skills being taught should be within the child's reach. Software should also be able to grow with the child and have numerous levels of difficulty.

⊙ **The teaching style of the software should be compatible with a child's needs**. There are four major categories of programs:

1. Drill and practice software that enables children to learn and recall basic information.
2. Tutorial software that provides in-depth teaching of a subject area.
3. Learning software simulations and strategy games that enable children to gain new information, but also allow them to apply what they know and learn.
4. Exploratory and reference products.

◉ **The software should provide immediate and positive (or neutral) feedback.** Children need to maintain a positive attitude toward learning when utilizing any educational product.

◉ **The educational approach of the software should be sound and free of content errors.** This can be a difficult area for parents to assess. Magazines featuring children's software reviews are good sources for parents.

◉ **The software should be technically and operationally sound and compatible with the home computer.** Concerns that should be addressed include whether or not the home computer has enough memory to run the program. Does it require any special computer additions or accessories—like a joystick, printer, color monitor, roller ball, CD-ROM, 3½" floppy, hard drive, etc.? Does the computer support the sound or graphics in the program?

Alsop wrote in his October 10, 1994, column "…business-oriented CD-ROM titles designed for individual use have languished…. The only serious market for business-oriented CD-ROMs are for reference works that are sold with a network license and installed on a network server or for more specialized applications for factory or other mission-critical use."

It may be true that businesses are not supporting the individual use of CDs in the workplace, but they are big proponents of multimedia training. Why? The answer is ROI, which stands for "return on investment." For example, in-house multimedia training can reduce the cost of training by eliminating travel expenses, instructor fees, facility charges, and the like. Furthermore, if easy access to training materials can increase the productivity of your current personnel, you may not need to hire as many new staffers as projected for next year's budget. That would mean you could also reduce your projected allotment for new salaries and new-hire training—a savings of money not yet spent, but a valid return on investment nonetheless.

To many companies, multimedia training seems to come with too hefty a price tag. But it is important to separate the one-time expenses of setting up a training program from the recurring costs of running it. The recurring costs tend to be much lower for multimedia than for live training. The initial expenditure for hardware and software can be seen in a more palatable perspective when it is translated into costs per trainee—it's sort of like amortizing an expense over long-term use.

And when it comes to those reference works that Alsop mentioned, be sure to consider the Newsworthy Factor and Hassle Factor. Lots of people use large volumes of printed materials on a daily basis. Such materials include medical and scientific journals, encyclopedias, and end-user documentation for machinery such as repair manuals. If you are one of these people, find out whether your resources are available on CD. If they are, make sure the data is current enough for your needs, and that the application has the search capabilities to find what you need.

EDS Unigraphics provides its end users with 55 volumes of information (that's 14,000 pages of documentation) all on a single CD. Not only does putting the data on CD save space, but end users can now find the information they need a lot faster.

Before you buy a CD, check out the license to apprise yourself of any limitations, restrictions, or additional fees. For example, some of the discs that provide marketing data have limitations on how much of the data may be used at any one time. Some applications assess additional charges for use over a certain limit. And don't forget that some phone discs expire after a specified number of lookups.

Sometimes an evaluation has to include technological considerations. What goes hand in hand with references? Resources. Once you find the reference material you're looking for, you might need some graphic, audio, and video clips to spice up the newsletter or presentation. First you'll have to decide what it is that you need. Do you need line drawings, black-and-white grayscale pictures, or color? The more complex the art, the more disc space is required. A CD-ROM offering color clips will offer fewer overall images per disc than a disc offering line art. The file format of the images must also be considered. Make sure the files are compatible with whatever program you'll be using.

What about the resolution? This is an issue for both still and moving images. For example, on the average 14-inch monitor, a 160×120–pixel video window in an 800×600 display measure only $1\frac{1}{2}$ inches square. If you enlarge the window, the image becomes distorted. But that's the low end of resolution. Full-screen, 32-bit broadcast quality is 640×480, with 30 frames per second. And in the middle you have half-screen at 640×240. Another consideration is the pixel depth, a function of the number of colors supported. Twenty-four–bit color may look best, but if your computer doesn't have enough power, the burden may slow down your processor.

Depending on your purpose, it may make a difference to you if the images are exclusive, limited, or public domain. You might not want to center an advertising campaign around an image if that image is in the public domain and other companies might be using it as well. Search-and-retrieval tools are also important. The greater the quantity of images, the more useful the disc will be if it offers some sort of search software. Many people find it useful to thumb through a booklet when searching for that perfect image. And finally, make sure the usage rights cover the uses you require. Some packages require royalties, copyright statements, and credits when used for certain purposes.

Many people in today's economy are working long hours. Some are even holding down two jobs. Add in family responsibilities, and you have little time left for shopping. Mail-order catalogs are big business. So too is television's Home Shopping Network. Catalogs and home shopping have always been great options for those who simply can't get around easily, whether due to infirmity or just a lack of transportation.

CD-based shopping catalogs are still in their infancy, but you can expect to see more of them soon. When they do begin to proliferate, look for catalogs that provide extra utilities. For example, look for a search capability so you can browse by category, price, or size, and for calendar reminders so you don't forget your anniversary or grandfather's birthday.

Buying CDs

CDs are showing up in locations where you routinely shop for specific interests or complementary goods and services. For example, you often see them in bookstores now. Microsoft Home titles are now being distributed by Ingram Book Company, the nation's largest wholesale distributor to the book trade, so you should be able to find these titles at leading book dealers nationwide. Look for CD titles in a special, new section such as "multimedia," or perhaps you'll find them in the appropriate subject category/shelf.

At the American Booksellers Association trade show in May, 1994, eighty CD-ROM publishers were listed in the catalog, and many more were actually on-site demonstrating titles. Booksellers are reportedly interested, although still a bit wary, and distributors such as Ingram know that it's just a matter of time and educating the booksellers before bookstores start handling CDs en masse. Technophobia and literary snobbism are also cited as obstacles to the acceptance of CDs.

Then there's the matter of educating the end users. Most bookstores don't have the means to provide demo stations. Just as individuals like to thumb through books before purchasing them, so too do they want to preview multimedia titles. There are, of course, other means of previewing CDs, including the demo and sampler discs mentioned in earlier chapters. If the publishers create the desire, the stores will undoubtedly stock the discs.

Ingram Book Company distributes books to over 30,000 bookstores, museums, shops, and other special and general retailers that carry books. And as I mentioned in Chapter 1, chances are good that CDs are already available (or soon will be) at your local Blockbuster store.

Handling CDs

People often ask about the shelf life of a CD and the data it holds. The laser used in a CD-ROM drive is a very low-powered one. Unlike tape, which wears out with use, reading a disc will not shorten its life span or harm it in any way. If a compact disc is properly manufactured, it will last for a very long time. Exactly how long nobody knows yet, because they haven't been around long enough to find out. What we do know is that if the edge of the disc does not get properly sealed, allowing oxygen to reach the metal surface, the disc will only last a few years at best. Standards and testing measures are evolving, and soon we will have discs that lasts more than one thousand years.

In the long run, how you handle and clean a disc may have some effect on the disc's life span, but this has not yet been proven. The basic rule of thumb is to be gentle with discs and don't use them for playing Frisbee.

If you would like some serious and detailed suggestions on handling discs, the following guidelines were prepared by the Compact Disc Reliability & Integrity of Media Working Group of the Special Interest Group on CD-ROM Applications and Technology (SIGCAT), chaired by Ron Kushnier. According to the group, these guidelines represent the current thinking of disc and drive manufacturers regarding the care and handling of CD-ROM discs. The validity and usefulness of most of these guidelines have not been substantiated by government testing and therefore are presented for information purposes only:

⊙ Wash your hands before contact with the disc. If available, wear lint-free cloth gloves, finger cots, or talc-free latex gloves.

⊙ Always handle the disc by the outer edge or the inner edge (the hole). Never touch the data surface.

⊙ If you must wipe the disc, do so with a soft, dry, lint-free cloth in a radial motion—that is, from the inner to the outer hub, not in a circular motion around the disc as you might do for a phonograph record. The most devastating scratches are those that occur along a circular arc of the disc. Scratches like these can obscure a long stream of pits.

⊙ Certain cleaning agents and solvents can damage the discs. Some of these include: gasoline, paint thinners, benzene, acetone, carbon tetrachloride, chlorinated cleaning solvents, ammonia, and household detergents that contain ammonia. Do not clean with a water-soaked cloth. The use of isopropyl alcohol, the ingredient in many commercial CD cleaning products, as well as certain waxes and acrylic liquids, is still questionable. Do not clean the label side of the disc.

⊙ Use of a CD-ROM caddy is highly recommended during transport and operation. Limit the amount of physical contact with the disc.

⊙ Discs like to "live" in the same conditions that people do. They don't like to be manhandled or to be exposed to temperature extremes, excess humidity, or high-intensity UV light.

Another frequently asked question has to do with traveling. Rest assured that once the data is on a disc, it won't come off, even when you pass through an airport checkpoint. Because the data is literally burned into the disc, neither magnets nor X rays have any effect on a compact disc.

Installing CDs

I prefer discs that don't clutter up my hard drive, but the issue is not so cut-and-dried. Installing certain files on your hard drive often makes the application run faster. Sometimes it's a trade-off between hard-disk space and performance speed. Indexes, for example, are placed on the hard drive to tell the program where to find the data on the disc. This, along with buffering, adds speed. The larger the buffer and the more detailed the index, the faster the application.

Some discs install operational files that are necessary to run the program. Such files might include the video or media player program. Without it, you wouldn't be able to see the video clips from the application. Often CDs install files that already exist elsewhere on a hard drive, but go unnoticed by the installation routine. A variety of utility programs (such as Repeat.Com) exist to help you find duplicate files so that you may delete them if you choose.

If a program has features that allow you to use bookmarks or save other user information, it has to be saved on the hard disk because you can't write to a CD. This doesn't necessarily mean that the program will take up lots of disk space by creating files on your hard drive. More likely it will create a directory or folder in which to store the files you create when you use the CD program.

Some CD titles give you installation options. A complete installation usually places entire indexes on your hard drive, whereas a semi or partial installation only copies over the most-used indexes. Occasionally you even get the option of a no-hard-drive installation, in which case the program runs entirely off the compact disc.

Networking CDs

In the October, 1994, issue of *Windows* magazine, Cheryl Currid touted the use of CD servers to solve the CD access problem. Whether for a single user or a network, if you use multiple CDs with any frequency, you'll soon tire of disc swapping in the drive, just as computer users tired of swapping floppy disks way back when. If you only have one drive, you have to swap. If you're in an office that's networked, there might be a few drives on the network, but chances are good that you have to call your colleague closest to a drive and ask him or her to insert a particular title for you. And as Currid points out, what happens when your colleague goes home and you're working late? Jukebox servers connected to the network could go a long way to solving this access problem, suggests Currid.

Back in June of 1992, *Multimedia/CD Publisher* reported that an estimated 26,000 CD-ROM networks were in use worldwide. The estimate was based on combined sales data for Online Computer System's Opti-net, CBIS's CD-Connection, and Meridian Data's CD-Net networking software packages.

Most CDs can be networked, but that doesn't mean you have the right or license to use them on a network. If you read the license printed on the package of the average CD purchased in a store, you'll find that you have the right for single-station use only. For example, the Knowledge Adventure Software License Agreement reads, "This software is licensed for use on a single computer in a single location."

The insert in my *Fractal Ecstasy* CD is a little more explicit. It says, "Deep River grants to you, the Licensee, a nonexclusive license to use the *Fractal Ecstasy* multimedia work (the 'Work') on one hardware system (that is, a system containing no more than one central processing unit and one CD drive) at a time."

If you look at a CD package and can't find such a notice, don't think your disc is exempt from the single-station restriction. The notice probably got thrown out with the box. Most publishers have not yet bothered to include software code to prevent network use without a license. So far, the honor system has prevailed. If you want to use a CD on more than one system at a time, or to put it on a network, you need a multi-user or network license.

You can network CDs in different ways. For example, you might have a dedicated server, i.e., a system that does nothing but handle data access requests from other systems on the network. Or you might have a peer-to-peer network, where you can access the systems of other people on the network.

The peer-to-peer network does have its drawbacks for CD users. Suppose your system is on the network and has the Phonebook CD installed. When a coworker down the hall accesses that disc in your drive from her desktop system, your system may be forced to do double duty. If you are busy working on another program, your system response time is likely to slow down and the coworker down the hall is likely to lose patience with the slow response time in accessing the disc as well.

A dedicated server provides a good alternative, and depending on the number of discs that need to be accessible on the network, you might want to use a tower or jukebox CD server. Another alternative is to daisy-chain several individual CD drives together. The latter option is slightly more expensive, but it is also more flexible, and if one drive breaks down you can remove it and reconnect the chain. If a jukebox breaks, the result is expensive downtime.

For users of LANtastic, Windows for Workgroups, NetWare Lite, 10Net, PowerLAN, and other peer-to-peer networks, software products such as Opti-Net can provide faster access to more applications and data stored on CD-ROM. By adding *data-caching* and *data-prefetching* to shared CD-ROM drives, Opti-

Net Lite can speed up access to CD-ROM applications by as much as 600 percent.

CD-ROM data-caching enables network users to store recently and frequently used applications and data in high-speed extended memory. From there it can be retrieved almost instantly. The cache temporarily copies into memory volumes of data from the CD-ROM disc. If the data hadn't been copied into memory, the read head in the CD-ROM drive would have to find and access the data over and over again.

Data-prefetching involves the use of algorithms that predict and retrieve the data that multiple users might request. The data is stored in the CD-ROM data cache. Prefetching is ideal when multiple users are contending for access to a single CD-ROM drive. Instead of thrashing about to respond to a random stream of small requests from many users, the drive sees and responds to an orderly stream of large requests.

Understanding Copyright Infringement

When I talked earlier in this chapter about using resources for graphic, video, and audio clips, I mentioned that you must be aware of any royalty or credit requirements, as well as copyright notices. The issue of copyrights, especially as it relates to the use of clips, bears some further discussion.

A copyright covers the expression of an idea, not the idea itself. But that doesn't mean you can take someone else's expression and alter it to make it your own. If you take an image and alter it, you could still be infringing on someone else's rights.

Suppose you have access to a color image of a vase full of red carnations sitting on a table covered with a floral print table cloth. The table is in front of a window and the lighting makes it appear that the sun is streaming in through the window, casting a shadow upon the table. If you take that image and alter its elements to make the carnations pink and the table cloth a solid blue, chances are that you're still infringing on the original copyright. If, on the other hand, you drew your own table, vase, and flowers, simply assembling them in a similar setting, you might have copied an idea but not stolen a copyright.

In this sample scenario, it is also important to note that if the original image is taken from a magazine, for example, and scanned into your computer, the mere act of scanning the original image is itself a copyright infringement.

These same principles apply to audio clips, as rap musicians found out when they tried to use unlicensed sounds from recordings within the body of their own creations. If you think that you're allowed to use small portions of someone else's work without permission or license, think again. It would also be a mistake to think that because you are only going to use it in-house, you need not get permission.

There are some exemptions to these copyright rules, but they are disappearing fast. The concept of "fair use" has been invoked as an exemption afforded to educators and nonprofit organizations. The basic premise was that educators using someone else's copyright (for example, by photocopying an article and distributing the copies to students) were not gaining any "commercial advantage" and so were not infringing. However, the argument has been advanced in recent lawsuits that if the use aids in one's professional status it might be construed as a commercial advantage.

Many issues regarding copyright and the protection of intellectual property are undergoing careful scrutiny and revision, often due to technological advancements. Meanwhile, it might be safest to use clips that come with a license for use, such as those I mentioned in Chapter 5. If you have special needs, you might want to hire the services of a clearance specialist, and I'll talk more about that in Chapter 14.

Chapter 12

Storing Memories
on Kodak Photo CD

In a brochure for a Seybold Photo CD seminar, Jonathan Seybold wrote, "Every once in a while a new standard comes along to transform the marketplace. Such has been our experience with Photo CD. Not only does it have application and provide value to traditional printing and publishing media; it also provides a bridge to new markets and new media."

Since June, 1992, wholesale photo finishers, retail photo stores, and commercial photo labs have offered Photo CD services. In his August, 1994, column in *Byte* magazine, Jerry Pournelle reported that over 13 million CD-ROM drives are Photo CD–compatible, and there are more than 30,000 places where you can drop off negatives and get back a Photo CD.

Initially, the Photo CD was dismissed by professionals as a new consumer toy, but publishers, prepress houses, and advertising agencies quickly caught on to the benefits. Photo CD represents a way to store images at low cost in a high-resolution format. You can now create four-color separations from a digital image for a fraction of what it costs to create traditional four-color separations.

The ability to use high-resolution pictures for playback on television and various computer platforms has led to an increase in interest and use in the home and business markets as well. Kodak Photo CD has not yet become the slide projector of the '90s, as originally predicted, but individuals are creating electronic photo albums and using their own images for clip art.

You can display pictures from a Photo CD on a television screen using a Photo CD, CD-i, or 3DO player. If you have a computer and the right software, you can also view your images on your computer screen, and use them with word-processing, desktop-publishing, and photo-imaging programs.

The process is really quite simple. You don't need a full-blown work-station to use Photo CDs. You can take your pictures same as always (you don't even have to use Kodak film) and let a finisher create a master disc for you. Then you just pop the disc into your player or CD-ROM drive and use the pictures you want.

The Photo CD scanning process automatically generates each image at five different resolutions. Any image can then be used for various applications with different resolution requirements, without the need for rescanning. You can use thumbnail sketches of images for quick viewing. You can import pictures in the Photo CD format (referred to as *PCD*) into variety of applications. There the images can be printed or edited, and stored in different formats that are native to those applications.

Photo CD has already become the de facto standard for digital images: once the specifications for Photo CD became public, the "open standard" made it desirable to software and content developers. More and more software pro-grams have become Photo CD–compatible. Besides Kodak's own software programs, more than 50 other applications are already Photo CD–compatible, including:

- ☉ Photoshop 2.5 from Adobe Systems Inc.
- ☉ Fetch 1.0 , PageMaker 5.0, and Photostyler from Aldus Corp.
- ☉ Compel 1.0a and MediaBlitz! 3.0 from Asymetrix Corp.
- ☉ CorelDRAW! 4.0 from Corel Corp.
- ☉ Photo Magic 1.0 and Picture Publisher 4.0 from Micrografx
- ☉ Word 6.0, PowerPoint 4.0, and Publisher 1.0 from Microsoft Corp.
- ☉ QuarkXPress from Quark Inc.

Kid's Studio, the 1994 CODIE award–winning storymaking program, gives kids a creative environment to write, narrate, and illustrate their own stories with Kodak CD images, clip art, sounds, and more. (Screen shot courtesy of Storm Software.)

What You Can Do with Photo CDs

Besides the imaging and publishing software programs I just mentioned, I've come across a few other programs for the home market that make interesting use of the Photo CD. One is *Kid's Studio* from Storm Software. This program makes it easy for kids to personalize their stories with their own photographs from a Photo CD. When the kids are done combining personal photos, pictures, words, sounds, and special effects to create their stories, they can print out their projects, view them onscreen, give diskette copies to family and friends, and even record them on videotape.

In addition to photos, kids can combine text, sound, and drawings, and they can incorporate stock art and shapes that come with the program.

This screen from *Family Tree Maker* shows the first page of an individual's Scrapbook. (Screen shot courtesy of Banner Blue Software.)

Another program for the home market is *Family Tree Maker.* Family trees are those scroll-like diagrams with names, dates, and connecting lines. They are cumbersome to draw by hand, but software programs are available to handle the task. Version 2.0 of *Family Tree Maker* goes a step further to include a Scrapbook feature. With Scrapbook, users can include family photos (up to 16,000 images per person), each with its own caption, date, and description.

Besides creating family trees with pictures in them, you can produce onscreen slide shows and album pages in a variety of layouts. And, most important to this chapter, these photos can be imported from a Photo CD. Just insert the disc in your CD drive and click on the picture you want to include. That's all there is to it. If you want to crop or rotate an image, you can do so from inside the *Family Tree Maker* program.

I've been hearing about all types of uses for Kodak's Portfolio CD. After having photos processed on Photo CD, students are creating interactive projects such as yearbooks by adding sound and interactive branches. Businesses are using the same methods to create presentations. These types of projects could be done on a regular CD-ROM using standard presentation or authoring programs, but they couldn't give you the cross-platform compatibility that Kodak's Photo CDs give you. For one relatively low production cost, the same disc can be displayed on a computer or television screen.

Professional Snapshots

In researching various Photo CD applications, I found that sometimes the Photo CD is used as the end product delivery medium. This is the case with Portfolio discs used for presentations of all sorts. At other times, the disc itself is used as an intermediate step between taking a photo and using it in some other medium, such as a magazine. In this section I'll provide some brief examples of both.

As I mentioned earlier, with Photo CD you can create four-color images for a fraction of what it costs to make traditional four-color separations. Businesses shell out a lot of money for all the color separations they need for printing brochures, newsletters, catalogs, annual reports, and other materials.

An article in the November/December, 1993, issue of *Computer Pictures* described a Seattle photo lab, Argentum, and the 16-page catalog job it did for a client. Using traditional color-separation methods, the job would have cost $26,000. By using Photo CD technology, they were able to cut costs by $6,000, saving the client 23 percent.

The costs for traditional four-color separations can be prohibitive for some. This was the case for Brent Stickels, a designer for No Fear, the San Diego–based clothing catalog. With Photo CD, No Fear can now afford to use quality color images. Stickels agrees that the color is not always true (often it is heavy on the blue and undersaturated), but he says that you just have to know where to compensate and how to adjust.

Quality has become an issue, but not necessarily a deterrent. In the November/December, 1994, issue of *Computer Pictures*, Bill Smith, president of Boston Photo Lab, was quoted as saying that the quality of a four-color separation from a Photo CD was still not up to the quality of the standard separation process.

I spoke with Mary W. Elings, a digital imaging consultant at Custom Process in Berkeley, California. She explained that the drum scan traditionally used to create four-color separations provides more highlight and shadow definition because it has a greater dynamic range. But highlight and shadow definition should not be a problem for most applications because the color differences are so slight. Unless you are working with very large images, these color differences will be barely noticeable.

The color problems involve very small degrees of color, and Elings believes that savvy users can handle the adjustments. In fact, she says that when you decide to produce your own color separations, you have to take on more responsibility. She compares it to desktop publishing, where you must be responsible for the typography—a responsibility that once was shared with a typesetter. Only a few years ago, most people didn't know the difference between 12-point Courier and 26-point Times Roman. As more people acquire and learn to use Photo CDs, they will learn more about working with color.

Elings also mentioned something else that I found quite interesting. She said that most service bureaus calibrate their Photo CD scanners daily to ensure color accuracy. If your computer hasn't been color calibrated lately (and whose has?), this could account for a variation in color between what is on the disc and what you see on your computer screen.

The combination of rapid processing and digital storage at multiple resolutions can solve a lot of problems. The Smithsonian Institution was in a hurry. It needed to assemble a photographic exhibition of each day's inaugural activities in The Museum of American History and release the photos to the press as quickly as possible. The Smithsonian's Office of Photographic Services sent out photographers to cover the events. The film was developed, scanned, and mastered onto a Photo CD. Pictures were added to the disc in multi-sessions until the limit of 100 images per disc was reached.

In another race against time, *Sports Graphic Number,* a leading Japanese biweekly publication, used Photo CD technology to acquire pictures of the 1994 World Cup soccer final. By the time the game ended on Sunday night, only 12 hours remained in which to get the images to Toppan's Itabashi Publications printing plant by press time.

Sports Graphic Number photographers were on hand to shoot the game on Sunday, July 17, 1994. The film was processed immediately. An editor and cameraman on-site selected six images to be scanned onto a Kodak Photo CD. The images were then copied from the disc onto a computer and sent over the phone lines via the Internet. At the printing plant, the images were downloaded from the Net and converted into CMYK (cyan-magenta-yellow-black) data for printing. They appeared in the next edition, right on schedule.

World-renowned photographer, Rick Smolen, has used the Photo CD as both a tool and a delivery medium. *From Alice to Ocean* is the title of an inter-active Photo CD presentation, a glossy adventure book of the coffee-table variety published by Addison-Wesley, an interactive CD-ROM title, and a photo-graphic gallery exhibit. The project was based on a 1980 book called *Tracks* by Robyn Davidson, who in 1977 made the rugged journey from the desert outpost of Alice Springs westward to the Indian Ocean, accompanied by four camels, a dog, and National Geographic photographer Rick Smolen.

Using the Photo CD technology helped Smolen create all four products with relative ease. Once the photos were mastered on Photo CDs, Rick was able to edit them using Adobe Photoshop and place them in Aldus PageMaker to produce the coffee-table book. The interactive CD-ROM program and Portfolio presentation was created using the same Photo CDs plus added audio, video, and graphics. The supersized print enlargements for the traveling gallery exhibit were made from the 16Base resolution of the selected images from the Photo CD.

Digital Video magazine of November, 1994, quotes Rick as follows: "We live in an age where images compete for attention. Rather than try to be more shocking or outrageous than my competitors, I want to be quicker, better, more thought-provoking." *Alice to Ocean* was named "Best interactive book/CD-ROM" by *Macworld* magazine. It won several other awards, including the 1993 Multimedia Awards Gold Medal for Technical/Creative Excellence: Best Motion/Still Imagery, and an Award of Merit for Best Information/Reference: Book Adaptation.

Professional photographers and stock houses are using Photo CD both as a tool and as a delivery method. And CD-ROM publishers are taking advantage of the high quality of photos mastered to Kodak Photo CDs. DiAMAR Interactive, publisher of the DiAMAR Portfolio series of digital stock photography on CD-ROM, has also released a CD-ROM titled *Understanding Exposure: How to Shoot Great Photographs*. This disc, based on a book by award-winning pho-tographer Bryan Peterson, contains over 500 photographs scanned using Kodak Photo CD technology.

Peterson demonstrates photographic theory by showing different photo-graphs of the same subject and explaining how exposure settings and lighting affects the results. When you think you've got a handle on it, you can experiment with different exposure settings on actual photographs, and immediately see the results on the disc. Not a bad idea before you go out and shoot your own film.

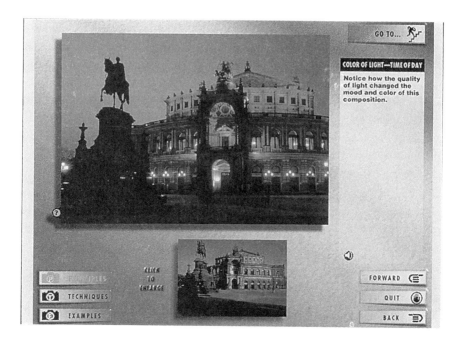

"Color of Light–Time of Day" is one of 75 topics covered by Bryan Peterson's *Understanding Exposure: How to Shoot Great Photographs* CD-ROM from DiAMAR. You can focus on principles, techniques, specific examples, or all three, and hear the author describe his techniques. (Screen shot courtesy of DiAMAR Interactive.)

Tools of the Trade

Kodak has come up with five different types of Photo CDs so far, and several different software programs to accommodate various uses. Kodak has even created software and hardware to allow you to press your own CDs. I'll spend the rest of this chapter talking about the different disc types and software for using them, and hold the discussion of mastering discs until Chapter 14. I'll also answer a few commonly asked questions in this chapter and tell you about the Kodak Picture Exchange.

Five types of Photo CD from Kodak. (Photo courtesy of Eastman Kodak Company.)

Two Master Discs

The Kodak Photo CD and the Kodak Pro Photo CD are both master discs. The first one is the standard disc, and it can hold up to 100 high-quality images from 35mm film, with five resolutions per image. The Pro Photo CD can handle film sizes up to 4×5 inches. Depending on the film size and number of resolutions (up to six), Pro discs can hold from 25 to 100 images. The Pro, aptly named, is often the choice of professionals. It is the best choice for museums that require an unprecedented degree of quality and for people working in high-end commercial imaging.

Photo finishers that provide Kodak Photo CD services can create a master disc from negatives, slides, and transparencies. Photo CDs are multisession-compatible, so you don't have to take in 100 pictures all at once to have them transferred. You can take in a roll at a time, if you want, and keep adding to the disc until it is full.

Each time you put pictures on a disc is called a "session," and for each session the mastering software creates an 18MB index so that the data can be read. This means that the more sessions you put on a single disc, the less room there is for pictures, because each added index takes up the space that could have been used by four more photos. If you are a computer user and you've created a "multisession" disc, you need a multisession CD-ROM drive to be able to read all the indexes.

Once your images are on disc, you can use various software programs to create presentations. Software is also available for creating catalogs and databases for image management and fast retrieval. But before we get into the software possibilities, I want to tell you about Kodak's Creation Station. It's a lot of fun and you don't need a computer to use it.

Creation Station

Those of you who do not feel computer-savvy, or who simply have no need for presentation programs and the like, might want to check out the Creation Station. The Creation Station is a kiosk. Consumers can use it to create enlargements and reprints of existing photos, and to enhance those prints with text, graphics, and borders.

The kiosks are just now beginning to ship to mass merchandisers, such as K-mart and Walmart, and to retailers who handle a lot of print enlargement processing business. The technology to create color laser prints from existing slides, prints, negatives, and Photo CDs has been available for some time, but has been in the exclusive hands of the vendors. They have been using the CopyPrint Station, which was designed for behind-the-counter use.

The same functionality used in the CopyPrint Station has been incorporated into the Creation Station. It too can work with a print, slide, negative, or Photo CD. You can add text and create custom graphic borders, and then print out the image in various sizes, including one 8 × 10 or nine wallet-size pictures.

The enhancement features are similar to those in the Create-It software for computers. The software also allows you to create simple presentations and "publish" them on a Portfolio disc. I'll tell you more about that in a moment.

Access

Access is the Kodak software that allows you to retrieve the images from a Photo CD. If you are using a third-party software program that is Photo CD–compatible (such as one of the imaging or publishing programs I mentioned earlier), you won't need to use Access. It does, however, allow you to display a contact sheet (a window with thumbnail images of all your photos), a feature that other software may or may not offer. You can set preferences for color range (from the top at 24-bit color down to 16 colors), and choose one of three image-display sizes in the contact sheet.

Portfolio Discs

A master disc acts solely as a storage medium. It is not interactive, and may only contain Kodak's image pack files (PCD files)—no sound, and no other image types. A Portfolio CD, on the other hand, was made to hold interactive presentations. It takes you beyond the realm of simple access to quality images, and moves you into a new medium for communications and creative expression.

Throughout this book I've been talking about interactive presentations and their use in business, at home, and at school. One of the benefits of using Portfolio CDs for on-the-road presentations, informational kiosks, trade show displays, and educational programs, is that you can play the disc on a television set using Photo CD, CD-i, and 3DO players. Businesspeople may especially like the portable Photo CD player that fits easily into a briefcase. Or you can play it on a Macintosh or Windows-based computer with compatible CD-ROM drives and Photo CD software. The software can be placed on the Portfolio disc, making one less requirement for the system.

PhotoEdge

Before you work out the presentation sequence, you may want to enhance or edit some of your photos. You can do this with any compatible software program, such as Adobe Photoshop, or you can use Kodak's PhotoEdge software for more basic image enhancement and correction.

PhotoEdge was designed especially for home users, business presenters, and other people who use photographs in their documents and presentations. Using PhotoEdge, you can crop images, zoom in for close-ups, adjust exposures, and sharpen or soften edges.

You can then print, copy, or export finished images and use them in other applications. When you are done editing your images, you can arrange your presentation using either Create-It or Arrange-It.

Create-It

The Create-It software program is for the Macintosh platform only. It was designed for people who want to create presentations, even if they have never before worked with a presentation software program. Because a number of such user-friendly programs are available for the Windows platform, and because those programs are Photo CD–compatible, it was deemed unnecessary to make a Windows version of Create-It. (Similarly, Kodak has not come out with high-end image editing software because Photoshop and others already exist.) If you want to make a Portfolio disc from Windows, you can use the Arrange-It program.

Using Create-It, you can design an interactive presentation and add text and sound to your images. You can use pictures from a Photo CD master disc as well as import images from other programs.

You create your presentation one frame at a time, selecting backgrounds, colors, and other elements; adding text, drawings and audio; and creating hot buttons to offer simple branching options.

In addition to making a Portfolio disc, you can use a Create-It presentation to make prints or transparencies. You can make color laser prints from your own printer, or go to a service bureau to make slides or resin-coated prints. Create-It is an ideal tool for families who own a Macintosh computer.

Arrange-It

Arrange-It is targeted for intermediate and advanced users who want to create presentations. With Arrange-It, you can design more sophisticated layouts and use multiple branching options and other features.

You can create menu branches, sequence images for playback, and link those images with audio clips. You can also use image files from other programs. Arrange-It comes with several utilities for converting images from applications that save in other formats, such as Microsoft PowerPoint.

After you've previewed your presentation onscreen, you can save it as a script file. Take the file along with the images and other content (i.e., any sound or graphic files you used) to a service bureau and have them master your Portfolio disc.

Create-It is a Macintosh program that allows you to create Portfolio disc presentations. (Screen shot courtesy of Eastman Kodak Company.)

If you use a lot of images that are not on a Kodak disc, you will need some means of exporting and carrying the files to the service bureau. Most bureaus can work from a SyQuest or Bernoulli cartridge drive, DAT tape, or magneto-optical disks.

In case you are planning to distribute a Portfolio disc for others to play on their computers, be sure to include the player software on the Portfolio disc in case the people to whom you give the disk do not have Kodak software. Player software can be included free of charge (just tell the service bureau).

For those of you who have your own in-house Kodak PCD Writer and the Build-It software, you can make your own Portfolio disc.

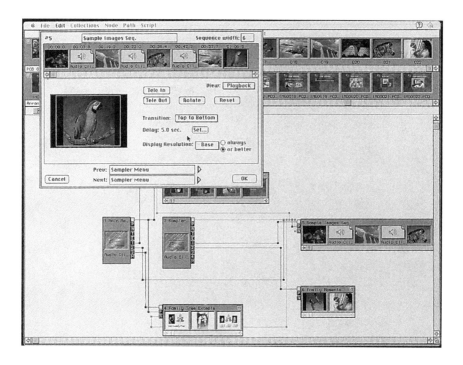

Arrange-It is a Macintosh and Windows program that allows you to create interactive Portfolio disc presentations. (Screen shot courtesy of Eastman Kodak Company.)

Catalog Discs

If you have a multitude of photos to keep track of, Photo CD Catalog will be the answer to your storage needs. I said "will be" because, as this book goes to press, the Catalog CD is just beginning to emerge in the consumer market. Westlight, a stock photo house, was one of the first to come out with a true Catalog CD.

The Catalog disc can store over 4,000 images, depending on which resolution you choose. Browser search and retrieval software is included on every Catalog disc so that anyone with a player can flip through the photo catalog without the need of any other software.

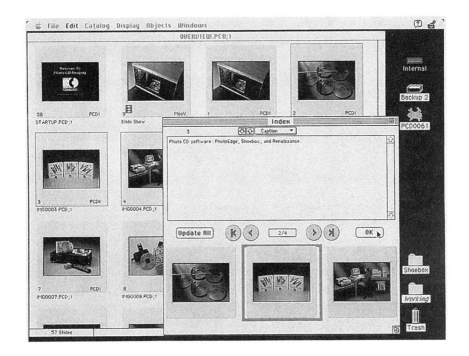

Shoebox is a front-end database program that allows you to manage hundreds of Photo CDs. (Screen shot courtesy of Eastman Kodak Company.)

Shoebox, Kodak's image manager software, and is often used to create a Catalog CD. It was designed to help commercial computer users manage thousands of multimedia titles stored on a desktop, including images stored on all types of Photo CD discs.

With Shoebox, you can index, catalog, and view thumbnail images, conducting your search by means of user-defined fields, keywords, and captions. When you find the image you're looking for, you can view it in any resolution, or copy, crop, export, and even print it. And you can make contact sheets.

A catalog can reference 30,000 or more files and have its own unique set of data fields. Users can also retrieve images from file formats other than Kodak's PCD format. They can retrieve QuickTime movies and WAV audio files as well.

Print Photo CDs

The Print Photo CD is another new Kodak disc type. So new, in fact, that it is just now beginning to be used by printers who work with color separations. Designed to support the prepress process, the disc is used to store all of the elements needed for a print job, including the film scans, layouts, and separations. To accomplish this, the Print Photo CD stores images in the CMYK format commonly used in the graphics industry.

Take It to the Bureau

Over 30,000 photo finishers and service bureaus across the country are offering a variety of Photo CD services, including the mastering of master and Portfolio discs. Many bureaus can also assist you in creating Portfolio presentations, with the costs varying by the amount of assistance you require. You can go to Custom Process, in Berkeley, California, for example, with nothing but your photos and an idea for a presentation. So even if you don't have a computer, you can still create Portfolio presentations.

The average cost of creating a master disc at a custom lab (notice I said "custom lab" because the work is done by photo professionals) is between $1 and $2 per image, depending on volume. The turnaround time is typically a day or two.

You can get your master disc for less money. I saw a message on the Internet that recommended a company called "LazerQuick" in Beaverton, Oregon, that charged only 59 cents per image. I phoned to verify, and the price per image is correct. They also charge $9.95 for the disc. If you bring back a disc for another session, then they charge the same price per image plus $4.75 for the session. I also heard that Fedco stores in the Los Angeles area charge only $14.99 to develop a 24-exposure roll of film and create a new Photo CD. They reportedly charge only 56 cents to add images to an existing CD. I couldn't verify these prices by phone, but my guess is that mass merchandisers will have pretty good prices. You should make some calls and locate a service provider who can meet your needs.

Creating a Pro Photo CD master disc is another matter, because it requires a different scanner. Each image is going to cost $15 to $20, and the turnaround time is about three days.

The cost of creating a Portfolio CD varies with the number of images, the complexity of the branching, and whatever additional services that may be required. You can safely assume that it is going to cost no less than a couple of dollars per image, and then some.

Some images may need retouching or sharpening. You can do that yourself by using imaging software, or you can have it done by a service bureau. Again, prices vary.

When I spoke to Mary Elings at Custom Process, she had a few tips to share:

⊙ Even though you may get better Photo CD results by using color negative film instead of transparencies or slides, you should stick with the film that you know the best. If you like shooting slides and you know how to get what you want in a shot, don't switch films. You might get a slightly larger dynamic range, but you might lose the shot.

⊙ If you just emptied an old drawer full of negatives and slides that you want to transfer onto a Photo CD, make sure they're clean and that the mounts are secure.

⊙ When you create a presentation, don't skimp on audio for the sake of a better image. The eye is much more forgiving than the ear.

⊙ Be aware of aspect ratios. You don't want to create an onscreen presentation and output it to slides only to find that some of your image or text has been cropped.

⊙ While contrast helps the eye, don't go to extremes. Light gray on top of dark blue is far better than stark white on a black background.

Common Questions and Answers

Which drives will work with Kodak Photo CD?   The Kodak Information Center maintains an extensive list of compatible drives, SCSI boards, drivers, and cable configurations. You can call Kodak for this information at (800) 242-2424, ext. 53. You can also download the list from CompuServe. It's in one of the CD-ROM Forum libraries.

What resolutions are used on a Photo CD?   Kodak Photo CD supports six levels of resolution. The first five levels are used on the Photo CD master disc.

The sixth level of resolution is used only for the Pro master disc. The first five levels of resolution are as follows:

- ◉ **128 × 192 pixels**   This is Base/16, also known as *small thumbnail* or *wallet*
- ◉ **256 × 384 pixels**   This is Base/4, also known as *thumbnail* or *snapshot*
- ◉ **512 × 768 pixels**   This is Base or Standard, comparable to TV quality
- ◉ **1024 × 1536 pixels**   This is Base*4 or Large, comparable to HDTV quality
- ◉ **2048 × 3072 pixels**   This is Base*16, also known as a *poster version*

Base/16 is one-sixteenth the resolution of the "Base" image, and 16Base (or Base*16) is sixteen times the resolution of "Base." These are not simply larger picture elements—they represent an increased number of scan lines.

4Base and 16Base (another way of referring to Base*4 and Base*16, respectively) images are compressed using Huffman encoding. Compatible software uses the decompression routine to pull the higher resolutions out of the image. You would typically need these higher resolutions if you want enlargements or if you intend to use an HDTV as a display device. The sixth level of resolution is available only on the Pro discs. At 4096 × 6144 pixels, this is Base*64.

Each PCD file contains all scans of an image. So from one PCD file you can extract an image in any one of the resolutions. The images are 24-bit color (that supports up to 16.8 million colors). For best viewing, your video card should also be 24-bit. However, you can get by with 256 colors; 16-bit is generally not adequate.

Which resolution should you use?   Lower-resolution images require less memory for handling. So if your system is struggling with memory management, try a lower resolution. Your system can also display lower-resolution images more quickly. The Base or Standard size images reproduce just fine in newsletters and similar publications. You can also change colors, retouch, and use Base images in animations.

How do Photo CDs work?   The gold layer of a Photo CD disc is painted with a thin film of photosensitive dye. The dye is interpreted as a pit, so an unused Photo CD is one big pit. The laser is then used to "bleach" the dye so that the bleached points reveal the shiny gold. The net result is a disc with dark and light spots interpreted as bits.

Are there any special tools for handling large image libraries?   The Kodak Professional Image Library, announced in 1993, is an automated compact disc database system with an online storage capacity of up to 100 compact discs of all types, including Photo CD, CD-ROM, CD-ROM XA, and CD-i. Off-line capacity for the Professional Image Library is an additional 2,400 discs. The Library is an excellent solution to the storage and management needs of stock photo agencies, museums, medical facilities, and other large organizations that produce and manage vast repositories of image-intensive data on disc.

The system includes the Kodak PCD professional jukebox. The jukebox can access as many as 100 Photo CD and CD-ROM discs. Jukebox manager software manages the stored media and directs the robotics operations.

You might think that it would take a long time to find something among 100 discs. But the search is pretty fast. Using Shoebox image manager software from the desktop, a user inputs the search criteria. Shoebox searches the database's defined fields, captions, and keywords, and displays thumbnail images of pictures that meet the criteria. The system can search approximately 1,000 images per second. Once you find the one you want, the jukebox manager software selects the appropriate disc, loads it into the drive, and reads the image file—all within a few seconds.

Where can you get Kodak product information?   To learn more about Photo CD products or other Kodak desktop color-imaging products, contact Eastman Kodak Company at (800) 242-2424, ext. 51, or (716) 724-1021, ext. 53.

You can also send inquiries to the following address:

Eastman Kodak Company
Kodak Information Center
Dept. E, 343 State Street
Rochester, NY 14650-0811

Information about Photo CD is also available on the Internet by anonymous ftp from ftp.cdrom.com:/cdrom/photo_cd, and from ftp.kodak.com:/pub/photo-cd.

For the location of the nearest reseller and other information about Photo CD products, you can call the Kodak Customer Assistance Center toll-free at (800) CD-KODAK or (800) 235-6325.

For the location of a service that will transfer negatives or transparencies to Photo CD discs, you can call the Kodak Customer Assistance Center at (800) 242-2424, ext. 36.

For information about drives that are compatible, call (800) 242-2424, ext. 53.

Kodak Picture Exchange

I can't end this chapter without telling you a little bit about a service called the Kodak Picture Exchange. Most, if not all, companies can benefit from using images, and if yours is one such company, you might find Kodak Picture Exchange a valuable resource. It may well answer the prayers of many art directors, public relations and advertising agencies, publishers, and design companies—people who depend on finding the right image for the job.

Kodak Picture Exchange is already offering online desktop access to over 100,000 images from 24 stock photography agencies. Subscribers connect via modem to a toll-free number and pay $85 per hour in connect-time charges. Once connected, they can search the Exchange database of images much the same way they would search their own Kodak catalogs, i.e., by searching for descriptive words or phrases.

The Exchange program has a number of useful tools to assist in the search, including a built-in thesaurus. Users can refine searches if the first criterion yields too many matches.

The major advantage of this system is that it allows buyers to search for images without having to rely on a researcher at a stock agency to guess what image they really want. And there is a clear advantage to conducting one search through images offered by several agencies instead of searching each agency's catalog separately. The service is available 24 hours a day, all year round.

After reviewing thumbnail images that meet your criteria, you can submit an online order form to request images from the agencies that own them. The stock agency then calls the buyer, they negotiate terms and fees, and the image is sent directly from the agency to the buyer. As an added benefit, buyers can download thumbnail images from the Exchange for no extra charge or pay $9 for a medium-resolution version of the image. This medium-resolution version can be used for layout and design purposes while the transaction is being completed.

Chapter 13

Becoming a CD-ROM Creator

Multimedia may be "hot," but that doesn't mean every application deserves the multimedia treatment. Adding music or video can be superfluous, gratuitous, and a waste of time and money. Initially, some companies have been put off by the cute multimedia applications of video e-mail and voice-annotated memos. They were deemed fun but frivolous, and inappropriate for serious business. But the landscape is changing, and both multimedia and compact discs are being put to very serious use.

As online data gathering and retrieval goes mainstream and we begin to amass vast quantities of customized data, individuals may choose to create their own CD-ROMs for personal archives and family projects. More and more people will create CD-ROM products for in-house business purposes, such as data storage or data dissemination to field offices. And some companies will market their products on compact disc.

Before you jump on the CD-ROM storage bandwagon, figure out how often you work with your data, and decide what you need:

⊙ Primary storage (used daily, must be speedy and easily accessible)

⊙ Nearline storage (transitional data, semi-archival, speed of access is not a consideration)

⊙ Archival storage (infrequently used)

CDs do not have to replace all other storage means. They can be used to complement and enhance your system, whatever it happens to be.

Access speed is usually an issue, so compare your options. Access time is a combination of the *seek rate* (the positioning of the head at the specified track) and *latency* (adjusting the drive speed for safe access). The seek rate for a hard drive can be as fast as 9 milliseconds. Bernoulli, SyQuest, and magneto-optical drives have seek rates usually under 40 milliseconds. CD-ROMs have the slowest seek rate, between 180 and 320 milliseconds.

But access doesn't end there. Once the data is found, it must be transferred back to your system so you can see it. The transfer rate of a single-speed CD-ROM drive is approximately 150K per second. Double-speed CD-ROM drives transfer at 300Kps, twice as fast. Quad-speed is 600Kps. Bernoulli and SyQuest drives, on the other hand, can transfer up to 2MB per second.

The interface between the drive and your system also affects storage transfer rates. IDE (integrated drive electronics) allow a maximum of 2–3MB per second. Standard SCSI-1 allows 5MB per second and the newer SCSI-2 standard provides for up to 20MB per second.

You should also consider the longevity of the media. Hard disks crash. Tapes wear, stretch, and break. The life span of a CD is unknown, but estimates range from 20 years to forever. The holographic option is fast approaching, but still way to costly for most users to consider at this time.

Using CD-ROM for storage has a variety of benefits. First, the discs require a minimal amount of physical space. Then there's all the time you save because you can retrieve data quickly and easily, assuming you have adequate software. Documents can't be misfiled, and clerical time is reduced because the data need not be refiled when you're done using it. Data can be shared and is secure. Data cannot be altered or erased from the disc. Finally, you can make copies inexpensively.

Discs are an inexpensive means of disseminating information. The government, for example, has to provide an inordinate amount of data to countless persons, organizations, and departments. The public has the right to know, and the information is available, but it has not been affordable until now. If you have a modem, you might find the information you need online. But rates are still high, and even on the Internet you need a certain amount of expertise to find what you want. CDs, on the other hand, are affordable for both the information provider and the seeker.

In a July, 1994, article titled "Kiosks Get the Word Out," *Presentations* magazine reported that Northeast Utilities uses CD-based kiosks in its Connecticut and New Hampshire offices to keep employees up to date on company news and information. The kiosk application is called EINSTEIN and stands for Employee Information News Service Terminal and Employee Interactive Network.

A moment ago I alluded to the fact that CDs provide a certain amount of security in that the data cannot be altered once it is placed on the disc. And that's a pretty good reason for using CDs. Another excellent security-related reason has to do with safeguarding sensitive information. Now that you can master discs in-house, you can secure data on-site without having to release it to outside sources for processing.

Compact discs may be a terrific way to market and distribute your goods and services. In today's economy, companies are looking for ways to leverage their assets, which means they need a way for large numbers of people to be able to see their assets. British Hulton Deutsch Picture Library provides a good example of a creative use of compact discs. Hulton Deutsch has created ten CD-ROMs with 100,000 images of more than 70,000 world-famous personalities.

Mass-market consumers are not clamoring for these images, but a strong vertical market exists among book, newspaper and magazine publishers, advertising agencies, and others who are always in search of the perfect illustration. The compact disc medium makes reaching this vertical market affordable.

Another good example of a vertical market for CDs was provided by Jerry Pournelle in his November, 1994, column in *Byte* magazine. He pointed out, "Many extremely important but highly technical journals have small circulations and consequently are very expensive to produce in traditional print media. The CD-ROM not only allows them to be produced at reasonable costs but also to include a great deal more supporting data. A single CD-ROM can contain years' worth of information."

Should You Do It?

There is certainly no shortage of good reasons to create a CD-ROM. In the first half of this book I describe dozens of CD applications of all types. If you think that you or your company should be using current technology, but you aren't sure if there is an appropriate application, try asking yourself the following questions:

- Would a CD-ROM be a more cost-effective means of publishing company documents such as annual reports, marketing brochures, catalogs, and product documentation? Would those documents communicate more effectively with multimedia?

- Might you be able to increase sales by providing interactive multimedia demonstrations of your products and services?

- Could you enhance the value of something that you are already distributing via another medium by distributing it on compact disc and adding "something extra" for perceived value?

- Could you boost your retail sales presence with an in-store kiosk or by providing free demo discs that the store might give out with every purchase?

- Could you cut training costs by developing CD-based training programs?

- Could you cut down on worker's compensation claims for back injury by trading in heavy sample and catalog cases for a portable CD player and a few discs?

- Could you increase your company's profile by designing a corporate kiosk for public display?

- Could you expand markets for your existing products by creating multimedia versions and cross-marketing?

- Does your company have assets that could be exploited in a compact disc application? Data that you could sell? (Maybe something along the lines of a demographic breakdown or trends analysis based on your business experience?)

Once you decide that you want to create a compact disc application, you need to draw up a budget. If your goal is to advertise or boost sales, evaluate the cost against projected sales. If using the compact disc medium is less expensive than prior methods, be sure to factor in the expected cost savings, both short- and long-term. Don't forget to consider the value of additional exposure, name recognition, and publicity that might be a by-product of your new CD-ROM.

If you're thinking about creating a commercial retail product, the risks may be greater. Evaluate the market, consider sales projections, and think carefully about the selling price. Don't forget to consider distributor percentages and other fees.

Until the market is better established, keep commercial production budgets as low as possible—$100,000 per CD-ROM title and $200,000 per game. Create as much of your own content as possible, then use royalty-free and public-domain materials. License as little as possible.

Considering Retail

You need more development money today than before. In the beginning, you could get a disc to market for less than $50,000. Today, development costs average no less than twice that amount—and that's just development. When it comes to marketing you can start talking millions. CD-ROM marketing expert Connie Connors, who works with clients such as Knowledge Adventure, said, "We tell our clients they'll need a million dollars to market a CD-ROM title."

The Connors quote appeared in Steve Ditlea's "The Big Apple Bites into CD-ROM," an article in the August, 1994, issue of *Upside*. In the article he also suggests, "One way around the expected product shakeout at the retail level would be to bypass stores as a primary outlet for multimedia CDs." The catalog approach has worked well for The Voyager Company, and its president, Bob Stine, says, "I wouldn't mind calling our catalog L.L. Voyager."

If you are considering the game market, the stakes are really high. According to an April 25, 1994, article in *U.S. News & World Report*, "Software based on new 32-bit technology—which delivers realistic video and quality sound—costs from $1 million to $2 million to develop. The reason: Video games are converging with Hollywood."

In the consumer market, a series idea is stronger than a single title. And broad-based appeal is important. It's still too early for narrow niche markets unless you have big bucks to spend on marketing and advertising. And check for market saturation before you begin. For example, there are probably enough dinosaur titles on the market to last quite a while.

Most successful titles appeal to a wide range of individuals of different ages and levels of expertise. The titles contain a mixture of media types, balanced and put to effective use. They also offer a variety of user activity. Such activities include watching demos, navigating through information, and playing a game.

Your product should be state-of-the-art in both its design and the technology it employs. Both the implementation and the content should work together to make your title engrossing. The competition is stiff and you want to be on par with the best. You also want to design your title to be robust enough to encourage repeated use (this is a must, at least until CD prices drop below $20).

Pricing the Sale

The ability to provide vast amounts of data on a single disc is one of the greatest assets of the medium. The more information on the disc, the more you can charge. But what if your customers don't need all that data? Will they pay for all the information when they need only a little? This is where the pay-per-use or pay-as-you-go strategy can prove useful.

Until now, most disc sales have been based on a flat fee per license. In most cases, you buy the disc and you have unlimited access to all the data. Unlimited access is one of the main decision factors for people deciding between online services and buying a disc. If the customer uses the disc frequently, the disc is more cost-effective than the online service, because charges for the online service exceed the purchase price of the disc.

On occasion, licenses to use CDs have access limitations. In addition to the single-user versus network license restrictions I mentioned in Chapter 11, I described one disc in Chapter 4, the *American Business Phone Book*, that limits access to a specific number of lookups. There are also discs, such as *MarketPlace Business*, whose usage is monitored in units. In this case, the purchase price buys the first 3,000 units. After that, you can use the disc only by purchasing blocks of 5,000 units. These are examples of beginning attempts to utilize a pay-as-you-go strategy.

If you are in the position to sell data, and that data is expensive to produce and its value is high, you should consider the pay-as-you-go strategy. If your price is too high, more people will be unable to afford the disc and you'll lose potential sales. If your price is too low, you'll lose money on the deal.

In Chapter 9 I talked a little about data encryption. In certain instances, encryption could provide a means for usage-based pricing. For example, suppose your service gathers specialized data on all of the Fortune 500 companies and you place all of this information on a single disc. You could design the application such that encryption codes are needed to unlock the data on each company.

Customers who only need data on one or two companies would be charged accordingly. Later, if they needed data on a third or fourth company, they would purchase the keys to unlock that data. Of course, you wouldn't have to design the application so that data is unlocked on a company-by-company basis. You could have codes that unlock any five companies, or codes that unlock all companies that match some specified characteristic.

Encryption as a means for usage-based pricing only works for certain types of applications, however. Online services typically charge for time of use, but that model doesn't always fit either. Some other type of metering (each time data is read or printed, for example) will have to be part of the solution. A few companies, including CD-MAX, Inc., Infosafe Systems, and Wave Systems Corporation, have already developed encryption and metering systems. Such technologies can often be licensed, so you do not necessarily have to come up with your own encryption and metering programs.

If you decide to use encryption as all or part of your solution, consider who will handle fulfillment. Someone has to be by the phone to take orders and give out the keys to unlock data. This too can be covered in-house, or outsourced to a third-party service provider.

Specifying Technology

For the most part, you will consider technical aspects during the design phase. Whether you use a 63-minute disc or a 74-minute disc is something that can be decided later. Selecting a method of compression will depend on the data and the type of application. So that too will be a part of the design process.

Another thing you can think about during the design phase is which platform to use. If you are developing an application for in-house use and your company uses only Macintosh computers, you will be developing a Macintosh-compatible disc. If your sales force already has brand-new, PC-compatible laptops with built-in CD-ROM drives, your new sales application should be designed for their use.

On the other hand, suppose management decides to redeploy those brand-new laptops to other departments and send the sales force out with hand-held CD-i or portable 3DO players. The issue of platform should be thought about in the design phase, but no decision should be etched in stone until the design phase is completed. (See Appendix A for a description of the various platforms and disc standards.)

What Will It Take?

One of the differences between in-house projects and those meant for the commercial marketplace is that the budget for in-house CDs does not hinge on projected sales. You won't be paying anyone sales royalties for in-house CDs. However, if you had to acquire licenses for your in-house CD, you could owe a royalty based on the number of units pressed.

Both in-house and commercial discs have to be manufactured, but manufacturing methods vary depending on volume. Packaging may be less of an issue for in-house applications. A budget for a commercial release has to include channel distribution fees and expenses for shipping and warehousing. And all budgets need a line item for contingencies. (Every project needs some padding.)

An article in the August, 1994, issue of *Multimedia Producer* reports that Graphix Zone spent approximately $500,000 to create the content and master disc for its ƒ *Interactive* title. About 30 percent of that amount was spent on hardware. The balance went to what Project Director Dave Nichols called "wetware," or human resources.

Because the ƒ *Interactive* project had to be completed in six months, extra personnel was brought onboard. The work was done by four three-member teams, each consisting of a creative writer, a graphic artist, and a 3-D animator or programmer. Additional personnel included a programmer, three managers, and an authoring expert who knew the ins and outs of the authoring program that was used. The sound and video was provided by ƒ's production company.

You'll need to spend money up front for equipment—for development machines, target playback machines for testing, digitizing boards, scanners, backup tape drives, and more. You may have some of this equipment on hand. What you don't have, you'll either have to borrow, rent, or purchase. If you plan to produce more than one title, the cost of equipment need not be absorbed by the first project alone.

Software expenses for the project are not limited to the authoring package or programming language. You may need search-and-retrieval engines, dictionaries, compilers, libraries, and playback engines. You will also need software for the data preparation—programs for editing audio, video, text, graphics, photos, painting, animation, and 3-D files. You might even need administrative and design programs for flowcharting and project management.

And then there's the content. If you are going to license any content, be sure that licensing fees are in your budget. Look for existing assets that can be recycled. Twenty to 25 percent of the material on the Oracle Corporation's annual-report disc was recycled from other projects.

Many clips, including video clips, are available on CDs and include rights for commercial use. If you can't find what you need there, try a stock footage house or photo agency. Another tip: obtain the rights to use a song and then find someone to perform it for you (perhaps MIDI-record it) instead of licensing the rights to an existing recorded performance.

Dave Berry of Electronic Arts said at a conference, "The formulas for calculating rights based on duration and visibility do not map well into the world of interactivity and nonlinearity." Companies like 3DO offer developers whole libraries of video and audio clips that have been cleared for use. Professional developers agree that if you only have $50,000 for licensing on a $150,000 project, you should generate your own content rather than obtaining a license to use content owned by someone else.

Don't shortchange yourself when budgeting for time. Most tasks, especially ones that are easy to describe, are more time-consuming than you might imagine. For example, under the heading "data preparation" alone are a whole host of tasks, including shooting and editing photos and video, writing and entering text, recording and editing audio, and drawing and rendering graphic images.

Other time-eaters include copyright searches and clearance negotiations, managing the beta testing program (which includes channeling feedback to appropriate team members), designing the package, and creating the documentation. And then there's the product testing. It always takes longer than anticipated, and one little bug can take days to correct.

Whatever you do, don't underestimate. For instance, if the text for your project is already available in a digital file, you may think that little time is needed for text preparation. But what about the time it takes to edit, format, and proofread the text? When you budget for time, add 10 to 20 percent for contingencies.

When you set up your schedule, include dates for interim deliverables and sign-offs. Obtaining approvals for incremental segments of a project can save you from having to start all over again from scratch when a customer wants changes or the program doesn't work as planned. Ideally, you should set aside extra time at the end of the project to make the minor adjustments that often are needed as a result of end-user testing. The last 10 percent of the development effort takes 25 percent of the total development time.

Every project needs a full-time core team headed by a project manager who is responsible for meeting schedules and budgets. This person is usually the liaison with the client or management (as the case may be), and should be intimately familiar with the project, understand where tasks overlap, and be able to assess critical milestones. This person is often the project designer as well.

Also on the core team is a graphic designer whose job is to design the interface and create the look and feel of the application. The lead programmer or authoring specialist is also a core team member. Depending on the type of application, the core team might include a scriptwriter. If you are creating an educational or training application, an instructional designer should be a part of the core team as well.

A project may require several programmers. Many multimedia presentation programs allow you to create applications without programming, but the powerful packages offer tools that allow users to program themselves. Typically, users can program by using a proprietary scripting language or by writing routines in a standard programming language such as C or C++.

During the data preparation phase, you need personnel to produce the actual data elements—to scan, digitize, retouch, render, record, and so on. You may choose to use outside services to clear copyrights, design the packaging, write the documentation, and handle other such tasks.

The more diversity of experience and perspective among the personnel working on a project, the better. A programmer, for example, may not have a feel for how different types of music can enhance a presentation. A scriptwriter may not have an appreciation of the psychology of colors. But no matter how diverse the members, they have to work together as a team.

Rockley L. Miller, president of Future Systems Inc. and editor and publisher of *Multimedia Monitor*, said in an interview in the IBM publication *Multimedia Today*, "A lot of the early design work and products out there have been driven by the computer side of the industry and, as such, they tend to reflect a database mentality.... Developers need to capture more from the artistic side—the side that says there needs to be continuity, a story line, an experience, and emotion."

Never look back. The state of the art is constantly changing, and you can't keep up. Don't look back unless you absolutely have to—unless looking back is guaranteed to improve the project. If you need to refuel in order to get off the ground, so be it. But if you're all fueled and ready to fly, go for it.

Great Idea, No Money?

I have heard many a conversation begin with, "I've got a really great idea for a CD-ROM title, but I don't have the money to put it together." Everybody has a great idea or two. Now, if you also have the content—either you created it or you have the rights to use it—then maybe you have something to talk about. There are ways to create a title and have someone else publish it.

One company that publishes other people's titles is Walnut Creek CDROM. If you know your way around the Internet, you will find that their author guidelines are available by anonymous ftp from ftp.cdrom.com in the file /pub/cdrom/author.txt. Walnut Creek deals primarily in straightforward distribution deals. You create the title on your own. When you're done, they add packaging, manufacturing, distribution, and marketing. As the creator, you receive a flat fee or a royalty per units sold, or some combination of the two.

An alternative is to make a deal with a big publisher who becomes involved in the development and production. Some publishers want to take over the production altogether, others want to provide funding, and some prefer only to oversee your production. Then the big publisher adds packaging, manufacturing, and marketing, paying you a flat fee for the production and a percentage of sales by way of a royalty. The amount of your royalty or fee varies, depending on the size of your investment. The greater your share of the investment, the greater your percentage should be.

In between there are a number of other arrangements. At the very least, you have to come up with an impressive prototype to sell your idea. Big publishers offer affiliate label programs, but, while they have money, life isn't necessarily easy for them. When an affiliate has a smash success, it usually parts company with the big publisher and becomes a big publisher in its own right. On the flip side, the big publisher stands to lose time and money if the affiliate's products don't do well.

How Do You Begin?

It all begins with analysis. Then, as you move into design, you start addressing issues such as hardware and software requirements, and the use of various media elements. At the end of the design phase you should have a detailed specification for the application as well as a prototype for hands-on assessment.

The more planning, the better. Wait until the last possible moment to do complex coding, and even then it is best to work in separate modules. As you go along, you may be required to make code changes, and it is easier to make such changes in specific modules. The analysis and design phases take up 40 to 50 percent of a development effort.

Start with a definition of your objectives and a description of your vision. This will give rise to a host of questions, the answers to which will play a large part in shaping your design.

Where will the application be used? In your office, a customer's office, at a trade show, in a store? Will lighting, noise, or physical space be an issue? Will the user be alone or assisted in the application's use? Is your application supposed to present information or demonstrate a product? If you're trying to make a sale, you will have to consider the amount of time a customer has to spend with the application, and you'll have to find a way to motivate customers to try out your application.

Describe your audience in as much detail as possible. Consider their level of expertise as computer users and their familiarity with the content. Demographic data may also play a role. The age of a user, for example, tells you a lot about the user's attention span. Above all, be sure that you know why users will want or need your application.

Describe user scenarios and take advantage of all opportunities to involve members of a target audience in the development of your product. If your product is a training title for in-house use, involve managers and field personnel who will be responsible for implementing and supporting its use. If you are developing a title for client use, solicit input whenever possible. And whether you are creating a title for in-house use or commercial distribution, make provisions for beta testing.

Exploring Design Issues

To communicate your design, you need to produce flowcharts, screen layouts, and verbal descriptions of the data itself and all the actions users could conceivably take to manipulate the data. Start out with broad strokes (starting from the main screen, where the user can choose to go) and work your way to the details (from the main screen the user can choose A, B, or C by clicking on the associated pictures). You'll end up with a detailed description of each screen, what it contains, and how it connects to other screens. You'll decide on buttons, menu options, screen transitions, and all sorts of other details before coding begins.

Be sure to consider the data types you wish to use. For example, if you need motion, you might want to use animation or video, or both. As you work out a design, plan for what you want, but keep alternatives in mind. You might not have the budget to shoot that video clip you envisioned, and you may not get a clearance to use that photo that would have been just perfect.

During the design phase, you need to take into consideration what type of hardware your end users have. For example, if your end users do not have MPEG video boards in their systems, that will affect how you use video. There are trade-offs. The choice of playback system will guide your design, and vice versa.

The minimum configuration determines how you use media in a variety of other ways as well. For example, when the processor speed is not sufficient, video appears jerky and large graphics are slow to appear onscreen. And video sequences that do not fill the entire screen should show broad action, as little details are lost in a quarter-screen window.

Hardware has to be taken into account during many design decisions. Decisions about color depth, screen resolution, and the selection of fonts are affected by hardware. When it comes to fonts, serif fonts (the ones with the extra squiggles) look great on a large screen, but they don't fare so well on small screens with low resolutions.

If the playing system can handle it, 24-bit color with a screen resolution of 1024×768 is great. More than likely, though, you have to design your application for a lower common denominator, probably 640×480 and 16 colors—maybe 256 colors if you're lucky. If you do get to use 24-bit color, beware the price you have to pay in disc space and the time it takes to load and display 24-bit color images onscreen.

Depending on your hardware specifications, you may want to design "scalable software." Here's how scalable software works: Instead of offering a program based on the lowest common denominator, your software assesses the playback system (perhaps during installation) and behaves accordingly. Your program can take advantage of high-performance hardware and still be capable of performing adequately on less powerful systems.

As you consider the playback system, you have to decide whether to design your disc for the Macintosh or PC platform, or both. You may need to create a separate disc, or you may have room for a hybrid disc. The decision you make about the platform must be made up front because it impacts all ensuing decisions and plans regarding file formats, editing programs, and authoring programs. What you decide about the platform also determines whether your program requires a media player. If it does require one, you might need a licensing agreement to include a media player, such as Apple Computer's QuickTime for Windows, with your product.

Concerns about file formats and licenses apply even if you are just doing document management, as many law firms are. You have to decide whether to use an index or go with a full-text retrieval system. Indexes make searches go a little faster, but indexing is a time-intensive task. If the input volume is high, it might be better to let the system do the hard work.

On the other hand, all the documents must be text files to have a full-text retrieval system. Scans of a text document saved as an image file cannot be retrieved in a full-text retrieval system. If you want to retrieve scanned documents, you have to provide some type of indexing and either license or program your own search-and-retrieval engine.

The prototype is the ultimate output of the design phase. You must be able to experience the application while it is still in development in order to assess its impact and uncover design problems. A prototype also allows you to identify technical and engineering issues.

As you build the prototype, you can experiment with response time, colors, screen resolution, and other design elements before making final decisions. Hopefully, developing the prototype will give you some clues as to what creating the real thing entails. Developing the prototype should help you make accurate projections of the resources you need to develop the application.

Examining Interface Elements

The interface is your one and only opportunity to put your best foot forward. If you can't engage the user's interest, or if the user can't figure out what to do, it's all over. A good interface with many enticing choices can draw the user in, but it must be intuitive. Nothing is more frustrating than knowing you have a choice and not knowing how to make it.

If you're creating a demo or sampler disc and your goal is sales, you must make it easy to explore what you have to offer. You also need to motivate your potential customers, first to explore and then to buy. According to Laurie Casey, director of VendorSystem Group at Rainbow Technologies Inc., "Graphical user interfaces tend to be more visually interesting and are more apt to stimulate sales." In her article about distribution in the September/October, 1994, issue of *CD-ROM Professional,* she also wrote, "Market studies show that there is a direct correlation between the quality of the user interface and the number of sales of products from 'locked' CD-ROMs."

If you are designing a stand-alone system such as a kiosk, where there is little opportunity for assistance, much less a phone to call tech support, the interface is more important than ever. Remember that you, as the creator, are not a typical user. Things that are basic or obvious to you may be completely foreign to the average end user. Even if the user knows how to navigate through the application, the process may be cumbersome and not responsive to the user's needs.

A letter to the editor in the October, 1994, issue of *NewMedia* magazine illustrates my point. "CD-ROMs are great. But some have too many levels to click through before you get to what you want," wrote Clarence Johnson, project manager with the U.S. Department of Commerce, National Institute of Standards and Technology in Gaithersburg, Maryland. "I have a history disc, and to see a particular battle I may have to start six levels below where I want to go. Sometimes I just quit." And that's the death knell, right there. The user quits.

Keeping the interface simple doesn't mean that you can't be creative. There is a fine line between going with the standards for the sake of making your interface intuitive or familiar, and doing something new. Another letter to the editor, again from the October, 1994, issue of *NewMedia*, addressed this issue. "Designwise, CD-ROMs are still in a primitive form; they aren't branching out yet," wrote Jeff Southard, a producer at Xronos Inc. in San Francisco. "There is a dependence on hierarchies, menus and buttons. Developers need to think up creative, new ways to let the user do the exploring. Some of the interfaces don't challenge the user to explore. It takes a lot of frontier products like *Myst* to show what we can really do with the medium."

I saw the following sentence in the November 1, 1994, issue of *PC Week*: "But there's a basic human-interface issue, particularly for kiosks where the last thing in the world someone expects to do is talk to it." The article was about voice recognition technology, but the quotation raises an interesting issue. What do people expect? Is it intuitive to speak to a kiosk? Probably not. Does that mean you shouldn't design one that way? Not necessarily. Designing an interface is one of those times when you have to tread the fine line between standards and creativity.

Pat Dunbar was the consultant who conceived of the annual report disc for Oracle. In an October, 1994, article in *Multimedia Producer*, Dunbar wrote, "A key design concept was to provide users with multiple paths through information." Assuming that the viewers of an interactive application range in experience and interests, it is important to provide alternative paths so users are not forced to pass through too many screens or menus to get what they want.

The fundamental issue for a user navigating in a hypermedia environment is knowing where he or she is, deciding where to go from there, and knowing how to get there. The user must understand and remember the conventions of the interface in order to navigate without becoming lost in "hyperspace."

Designers should strive to keep the content in the foreground and the system's mechanics in the background.

When it comes to navigation, main topics should be easy to access from many different locations. Paths should have two-way options to allow for backtracking, and the user should be able to exit the program at any time.

In order to browse and navigate comfortably, users should be able to conceive of the information space as a whole. The concepts of space or time provide easy structures. For spatial orientation, programs might include maps and territories, both global and local. Maps and other spatial representations let users see where they are, where they've been, and where they're going. Another way to keep users from getting lost is to use overlapping windows, but too many windows can clutter the screen.

Besides standard tools such as a table of contents and index, guides can be used to assist with navigation and provide information. Guides might be visual representations of real people, or characters created especially for the presentation.

An interface does more than just help users navigate, it defines the look and feel of an application and can make its usage more intuitive. There are dozens of guidelines you can follow to create a good interface. For example, visual cues are excellent, but they shouldn't be heavily dependent on color coding because more people than you think are color blind to some extent.

Take advantage of what comes naturally. The eye normally rests first on a graphic, then on text. In English, we read from left to right, and that's why you so often see text to the right of an image, not the other way around. A screen transition that wipes from right to left generally implies forward movement. Left to right implies backward movement.

Care must be taken to examine cultural meanings and implications, and even when care is taken there can be much confusion. For example, does a "+" represent addition, a hospital, or a church? The same confusion exists in interpreting colors. Does red imply heat, danger, or anger?

Subliminal cues direct your eye and interest. Well, many aren't exactly subliminal, although they are subtle. Symbols can indicate the end of a sequence, or a continuation. Shading can indicate whether or not a button is already pressed down. Whatever your design characteristics are, be consistent.

If your application might be used for large group presentations in auditoriums, don't use a font that is too small to be read by people sitting in the back of the room. And sound cues don't work well in noisy rooms.

Text should be a clear solid color, generally light on a dark background. Try not to use ALL CAPS, since a string of capital letters is much harder to read than a combination of upper- and lowercase letters. Extra thin or extra fat type styles can also be problematic, and shadows and shading should be used judiciously. Text should never take up more than 60 percent of the screen.

Strive for consistency in the placement, size, shape, and color or your design elements. For example, a menu should always appear in the same location, and the button that takes you back to a specific screen should always look the same, no matter where you are.

Optimize for speed. Four seconds is about the longest a user can wait before becoming antsy. You can use sound or another image as a diversion if necessary.

Forward and backward arrows for turning "pages" with lots of long scrolling text screams "book!" but if the book metaphor is what your application needs, then you should consider adding a print function.

Sound can be used to enhance the emotional response or create moods, but it can also become intrusive. If it's appropriate to the design, I try to provide an option for turning off the sound so the user can do that if he or she wants to.

Don't clutter up the screen. A viewer's focus may become fragmented. If you want the viewer to focus on something specific, try to limit the intensity of other elements on the screen.

There is such a thing as too much. Animations, morphing, and other special effects are overkill if they do not specifically relate to the content or help achieve a design goal.

Before you make interface design decisions, know your audience and understand how, when, and where it will use the program. A lot of design decisions are just a matter of common sense, if you think about it. Yes, there are some design rules of thumb and common-sense questions to guide the process, but they are no substitute for professional expertise.

If you do not have a staff with the experience to produce your application, consider hiring a consultant or employing the services of a production house. In the next chapter I'll wrap up with some talk about production as it relates to both in-house manufacturing and working with outside service providers.

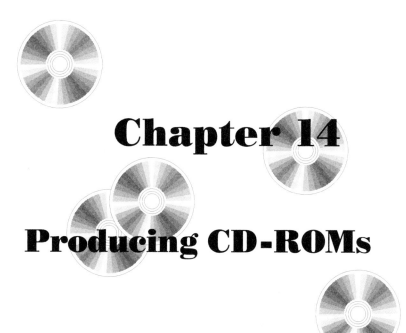

Chapter 14

Producing CD-ROMs

When you have completed the initial design specifications, and perhaps even a prototype, you might be able to move right into production, depending on what decisions you made with regard to media assets. Media assets are the specific graphics, text, sound, video, etc. that are used in an application. For every media asset that you do not plan to create yourself from scratch, or that comes from a resource that includes usage rights, you need to find the copyright holder and negotiate a license for its use.

Obtaining Clearances

You must have a license to use other people's property, so it's wise not to proceed too far into production until you have all the licenses you need. You do not need permission to use all properties, however. For example, if the property is in the public domain, you are not likely to need permission to use it, but even that determination is not always clear-cut. For example, a recording may be covered by more than one copyright, each expiring at a different time.

When you find something you want to use, a song for instance, decide if you want the song itself or a particular recording of the song. If you want to record your own performance of the song, you only need a license from the song's publisher. However, if you want to use an existing commercial recording, you need permission from the publisher and the record company. You may also need permission from the songwriter and the performing artist who made the recording.

Sometimes it's not so easy to figure out who has which rights. When Stuart Weg was working as an electronic media editor at Macmillan's, he found out how muddy the waters can become when evaluating the concept of "author." "With a book, two or three names appear on the cover and they wrote the book," said Weg. "When you are putting 1,400 stills and half an hour of video clips and ten minutes of animation on a platter, who wrote that?"

Another crucial detail is making sure that the person or company with whom you are negotiating actually has the authority to grant you the rights you need. For example, you might find a photo in a magazine, attempt to negotiate with that publication, and then discover that the magazine itself only has a license to run the picture in a specific issue. Perhaps the copyright ownership of the photo itself is in the hands of the photographer or a stock photo agency.

To complicate matters further, sometimes even the individuals involved are unaware of who owns what (perhaps because the legal staff always handles those things). Grievances and lawsuits often result. The April 27, 1994, *Wall Street Journal* reported on one such grievance. It seems that the writer who interviewed Fidel Castro in 1967 for *Playboy* magazine accused *Playboy* of "electronic piracy" when the interview was used on the *Playboy Interviews* CD-ROM. *Playboy* reportedly offered the author $100 after the fact, but the offer was rejected.

Besides the property itself, the content of the property may require usage licenses. For example, individuals often have some control over how their likenesses are used, so you may require a model's release as well as a copyright license to use some photos. And people's personal property is also protected. For example, suppose you wanted to use a picture of my home that happened to include the brass statue sculpted by my grandmother. Whether or not it's registered, the sculpture is a work of art and is protected by copyright law. You could not use the photo without both my permission and the permission of my grandmother—i.e., without a license.

Trademark protection can also come into play. At the start of this chapter I suggested that if you draw something from scratch, you own the copyright. But if you draw a picture of Mickey Mouse and use it commercially, Disney will sue. Nor can you write a story called "Mickey Mouse Goes to Moscow." Trademarks protect words, symbols, names, and other means of identifying goods and services. You may not use copyrighted works or trademarks without a license and/ or proper attribution.

An editorial in the April/May, 1994, issue of *Computer Artist* reports on a lawsuit between FPG International (a major stock photo agency) and *Newsday*, a daily newspaper. *Newsday* used a photo without permission or license, altered the image, and credited it as a "*Newsday* computer illustration." Even if the original image is altered to such an extent as to make it unrecognizable, altering an image to any extent is an infringement of the original copyright.

In that same editorial, FPG International suggests caution when using photo clip CDs that come with the right to use the images in any way, including advertising. The right to use an image in any way does not necessarily include the right to use any trademarks that are a part of the photograph's content. The editorial gave the example of a picture featuring cars from a specific manufacturer. The unnamed car manufacturer said it would sue for trademark infringement if the photograph was used in an advertisement.

Problems with usage are not limited to advertisements and other money-making propositions. Your simple act of scanning an image and altering it violates two rights protected by copyright law, the right of the copyright holder to make copies and create derivative works.

You can contact rights owners yourself or hire the services of a clearance house. Experts can offer inside knowledge, contacts, and experience. They know when it's necessary to contact performers, writers, musicians, and other participants, such as stunt performers who are often overlooked. And ownership isn't the only issue. Other considerations include territories and the duration of the license.

Jill Alofs, founder of Total Clearance, offers the following three tips for using media that others have created:

- Determine your budget limitations before you begin looking for clips. Be realistic about your budget and flexible about your needs.

- Don't wait until the last minute. Start your content search early. Give yourself as much time as possible so that you can find the best clip or consider alternatives if your first choice doesn't fit the budget.

- Think clearly and comprehensively about how you want to use the property you seek to license. Think with the future in mind.

Clearance specialists charge by the hour or sometimes by the project. Weigh your options carefully. As they say, ignorance of the law is no excuse, and injunctions are costly whether or not the offense was intentional.

Preparing Data

Data preparation is the next step in the production process. If you're creating your own media, preparation includes shooting photos and video, then editing the images and incorporating them into your screens. It also includes composing music and recording music, narration, and sound effects, and then editing those elements. Even if you are licensing media instead of creating it, you will have to edit the elements to make them work in your application. You may need animators, typographers, and content experts to create your media assets.

You might think that, with all the technological advances and "user-friendly" tools, you can handle data preparation in-house. Sometimes you can. Rob Stuart, communications coordinator for Cushman & Wakefield's regional Atlanta office, wrote a personal experience piece for the October, 1994, issue of *PC World* in which he described how the company used video in its client presentations—presentations that until then had been basically text and images. With the purchase of a video capture board, they were able to shoot video with a camcorder and record it on a PC using Video for Windows software. Now they had motion video clips, plus the ability to create still images by isolating in single video frames if they wanted to. No longer did they have to shoot rolls of film, have them developed, and then scan them into computer files.

The results for the Cushman & Wakefield office were positive. "Since [incorporating video], we've won 20 to 30 percent more bids," Rob Stuart wrote. "In addition, we save at least $500 a month because we don't have to pay for slide preparation. And we no longer write proposals, copy them, and put them in binders. Instead we just print the presentation screens to a color printer. We can keep customizing the presentation right up until the meeting, and no one has to work all night making copies."

Whether you intend to create media from scratch or repurpose other media, data preparation should be carried out by specialists. If you have media professionals in-house, terrific. If not, get help because only professionals understand all the consequences of working with media. For example, consider what's involved in storing images. When you capture images on video, you create raster images that eat up hundreds of megabytes of disk space. Both television-quality and animation video is displayed at a rate of 30 frames per second. Therefore, unless you know how to compress the images, one minute of television-quality video will use approximately 2GB (that's two billion bytes) of storage space.

Each media type has its own issues. MIDI files, for example, save a lot of space compared to the digital audio files used for narration. One minute of 16-bit MIDI sound takes up only about 200K of storage space, while one minute of digital audio requires approximately 10MB. MIDI is also less expensive to produce and easy to edit.

The space requirements for rasterized graphics (bitmap images) depends on the size of the image, the number of colors, the file format, and the compression method. Changing the screen size or resolution requires image-processing software. Vector graphics are made with CAD or draw programs. They take less disk space but sometimes take more time to appear on the screen. How much disk space is required depends on the size and complexity of the image, and again on the file format.

Whoever handles the graphics for your project should be familiar with all the different file formats. Handling graphics can be a time-consuming process! You should make calculated decisions at the beginning in order to avoid mid-stream file conversions later on. It is also a good idea to use discrete elements in graphics so that common aspects can be reused. For example, the background should be separate from the buttons on the main screen so that you can reuse the background in other screens where the buttons are different.

Choosing an Authoring Program

In an article about multimedia authoring in the June, 1994, issue of *Presentations* magazine, Carlos Domingo Martinez groups authoring tools into four categories: traditional presentations, multimedia presentations, multimedia authoring, and high-end authoring systems. He is quick to point out that the four categories overlap a great deal.

The main difference between traditional and multimedia presentations is that traditional presentation programs were not conceived with multimedia in mind. As such, they do not offer the additional tools that are a part of multi-media presentation programs, such as time-based event sequencing and path animation.

Multimedia authoring programs, says Martinez, add production capabilities such as SMPTE time-coding for video output, cue sheets, and more advanced editing tools. Some have scripting capabilities. By contrast, high-end authoring systems are used for more complex applications, and are ideal for computer-based training and kiosk applications. High-end products must have scripting tools, and many can be controlled by external program code written in other programming languages.

Many considerations will affect your choice of authoring tools. If your application requires touch screens, for example, then your software package must be able to support them. If you are going to collect user data, the package has to support that function as well. You need to consider whether or not you will need to distribute a player engine with your application. (A player engine is software that allows you to play/run an application or clip without installing the software program used to create it.) Does the production software package provide one, and if so, is it royalty-free? Yet another important consideration is whether the package supports cross-platform development.

Sometimes an authoring package offers too much. For example, if you are designing an archival system with primarily text and graphic data, all you probably need is software for indexing and viewing the data, and perhaps a relational database–type structure and powerful search engine as well. When it comes to building full-text retrieval databases for CD-ROMs, you can program your own or use a specialized authoring package. Some packages allow you to create massive databases and then spin off smaller sub-databases as separate CD-ROM titles that look exactly like the original.

Features to consider in an authoring software package include the following:

- The ability to connect to a database
- A precoded training module for student registration and the gathering of student test data
- A flowcharting tool
- Data editors
- A scripting language for more control
- Multiplatform compatibility

In addition to authoring software, you might use a number of other tools in the data-preparation phase. For example, you might use a 3-D drawing and rendering program to create a 3-D image for the title. Or you could use stand-alone programs for editing animation, video, and audio, not to mention image-enhancing programs such as Photoshop.

Testing Your Application

You'll want to create a one-off for testing purposes before you commit to a larger manufacturing run. A *one-off* is a single, individually mastered disc. If you have a CD recorder, you'll probably create your one-off in-house. If not, a service bureau can make one for you (I'll talk more about that at the end of this chapter). Before creating the one-off, be sure to check the interface and make sure that all buttons and menu items are functional. Verify the data to make sure that it is both accurate and properly displayed.

When you're satisfied that the one-off functions properly, you can press enough copies for real testing. You want to make sure that your application is stable and functions reliably. The more people that test your application, the better. One person cannot test a program accurately, because no matter how many times the tester goes over the program, he or she will do it in a similar way each time. Make sure your tester group includes both novices and pros. This way, you can check ease-of-use and see whether the application meets its intended objectives.

Working with a Production Studio

Producing interactive compact disc applications in-house is a big job. If you do not have the staff to handle such a project or are not prepared to hire additional staff for the job, there is another alternative: You can hire the services of a production studio. Throughout this book I have mentioned applications that were designed and produced by production houses, including Spinnaker Communications (creator of the FEMA training application), Prism Studios (architect of the Dayton-Hudson's holiday gift kiosk), Mammoth Micro Productions (producer of the Oracle annual report disc), and Big Hand Productions (producer of The Preview Machine, the Mercedes-Benz sales program, the EDS proposal, and many other applications).

I talked at great length with members of Big Hand Productions to find out how one might best work with a production house. Kimberly Rispin, the press and marketing manager, synthesized the team's answers. I asked them what to consider when deciding whether to create CD applications in-house or go to a production company. There was one singular and most emphatic answer: "First and foremost, you need to have the appropriate staff in-house to design, produce, and author the program." You must have a staff—not just one lone expert. An experienced video producer isn't likely to know if a program can be optimized to gain more speed or space. Similarly, a programming expert may know little about graphic design.

Without experts in each area, you can end up with a product that might run, but doesn't work. "Many of those programs are not interesting, don't look nice, are confusing, have technical problems, work too slowly, don't meet the objectives of increasing sales or cutting down on training time, and so on," they said.

I also asked what you should know before going to a production house and what you can expect when you get there. First, they suggested that you should have a good understanding of the production process; and second, you should be prepared to roll up your sleeves. "They can't just write us a check and walk away, expecting to get a disc back that they're going to be happy with," I was told. "A studio typically relies on the organization that has hired it to be the content or information expert. This can mean as little as dropping off a box of company slides, brochures and a video, to spending hours researching the company's archives to find just the right product shots, video clips, etc., to over-seeing or writing scripts for professional voice talent. Depending on the project and the topic, your involvement in the information gathering process may be minimal or incredibly significant."

Being prepared also means making certain decisions before you meet with the production studio. Define your objectives and have a clear understanding of your target audience. You do not have to decide on which platform to use. "Your project objective and target audience, once clarified and nailed down, should dictate what platform(s) are most appropriate for your project. The studio you are working with should be able to help you with this. Unfortunately, you should be warned that some studios may be biased toward or against certain types of CDs or platforms. It's good to select a studio that has experience producing for several different platforms, so they can tell you the pros and cons of each."

Some companies hire a production studio to augment their own in-house staff. This sometimes works, but only to a limited extent. Sometimes in-house personnel have experience that seems related but doesn't really translate to CD-ROMs. One example cited was that of a graphics designer who works in the print medium. That designer may not have the expertise to produce images that translate well on a CD platform.

Another example cited by Big Hand Productions relates to shooting video for different purposes. "We have worked with many companies that shoot their own custom video in-house, and we incorporate that footage into their interactive program. We do, however, send an interactive producer over to work with the company's video producers to help them create video that will work the best in an interactive program. This can be very different from producing linear video that goes to broadcast or tape. The same is true if you want to use your in-house script writers. Some writers are able to adapt their writing skills to interactive formats and others don't seem to get it. They are too accustomed to writing for a traditional beginning, middle, and end, not writing sections of information that may be accessed in any of a million different order combinations."

What should you expect from the studio? "To be on target, on time, and on budget with the project," they replied. Of course, if you are not clear about your target audience and objectives, you may have to make midstream changes, and that will cause delays beyond the studio's control.

Finding a studio with a reputation for staying on time and within budget is important, but it's not the only thing to consider. Before you settle on a studio, you need to have a meeting of the minds and find out whether you are comfortable with the studio's design philosophy. For example, the leadership of Big Hand Productions believes that the competition for your CD project is akin to HBO or MTV. "We design our programs to have a TV look, not a computer look," they said. If you have a different philosophy or style, you had best discuss it up front.

Another interesting issue is whether or not a production studio should also sell you the hardware. Big Hand Productions prefers to work independently of specific platforms and manufacturers. "This way, at any given time, we can recommend the best computer or brand of touch screen for our clients based on their specific needs. We stay abreast of the market and emerging technologies, and our clients do depend on us as a resource. We have vendors that we can refer clients to, knowing that they will provide them with good-quality products and services."

Finally, I asked Big Hand Productions to describe the perfect client from the perspective of a production studio. The company had four wishes:

⊙ **A client with a multimedia budget and long-term plans.**   "We love it," they said, "when we have the opportunity to develop a long-term relationship with our clients. If they have a budget for the year or more, and we can become partners with them in helping to solve training or presentation problems or other challenges with the use of multimedia, then we are really doing our job as a vendor and, more importantly, as a strategic business partner."

⊙ **A knowledgeable client.**   "We have historically spent quite a bit of time educating our clients about multimedia in general, and then more specifically about the process of producing interactive multimedia titles. More and more of our new clients are educated about multimedia, so we can spend less and less time educating, and more time creating."

⊙ **A client who knows the objectives of their project.**   "Many companies are setting aside budgets for multimedia projects for the first time. Some know exactly what they want from it, while others know that they need to stay on the leading edge and simply don't want to be left behind. A project can only be successful if the end-user, or consumer, is considered in each step of the design and production, whether it's a children's title or a corporate presentation."

⊙ **A client who trusts us to do the best job possible for them.**   "If a client has clearly and concisely communicated to us what they need and given us the materials that we need, then they need to go away for a little while and let us do our 'magic.' To design the best project possible, our artists need some room to be creative. But we do need a client to be available when we have questions."

Manufacturing Your Discs

If you hired the services of a production studio, the studio will probably also handle your manufacturing needs. They won't do the manufacturing themselves, but usually they'll create the master disc and set you up with a manufacturer. What if you are developing the application in-house? How do you go about finding and working with a manufacturer?

As I mentioned earlier in this chapter, you can do your own manufacturing in-house if you have a CD recorder. You can certainly master your own test discs and, depending on volume requirements, you may even be able to press all the discs. However, because of the time it takes and the cost of blank discs, pressing the discs yourself only makes sense for quantities under 50—especially if you have a single-speed desktop CD-R machine. If you happen to have the Kodak PCD Writer 600 and the Disc Transporter attachment, you can press 75 discs overnight without having to be there.

The PCD Writer 600 can fill a whole disc in about 10 minutes. (Photo courtesy of Eastman Kodak Company.)

Before you can press discs, you have to format the data for placement on the disc, a process called premastering. *Premastering* means to convert the data into the CD-ROM image. *Mastering* is the second step, where that image is actually recorded on the disc. You can record the image onto a tape or other medium and transport it to a one-off service bureau or replication company.

Ideally, premastering software should allow you to test the application before you actually master it. If you are only writing a single disc, being able to test the application is not quite as critical, because the most you could lose is the cost of a single disc and an hour or so of time.

You should also be able to specify how you want the data laid out on the disc. This is important because you want to place the data likely to be accessed most often on the inside of the disc. Accessing data on the inside is faster than reaching data on the outlying edges.

Also make sure that the mastering software supports the recording of different disc formats and standards. If you are working with multimedia, you'll

The Disc Transporter automates disc pressing. The drive bay you see here is actually the bay on the PCD Writer, placed behind the Disc Transporter machine. Used in conjunction with the PCD Writer 600, you can press 75 discs overnight. (Photo courtesy of Eastman Kodak Company.)

certainly need the CD-ROM XA standard, but if you also want to create Video CDs, CD-i discs, or even Photo CDs, check to see that they are supported, too. For example, if you want to create Portfolio Photo CDs, you need Kodak's Build-It software, a Sun computer, and a Kodak PCD Writer. PCD Writers are also capable of mastering other disc formats using Kodak's MultiWrite or DirectWrite software.

Yet another consideration is single-session, incremental-session, and multisession capabilities. *Multisession* allows you to add data to the CD-ROM in stages instead of filling the disc all at once. An *incremental session* is a compromise that fools the recorder into letting you add files at different times. You can take a break in between increments, but the session is not closed until you say so. Of course, you can't read the disc until the session is closed, either. Once closed, the session is treated as though it were a single session.

Single session can be read by all CD-ROM drives, but it has drawbacks. The most obvious is the potential for wasted space if you don't have enough data to fill the disc. Less obvious, but more restrictive, is the fact that you can't mix

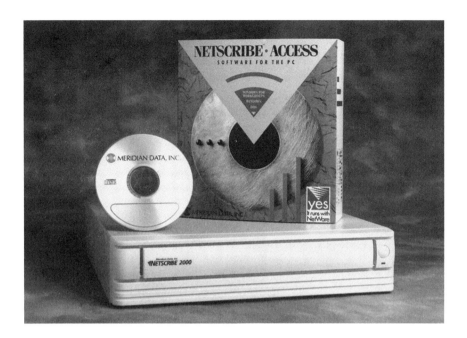

Netscribe 2000 is an integrated controller that provides shared access to a CD recorder over standard Ethernet networks. The unit includes client/server software for transparent CD writing and reading with DOS, Windows, and Macintosh computers. (Photo courtesy of Meridian Data, Inc.)

data types on a single-session disc. For every session there is a file index on the disc. Singles-session drives can only see the first index. Multisession drives can read later indices.

If you are planning to create hybrid discs that can be read on both Macintosh and PC drives, you have to do your publishing from a Mac system. If you need to access data from across the network, be sure your premastering package supports that need. To use CD-R on a LAN, the CD-Recorder must be properly connected. Netscribe Access from Meridian Data is one package for accessing data across a network.

Most recorders come with mastering software, so the factors I just discussed may limit your hardware choices. But there are other hardware-related factors to be considered as well, including price, speed, size, internal or external mounts (recorders are now available that fit inside a desktop system's drive bay), and the manufacturer's reputation.

Single-speed recorders work in real time, so a full CD-ROM takes a little over an hour to record. Double-speed recorders work twice as fast, so that same disc takes only half an hour. Quad speeds take 15 minutes, and the newest 6x recorders (such as the Kodak 600 I mentioned earlier) take about 10 minutes per disc. But don't get carried away too fast. Mastering a disc requires a continuous stream of data and fast recorders want that data more quickly.

What this means is that if you want to use a fast recorder you need a fast, powerful computer system with a lot of memory. A second consideration has to do with speed and errors. For some reason, the faster the mastering process, the more data errors are likely to occur. So, faster is not always better. If you want a fast recorder, see if it also offers you the option to record at slower speeds.

Some recorders can be daisy-chained or set up in towers so you can record more than one disc at a time. Beware of daisy chains, though. When one link breaks down, the rest fall as well. This does not seem to be a problem with towers.

If you do not have the appropriate equipment in-house, or you want to press more than 50 to 75 discs, find an outside service bureau. A one-off service is just right for jobs requiring a few hundred discs. The service costs a little more, but you save time and wear and tear on your desktop recorder. A service bureau should be able to work from a master disc; alternatively, you can provide the data on tape, SyQuest or Bernoulli cartridges, or a magneto-optical disk.

To manufacture an application disc in even greater quantities, you need a professional replication service. Full-service companies such as Metatec offer disc replication, package printing, and such fulfillment services as warehousing, shipping, and tracking.

When you select a company to handle your needs, ask yourself these questions:

- ◉ What is the company's reputation and area of specialization? (Some companies specialize solely in CD processing.)
- ◉ Are fulfillment services provided around the clock?
- ◉ Do they provide pressing, printing, and fulfillment? If so, are the services integrated with centralized tracking? (The company might actually be three separately run sister companies.)
- ◉ What is the turnaround time for your type of job, and does that meet your requirements?
- ◉ Will the company handle the premastering and mastering of the CD, as well as replication?

Make sure that the company you select is experienced in all facets of whatever services you need to retain. For example, if the company is going to print or paste artwork directly on the disc, make sure it has experience with this procedure. The company should be well-versed in the inks and glues that are safe and know which ones eat holes in discs. This may seem all too obvious, but the point is that experience counts a lot. And it counts for all phases of your product development, production, and manufacturing.

Appendix A

Compact Disc Technologies

Compact discs are mastered by using a pinpoint beam of light to burn pits into the CD's surface. That's why some people refer to "burning a disc" when they speak of creating one-offs or small quantities of discs. To manufacture large quantities of discs, a glass master is produced and used to stamp the rest of the discs.

To read a compact disc, laser light is reflected off the surface onto a photo-detection device that interprets the presence or absence of light as 1s and 0s (binary code). The discs are made of durable, heat-sensitive, reflective metal. Discs are encased in a thin, plastic coating to withstand handling.

Technical specifications for the way in which a CD is formatted account for the differences between various types of CDs. The use of various encoding and decoding schemes also accounts for different CD types. When a new specification becomes an approved standard, a specification book is published. The Red Book and Yellow Book standards, for example, get their names because the specification books for these standards had red and yellow covers, respectively.

Disc Formats

Here are the standard disc formats:

Compact Disc Digital Audio (CD-DA)   CD-DA, also known as Audio CD, was introduced by Sony and Philips in 1982 as a medium for digital music recordings. The discs can hold up to 74 minutes of CD-quality audio and are made according to Red Book specifications.

CD-ROM and CD-ROM XA   CD-ROM was first introduced in 1985 as a mass storage solution for computer-readable text. As the technology evolved into CD-ROM/XA, it was adopted by a number of video game companies. The XA prototype was first unveiled in September of 1988 to show high-quality compressed audio and data mixed on a disc.

The XA (*eXtended Architecture*) technology offered improved drive performance. With this technology, graphics, video, and audio are interleaved on a single continuous file stream. Decoding the compressed audio is handled separately by the hardware, leaving the processor free to pass the video and graphic data directly to the application. Software designed for XA drives cannot be played on plain CD-ROM drives. These discs are made according to Yellow Book specifications.

CD-i   CD-i stands for *compact disc-interactive*. Codeveloped by Philips and Sony, it uses a Motorola 68000 microprocessor but is styled to look like a VCR or audio CD player. It is a stand-alone, self-contained unit that can be connected to any existing television or stereo system. CD-i players can also play Audio CDs and CD+G discs, as well as Kodak Photo CDs. CD-i players with the full-motion video (FMV) option are Video CD–compatible and can play MPEG-1 files as well.

CD-i was originally intended to be the standard platform for TV-based interactive multimedia. When announced in 1987, CD-i did not have full-screen, full-motion video. In September, 1988, they achieved quarter-screen video; and by May, 1989, a CD-i disc could hold 74 minutes of VHS-quality, full-screen, full-motion video with CD-quality audio.

At the time, CD-i did not achieve mass acceptance. Today it has re-emerged as an important technology. With its new digital video capability, CD-i is often the platform of choice for multimedia kiosks and corporate applications. And it may still be a contender for the standard in TV-based multimedia. These discs are made according to Green Book specifications

Photo CD   The best media for displaying photographic images on TV sets and computers. Just take your film to the local processing house to create your own Photo CDs. A Photo CD player attaches directly to the television and can also be used to play audio CDs. With the right software, Photo CDs can be run on computers with CD-ROM XA-compatible drives. CD-i and 3DO players are also Photo CD–compatible.

Mastering Photo CDs is a little different from the other CDs, in that the laser is not used to burn actual pits into the disc's surface. The gold layer of a Photo CD is painted with a thin film of photosensitive dye. The dye is interpreted as a pit, so an unused Photo CD is one big pit. The laser is then used to "bleach" the dye so that the bleached points reveal the shiny gold. The net result is a disc with dark and light spots interpreted as bits.

Video CD   Video CDs, sometimes called VCD and related to KaraokeCDs, are used for linear video and have only limited interactive capabilities. Like audio CDs, they have a maximum playing time of 74 minutes. These discs are made according to White Book specifications, using MPEG-1 video compression as defined by the Moving Picture Experts Group. While some video-compression techniques such as QuickTime and Video for Windows are software-based, today MPEG-1 requires special chips to decode the data. In the future, faster chips such as the PowerPC may someday play it without needing a special MPEG chip. Video CDs can be played on Video CD players, 3DO players, and CD-i players with MPEG video adapters. In addition, some audio CD and CD-ROM players can be upgraded with add-on components.

CD-R   CD-R stands for *compact disc recorder.* This standard makes it possible to "write" discs that can be read by standard CD-ROM drives. CD-R is based on Orange Book Part II specifications.

File Systems

You may also hear discs referred to as ISO 9660, HFS, or hybrids. These terms are not disc formats, but refer to which standard file system was used in making the disc. The ISO 9660 specification is the lowest possible common denominator that allows discs to be read by both PC and Macintosh platforms. I say "lowest common denominator" because the ISO 9660 does not support things like long file names or Macintosh icons.

HFS (*hierarchical file system*) does support the Macintosh interface conventions, and this format is used only for discs to be played on a Macintosh platform.

If you want your disc to be compatible with both the PC and Macintosh platform, you might choose to create a *hybrid HFS-ISO* disc. This disc really contains two separate versions, one for each platform. In terms of storage space, hybrid discs only allow half a disc for each version of an application.

Other Terms and Platforms

You will hear a variety of other names and terms that relate to compact discs. Sega and Nintendo, for example, are platforms (or players), not disc formats. Sega and Nintendo players were once only capable of using cartridges. Today they have compact-disc compatibility.

3DO describes both the disc and the platform. The platform is based on a 32-bit RISC (reduced instruction set computing) processor, twin custom-designed graphics animation processors, and a double-speed CD-ROM drive. 3DO players offer high performance, especially when it comes to playing 3-D graphics. Audio CDs, CD+G, and Photo CDs can all be played on a 3DO machine.

CDTV was not a disc type. Commodore Dynamic Total Vision was the name for Commodore's stand-alone compact disc player. It was pulled from the market when Commodore went out of business. It looked sort of like a VCR but was essentially an Amiga computer with a CD-ROM drive. Meant to be a reference device, CDTV was designed to appeal to consumers who were computer-shy. The platform never gained consumer acceptance.

VIS was a short-lived endeavor that began in 1992 when Tandy launched VIS as a family-oriented educational entertainment product. The system used the Microsoft Modular Windows operating system, hoping that developers would support the platform, but it never gained enough market share.

CD+G discs were basically audio CDs with some added graphics. They were designed to be played on audio CD players with a graphics upgrade, on special CD+G players, or on video laser disc players, but never gained much popularity. Neither, it seems, did the players. CD+G is used extensively for Karaoke in Japan and the United States.

Index

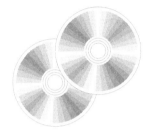

N

Nadeau, Michael, 184
Naked Gun (Philips Media Video CD Group), 131
National Parenting Publications Award for Best Software winner, 119
National Portrait Gallery (Abt Books), 106
National Trade Data Bank (Office of Business Analysis), 100
NautilusCD (Metatec), 162
Netscribe 2000 (Meridian Data), 267
NetWare Lite, CD-ROMs for networks using, 214
Networking CDs, 213–15
New England Journal of Medicine (Creative Multimedia), 99
New Family Bible, The (Time Warner Interactive Group), 149–50
New Grolier Electronic Encyclopedia, The, 20
New Prescription Drug Reference Guide (Creative Multimedia Corporation), 155
New Wave Hookers, 174
NewMedia InVision Awards winners, 110, 113, 120, 169
Newsletters on CD-ROM, 97
Newspapers on CD-ROM, 97
Newsweek Interactive (Newsweek), 158, 178
Newsweek on CD-ROM, 158
NFL's Greatest Plays (Turner Home Entertainment), 139–40, 193
Nichols, Dave, 244
Night Before Christmas, The (Discus), 122
Nightwatch Interactive, 174
1992 Occupational Outlook Handbook, 149
1992 NFL Season (Compton's New Media), 140
Nintendo as main platform for children, 12
Nintendo Ultra, 184
Nonfiction, CD-ROMs for, 146–49
Norman, Donald, 147
NoteStation (MusicWriter), 110, 112, 195
Nuclear Science Abstracts (Dialog OnDisc), 99
Nugen, Jack, 110

O

Office, CD-ROMs in. *See* Business, CD-ROMs in
On Evolution (The Voyager Company), 147
"One-off"
  creating, 83, 271
  defined, 261
Online services
  getting news from, 93
  owning CD-ROM-based materials versus using, 102–3
  popularity of, 8
  searching tools on, 191

Onsi, Pat, 101
Optical character recognition (OCR), 82
Opti-net (Online Computer System), 213
OptiNet Lite, 214–15
Oracle Corporation's CD-ROM annual report, 53–54, 244
Oxford English Dictionary (Tri-Star Publishing), 20, 74

P

PageMaker 5.0 (Aldus), 218
Paperwork Reduction Act, 84–85
Parent's Choice Award winner, 120
Parents selecting CDs for children, guidelines for, 207–8
Passage to Vietnam, A (Against All Odds Productions), 157
Patents, CD-ROMs in, 80–81
Paul, Fredric, 136
PC
  broadband service through, 196–97
  as social instrument, 198
  and television as the two central appliances of the future, 180
PC Library (Allegro New Media), 76
PCD Writer 600 (Eastman Kodak), 83, 229, 264–66
Pearson Senior High School, "information everywhere" approach of, 29–30
Pediatric Infectious Disease Journal (Creative Multimedia), 99
Peer-to-peer network, 214
Penthouse Interactive, 174
People v. O. J. Simpson: An Interactive Companion to the O. J. Simpson Trial (Turner Home Entertainment, CNN, and Intellimedia Sports), 161–62, 181
People Who Lead (PERC Macromedia Group), 89
Personal productivity, CD-ROMs for, 170–73
Perugi, Mike, 66
Pete Townshend Live, 137
Peter Gabriel: All About Us (Philips), 136–37
Peterson, Bryan, 223–24
Petzold, Charles, 189
Philosopher's Index, The (Dialog OnDisc), 98
PhoneDisc USA (Digital Data Associates), 61, 97
Photo CD (Eastman Kodak), 1, 11
  benefits of, 217–18
  business use of, 51, 221
  capabilities of, 219–21
  data storage on, 234
  Dayton's, Hudson's, and Marshall Field's stores use of, 108–10
  development by Kodak of, 5–6